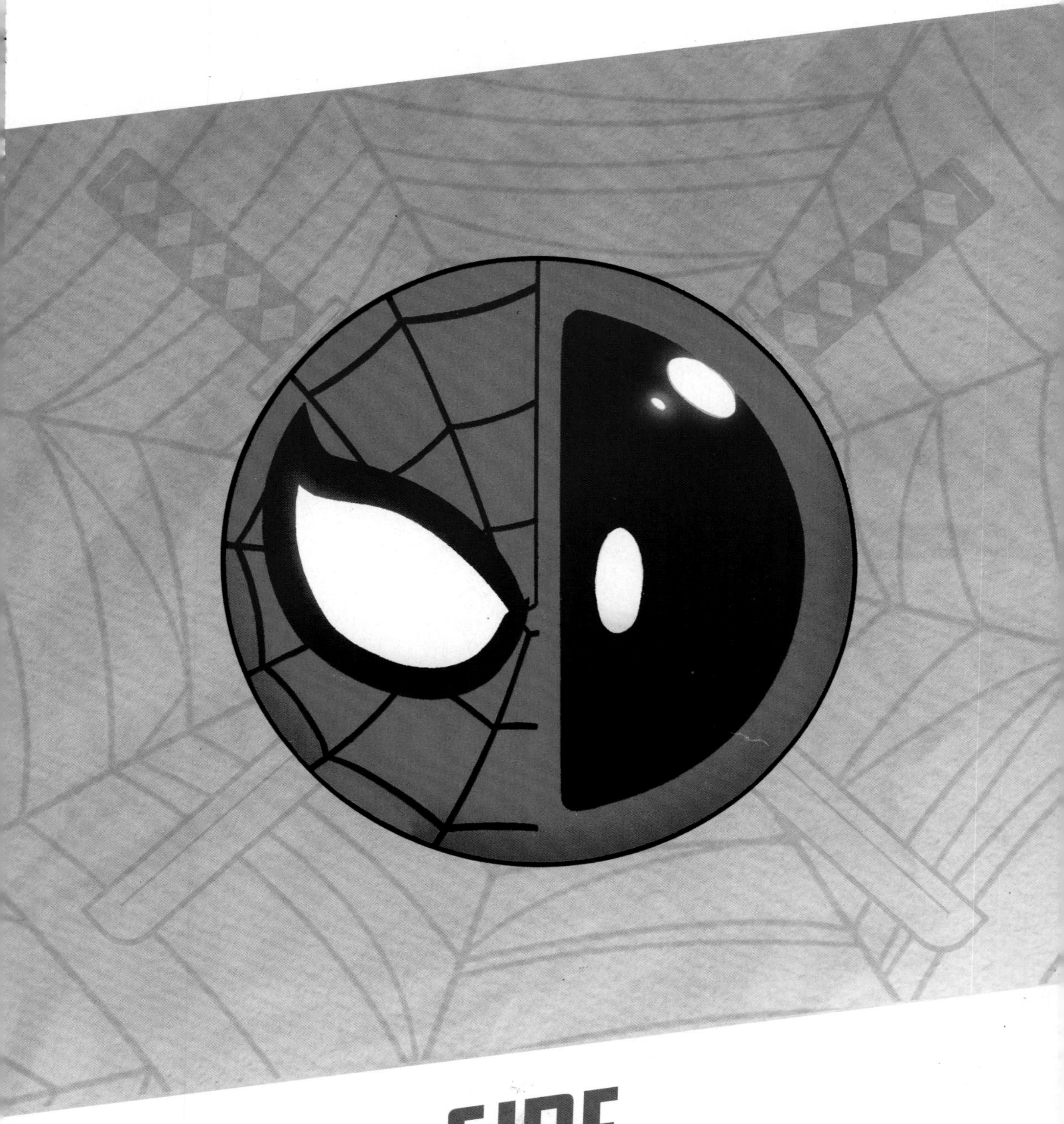

SIDE PIECES

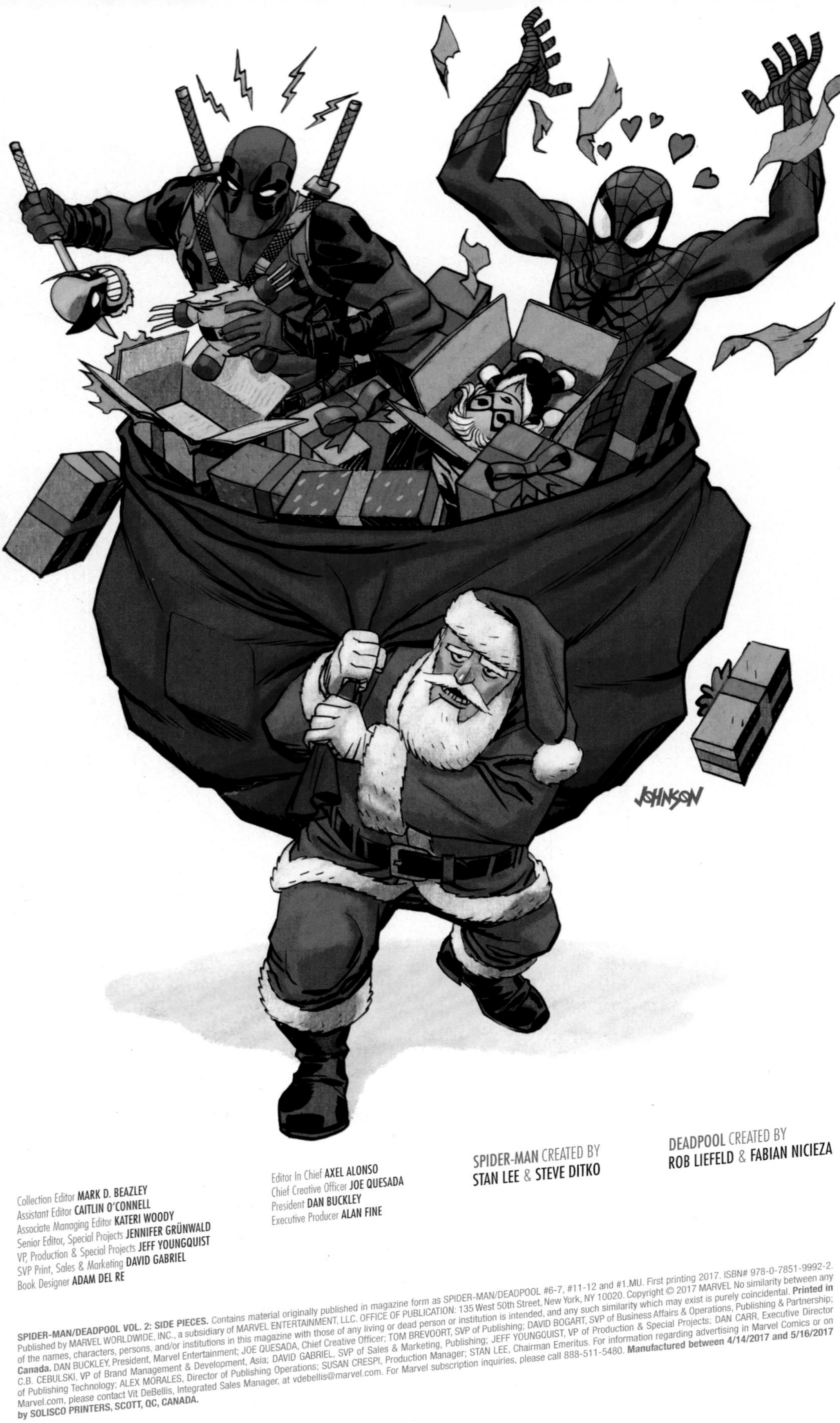
JOHNSON

SPIDER-MAN CREATED BY
STAN LEE & **STEVE DITKO**

DEADPOOL CREATED BY
ROB LIEFELD & **FABIAN NICIEZA**

Collection Editor **MARK D. BEAZLEY**
Assistant Editor **CAITLIN O'CONNELL**
Associate Managing Editor **KATERI WOODY**
Senior Editor, Special Projects **JENNIFER GRÜNWALD**
VP, Production & Special Projects **JEFF YOUNGQUIST**
SVP Print, Sales & Marketing **DAVID GABRIEL**
Book Designer **ADAM DEL RE**

Editor In Chief **AXEL ALONSO**
Chief Creative Officer **JOE QUESADA**
President **DAN BUCKLEY**
Executive Producer **ALAN FINE**

SPIDER-MAN/DEADPOOL VOL. 2: SIDE PIECES. Contains material originally published in magazine form as SPIDER-MAN/DEADPOOL #6-7, #11-12 and #1.MU. First printing 2017. ISBN# 978-0-7851-9992-2. Published by MARVEL WORLDWIDE, INC., a subsidiary of MARVEL ENTERTAINMENT, LLC. OFFICE OF PUBLICATION: 135 West 50th Street, New York, NY 10020.

Printed in Canada. DAN BUCKLEY, President, Marvel Entertainment; JOE QUESADA, Chief Creative Officer; TOM BREVOORT, SVP of Publishing; DAVID BOGART, SVP of Business Affairs & Operations, Publishing & Partnership; C.B. CEBULSKI, VP of Brand Management & Development, Asia; DAVID GABRIEL, SVP of Sales & Marketing, Publishing; JEFF YOUNGQUIST, VP of Production & Special Projects; DAN CARR, Executive Director of Publishing Technology; ALEX MORALES, Director of Publishing Operations; SUSAN CRESPI, Production Manager; STAN LEE, Chairman Emeritus. For information regarding advertising in Marvel Comics or on Marvel.com, please contact Vit DeBellis, Integrated Sales Manager, at vdebellis@marvel.com. For Marvel subscription inquiries, please call 888-511-5480. **Manufactured between 4/14/2017 and 5/16/2017 by SOLISCO PRINTERS, SCOTT, QC, CANADA.**

10 9 8 7 6 5 4 3 2 1

MARVEL COMICS
BEGRUDGINGLY PRESENTS...

PETER PARKER WAS BITTEN BY AN IRRADIATED SPIDER, GRANTING HIM AMAZING ABILITIES, INCLUDING THE PROPORTIONAL SPEED, STRENGTH AND AGILITY OF A SPIDER, AS WELL AS ADHESIVE FINGERTIPS AND TOES. AFTER LEARNING THAT WITH GREAT POWER, THERE MUST ALSO COME GREAT RESPONSIBILITY, HE BECAME THE WORLD'S GREATEST SUPER HERO! HE'S...

THE WORLD'S GREATEST SUPER HERO!
The AMAZING SPIDER-MAN

AVENGER...ASSASSIN...SUPERSTAR! WADE WILSON WAS CHOSEN FOR A TOP-SECRET GOVERNMENT PROGRAM THAT GAVE HIM A HEALING FACTOR THAT ALLOWS HIM TO HEAL FROM ANY WOUND. DESPITE EARNING A SMALL FORTUNE AS A GUN FOR HIRE, WADE HAS BECOME THE WORLD'S MOST BELOVED HERO. AND IS THE STAR OF THE WORLD'S GREATEST COMICS MAGAZINE (NO MATTER WHAT THAT JERK IN THE WEBS MAY THINK). CALL HIM THE MERC WITH THE MOUTH...CALL HIM THE REGENERATIN' DEGENERATE...CALL HIM...

DEADPOOL

SCOTT AUKERMAN, GERRY DUGGAN,
PENN JILLETTE, NICK GIOVANNETTI AND PAUL SCHEER
& JOSHUA CORIN
Writers

REILLY BROWN, SCOTT KOBLISH,
TODD NAUCK & TIGH WALKER
Pencilers

RICK MAGYAR, LE BEAU UNDERWOOD, SCOTT HANNA,
SCOTT KOBLISH, TODD NAUCK & TIGH WALKER
Inkers

JASON KEITH, VAL STAPLES, GURU-eFX & RACHELLE ROSENBERG
Colorists

VC'S JOE SABINO
Letterer

MIKE DEL MUNDO (#6), DAN PANOSIAN (#7), SCOTT KOBLISH & GURU-eFX (#11)
AND DAVE JOHNSON (#12 & #1.MU)
Cover Art

DEVIN LEWIS
Associate Editor

ALLISON STOCK
Assistant Editor

JORDAN D. WHITE & NICK LOWE
Editors

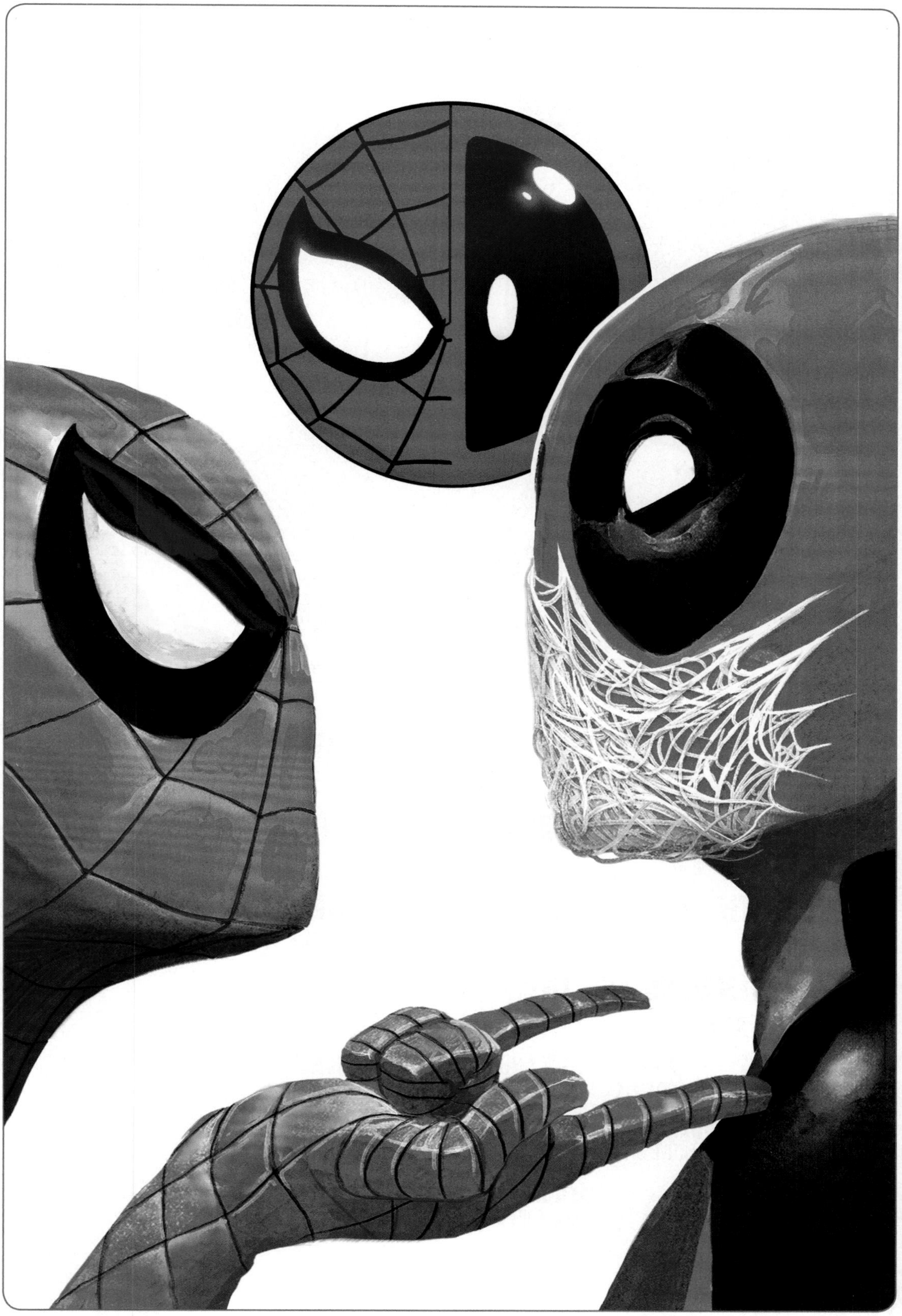

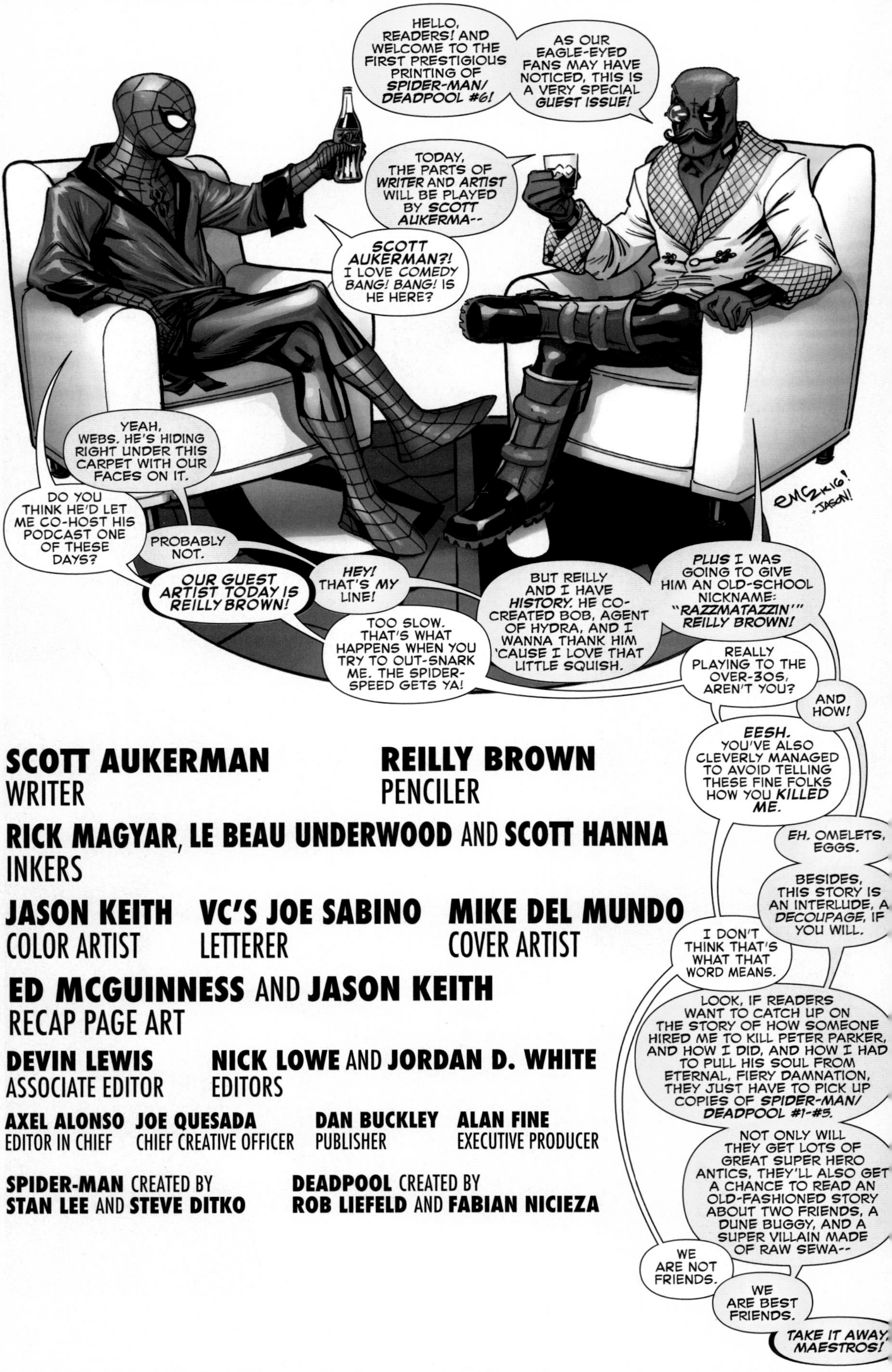

HELLO, READERS! AND WELCOME TO THE FIRST PRESTIGIOUS PRINTING OF *SPIDER-MAN/ DEADPOOL #6!*
AS OUR EAGLE-EYED FANS MAY HAVE NOTICED, THIS IS A VERY SPECIAL *GUEST ISSUE!*
TODAY, THE PARTS OF *WRITER* AND *ARTIST* WILL BE PLAYED BY *SCOTT AUKERMA--*
SCOTT AUKERMAN?! I LOVE *COMEDY BANG! BANG!* IS HE HERE?
YEAH, WEBS. HE'S HIDING RIGHT UNDER THIS CARPET WITH OUR FACES ON IT.
DO YOU THINK HE'D LET ME CO-HOST HIS PODCAST ONE OF THESE DAYS?
PROBABLY NOT.
OUR GUEST ARTIST TODAY IS REILLY BROWN!
HEY! THAT'S *MY* LINE!
TOO SLOW. THAT'S WHAT HAPPENS WHEN YOU TRY TO OUT-SNARK ME. THE SPIDER-SPEED GETS YA!
BUT REILLY AND I HAVE *HISTORY.* HE CO-CREATED BOB, AGENT OF HYDRA, AND I WANNA THANK HIM 'CAUSE I LOVE THAT LITTLE SQUISH.
PLUS I WAS GOING TO GIVE HIM AN OLD-SCHOOL NICKNAME: *"RAZZMATAZZIN'" REILLY BROWN!*
REALLY PLAYING TO THE OVER-30S, AREN'T YOU?
AND HOW!
EESH. YOU'VE ALSO CLEVERLY MANAGED TO AVOID TELLING THESE FINE FOLKS HOW YOU *KILLED ME.*
EH. OMELETS, EGGS.
BESIDES, THIS STORY IS AN INTERLUDE, A *DECOUPAGE,* IF YOU WILL.
I DON'T THINK THAT'S WHAT THAT WORD MEANS.
LOOK, IF READERS WANT TO CATCH UP ON THE STORY OF HOW SOMEONE HIRED ME TO KILL PETER PARKER, AND HOW I *DID,* AND HOW I HAD TO PULL HIS SOUL FROM ETERNAL, FIERY DAMNATION, THEY JUST HAVE TO PICK UP COPIES OF *SPIDER-MAN/ DEADPOOL #1-#5.*
NOT ONLY WILL THEY GET LOTS OF GREAT SUPER HERO ANTICS, THEY'LL ALSO GET A CHANCE TO READ AN OLD-FASHIONED STORY ABOUT TWO FRIENDS, A DUNE BUGGY, AND A SUPER VILLAIN MADE OF RAW SEWA--
WE ARE NOT FRIENDS.
WE ARE BEST FRIENDS.
TAKE IT AWAY, MAESTROS!

SCOTT AUKERMAN
WRITER

REILLY BROWN
PENCILER

RICK MAGYAR, LE BEAU UNDERWOOD AND **SCOTT HANNA**
INKERS

JASON KEITH
COLOR ARTIST

VC'S JOE SABINO
LETTERER

MIKE DEL MUNDO
COVER ARTIST

ED MCGUINNESS AND **JASON KEITH**
RECAP PAGE ART

DEVIN LEWIS
ASSOCIATE EDITOR

NICK LOWE AND **JORDAN D. WHITE**
EDITORS

AXEL ALONSO
EDITOR IN CHIEF

JOE QUESADA
CHIEF CREATIVE OFFICER

DAN BUCKLEY
PUBLISHER

ALAN FINE
EXECUTIVE PRODUCER

SPIDER-MAN CREATED BY
STAN LEE AND **STEVE DITKO**

DEADPOOL CREATED BY
ROB LIEFELD AND **FABIAN NICIEZA**

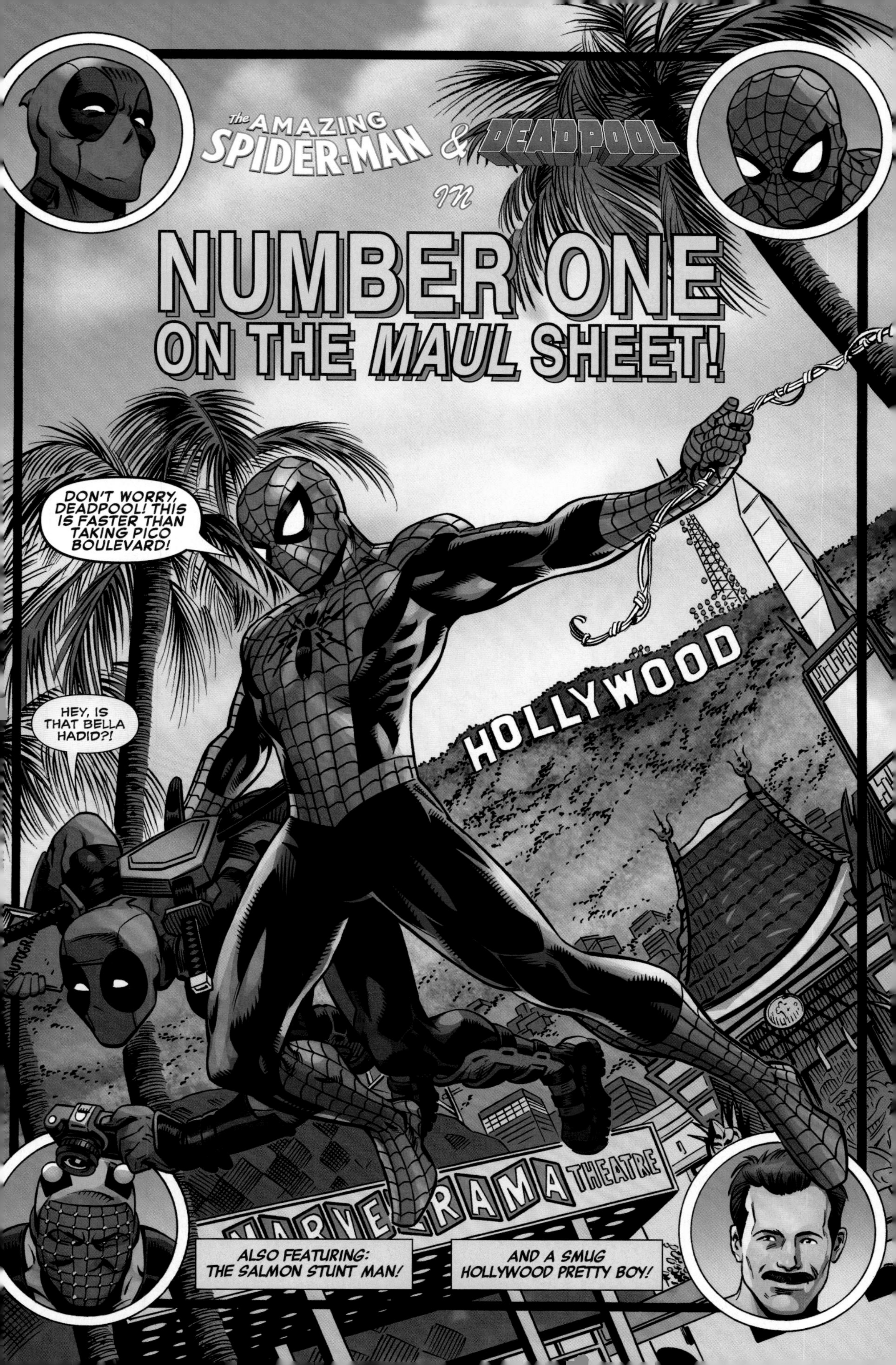
The AMAZING SPIDER-MAN & DEADPOOL
IN
NUMBER ONE ON THE MAUL SHEET!
DON'T WORRY, DEADPOOL! THIS IS FASTER THAN TAKING PICO BOULEVARD!
HEY, IS THAT BELLA HADID?!
HOLLYWOOD
AUTOGRA
THEATRE
ALSO FEATURING: THE SALMON STUNT MAN!
AND A SMUG HOLLYWOOD PRETTY BOY!

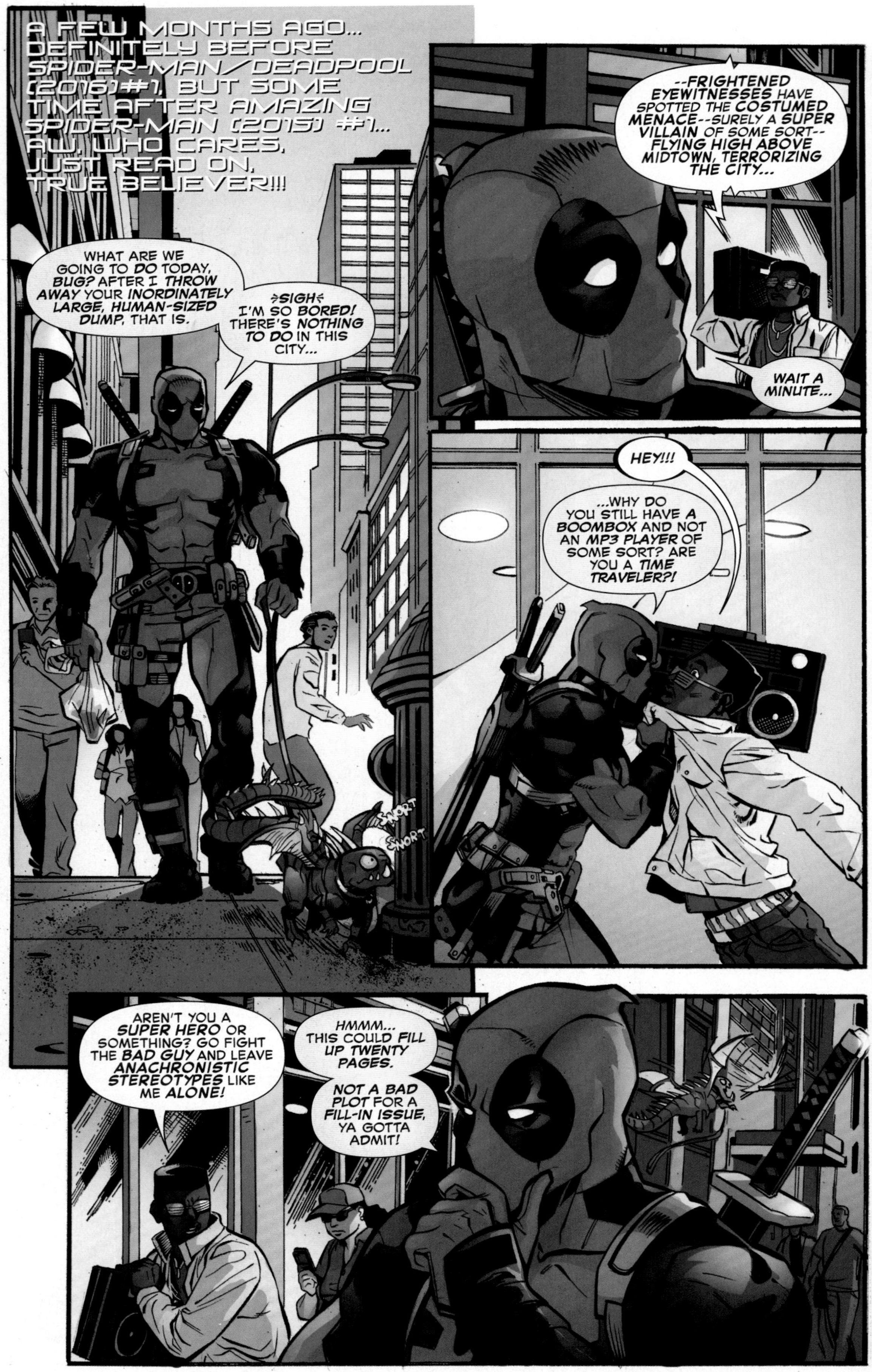

A FEW MONTHS AGO... DEFINITELY BEFORE SPIDER-MAN/DEADPOOL (2016) #1, BUT SOME TIME AFTER AMAZING SPIDER-MAN (2015) #1... AW, WHO CARES, JUST READ ON, TRUE BELIEVER!!!
WHAT ARE WE GOING TO DO TODAY, BUG? AFTER I THROW AWAY YOUR INORDINATELY LARGE, HUMAN-SIZED DUMP, THAT IS.
SIGH I'M SO BORED! THERE'S NOTHING TO DO IN THIS CITY...
SNORT
SNORT
--FRIGHTENED EYEWITNESSES HAVE SPOTTED THE COSTUMED MENACE--SURELY A SUPER VILLAIN OF SOME SORT--FLYING HIGH ABOVE MIDTOWN, TERRORIZING THE CITY...
WAIT A MINUTE...
HEY!!!
...WHY DO YOU STILL HAVE A BOOMBOX AND NOT AN MP3 PLAYER OF SOME SORT? ARE YOU A TIME TRAVELER?!
AREN'T YOU A SUPER HERO OR SOMETHING? GO FIGHT THE BAD GUY AND LEAVE ANACHRONISTIC STEREOTYPES LIKE ME ALONE!
HMMM... THIS COULD FILL UP TWENTY PAGES.
NOT A BAD PLOT FOR A FILL-IN ISSUE, YA GOTTA ADMIT!

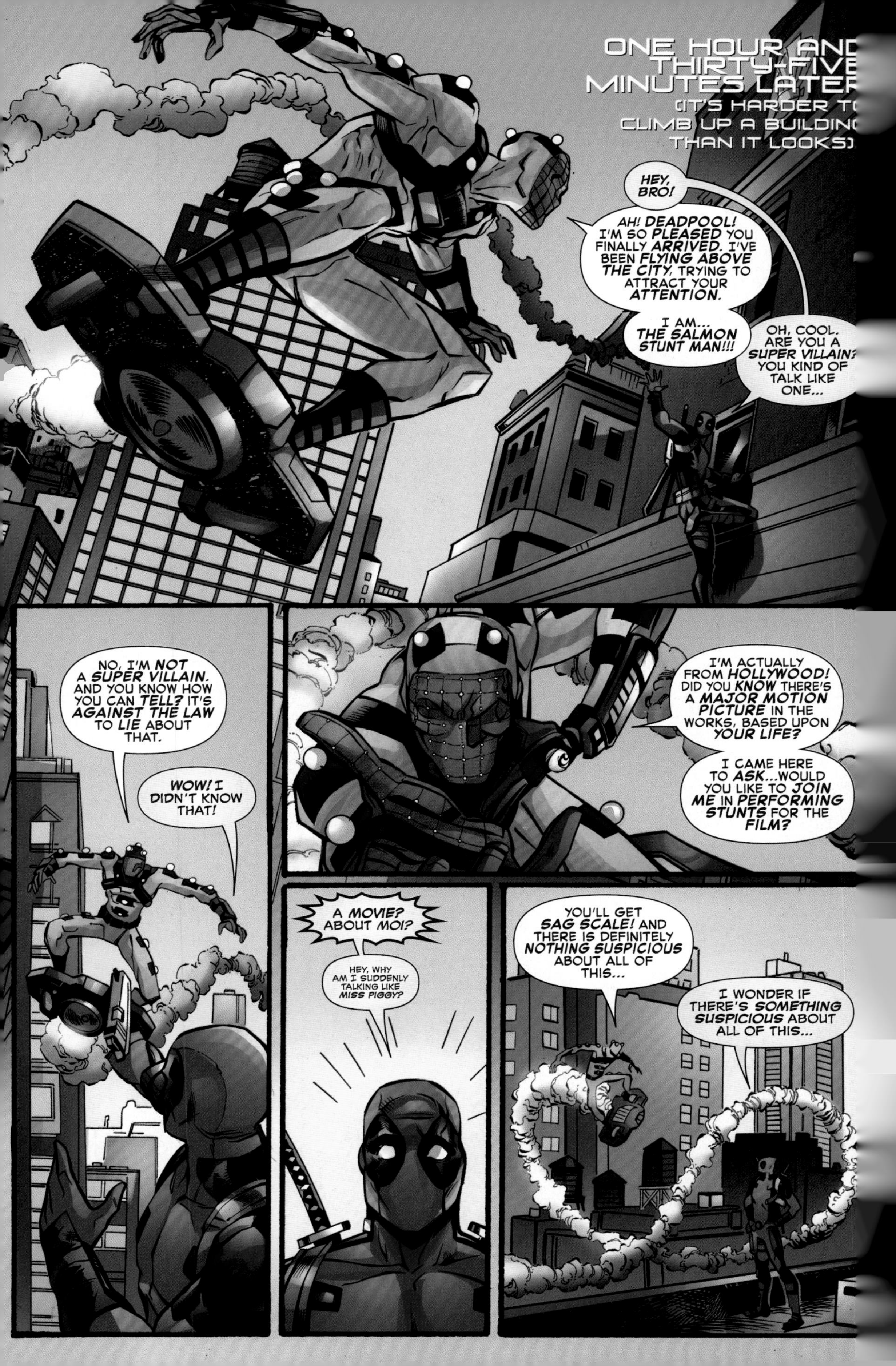
ONE HOUR AND THIRTY-FIVE MINUTES LATER
(IT'S HARDER TO CLIMB UP A BUILDING THAN IT LOOKS)
HEY, BRO!
AH! DEADPOOL! I'M SO PLEASED YOU FINALLY ARRIVED. I'VE BEEN FLYING ABOVE THE CITY, TRYING TO ATTRACT YOUR ATTENTION.
I AM... THE SALMON STUNT MAN!!!
OH, COOL. ARE YOU A SUPER VILLAIN? YOU KIND OF TALK LIKE ONE...
NO, I'M NOT A SUPER VILLAIN. AND YOU KNOW HOW YOU CAN TELL? IT'S AGAINST THE LAW TO LIE ABOUT THAT.
WOW! I DIDN'T KNOW THAT!
I'M ACTUALLY FROM HOLLYWOOD! DID YOU KNOW THERE'S A MAJOR MOTION PICTURE IN THE WORKS, BASED UPON YOUR LIFE?
I CAME HERE TO ASK...WOULD YOU LIKE TO JOIN ME IN PERFORMING STUNTS FOR THE FILM?
A MOVIE? ABOUT MOI?
HEY, WHY AM I SUDDENLY TALKING LIKE MISS PIGGY?
YOU'LL GET SAG SCALE! AND THERE IS DEFINITELY NOTHING SUSPICIOUS ABOUT ALL OF THIS...
I WONDER IF THERE'S SOMETHING SUSPICIOUS ABOUT ALL OF THIS...

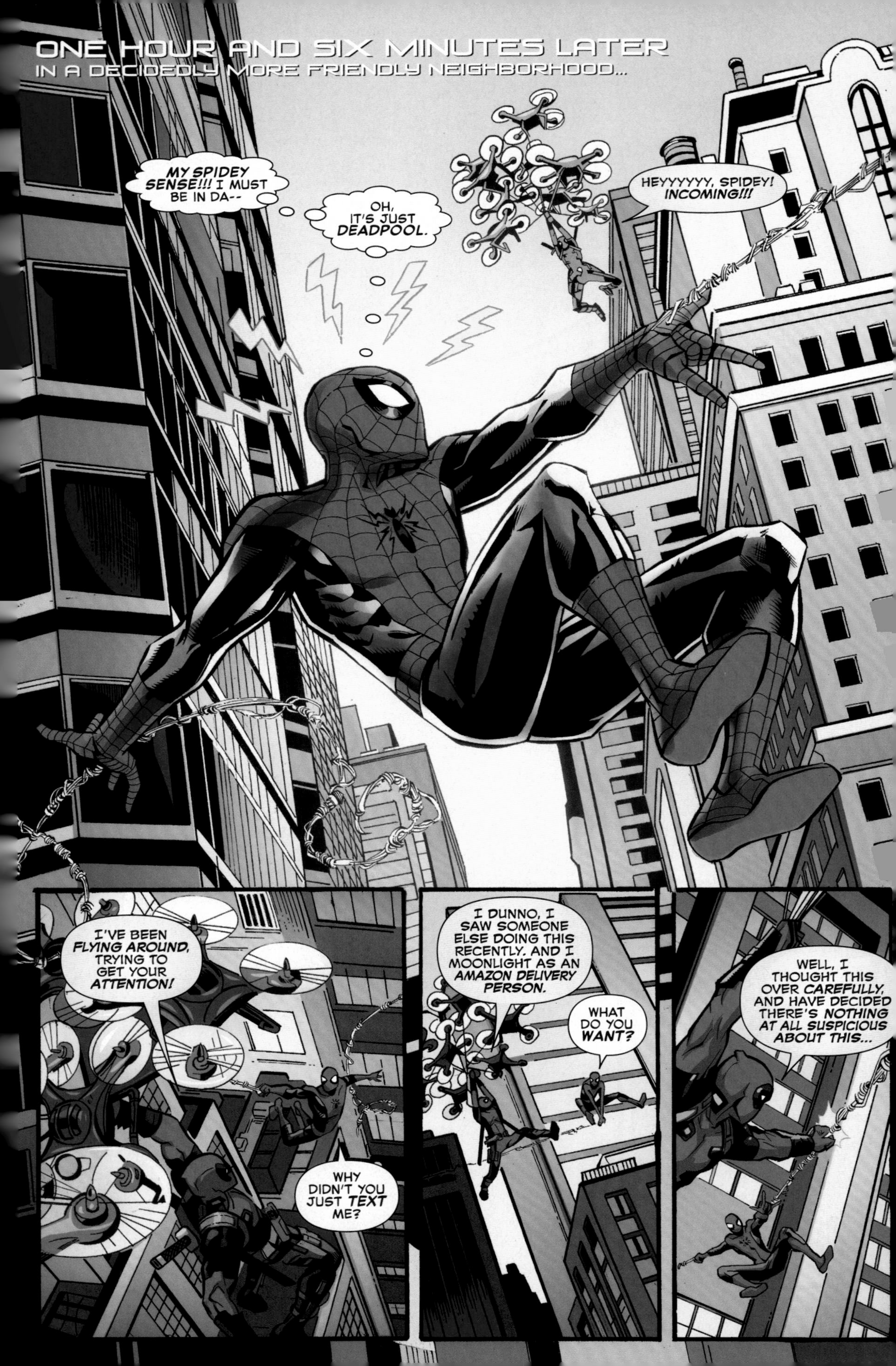
ONE HOUR AND SIX MINUTES LATER
IN A DECIDEDLY MORE FRIENDLY NEIGHBORHOOD...
MY SPIDEY SENSE!!! I MUST BE IN DA--
OH, IT'S JUST DEADPOOL.
HEYYYYYY, SPIDEY! INCOMING!!!
I'VE BEEN FLYING AROUND, TRYING TO GET YOUR ATTENTION!
WHY DIDN'T YOU JUST TEXT ME?
I DUNNO, I SAW SOMEONE ELSE DOING THIS RECENTLY. AND I MOONLIGHT AS AN AMAZON DELIVERY PERSON.
WHAT DO YOU WANT?
WELL, I THOUGHT THIS OVER CAREFULLY, AND HAVE DECIDED THERE'S NOTHING AT ALL SUSPICIOUS ABOUT THIS...

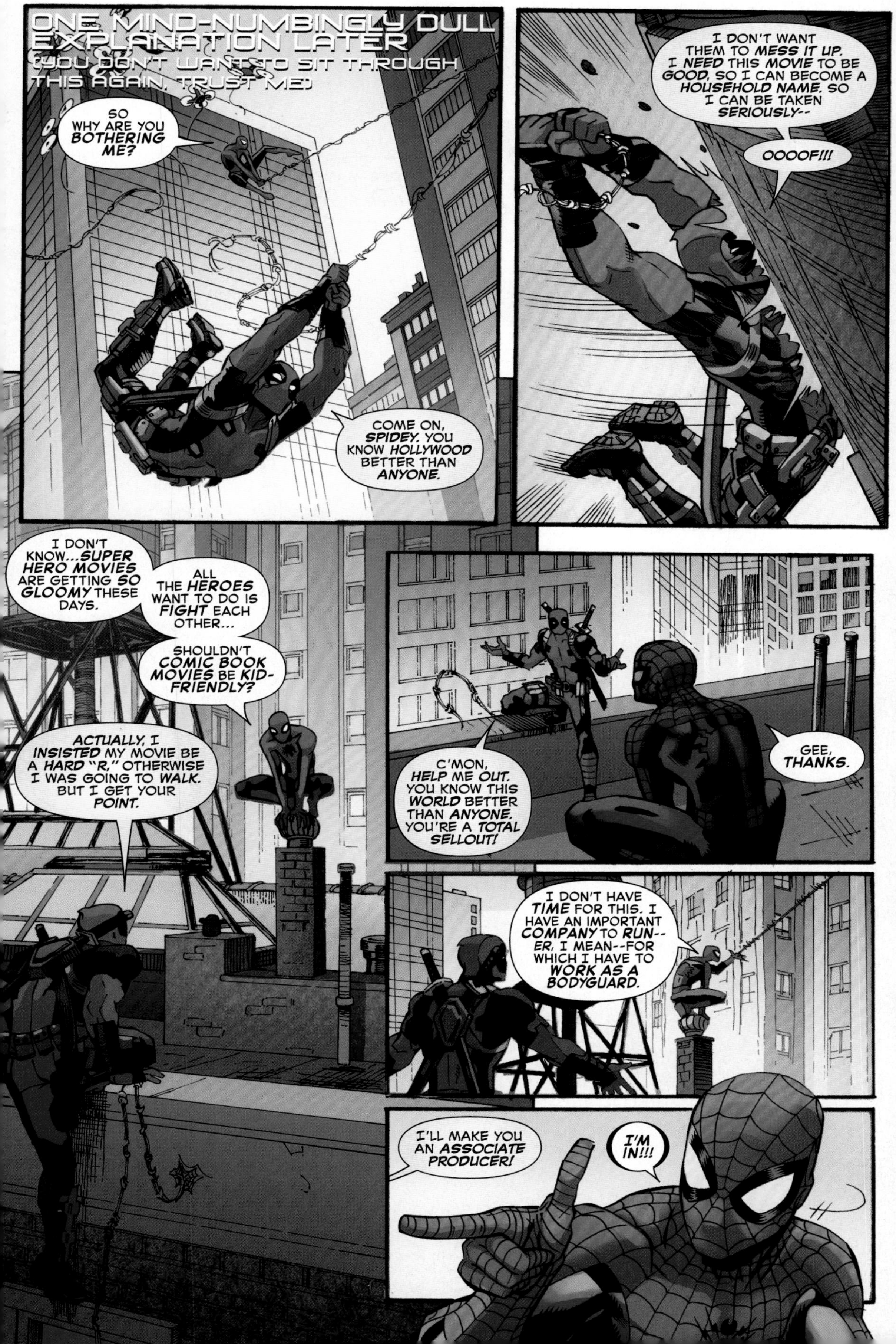
ONE MIND-NUMBINGLY DULL EXPLANATION LATER
(YOU DON'T WANT TO SIT THROUGH THIS AGAIN, TRUST ME.)
SO WHY ARE YOU BOTHERING ME?
COME ON, SPIDEY. YOU KNOW HOLLYWOOD BETTER THAN ANYONE.
I DON'T WANT THEM TO MESS IT UP. I NEED THIS MOVIE TO BE GOOD, SO I CAN BECOME A HOUSEHOLD NAME. SO I CAN BE TAKEN SERIOUSLY--
OOOOF!!!
I DON'T KNOW...SUPER HERO MOVIES ARE GETTING SO GLOOMY THESE DAYS.
ALL THE HEROES WANT TO DO IS FIGHT EACH OTHER...
SHOULDN'T COMIC BOOK MOVIES BE KID-FRIENDLY?
ACTUALLY, I INSISTED MY MOVIE BE A HARD "R," OTHERWISE I WAS GOING TO WALK. BUT I GET YOUR POINT.
C'MON, HELP ME OUT. YOU KNOW THIS WORLD BETTER THAN ANYONE. YOU'RE A TOTAL SELLOUT!
GEE, THANKS.
I DON'T HAVE TIME FOR THIS. I HAVE AN IMPORTANT COMPANY TO RUN-- ER, I MEAN--FOR WHICH I HAVE TO WORK AS A BODYGUARD.
I'LL MAKE YOU AN ASSOCIATE PRODUCER!
I'M IN!!!

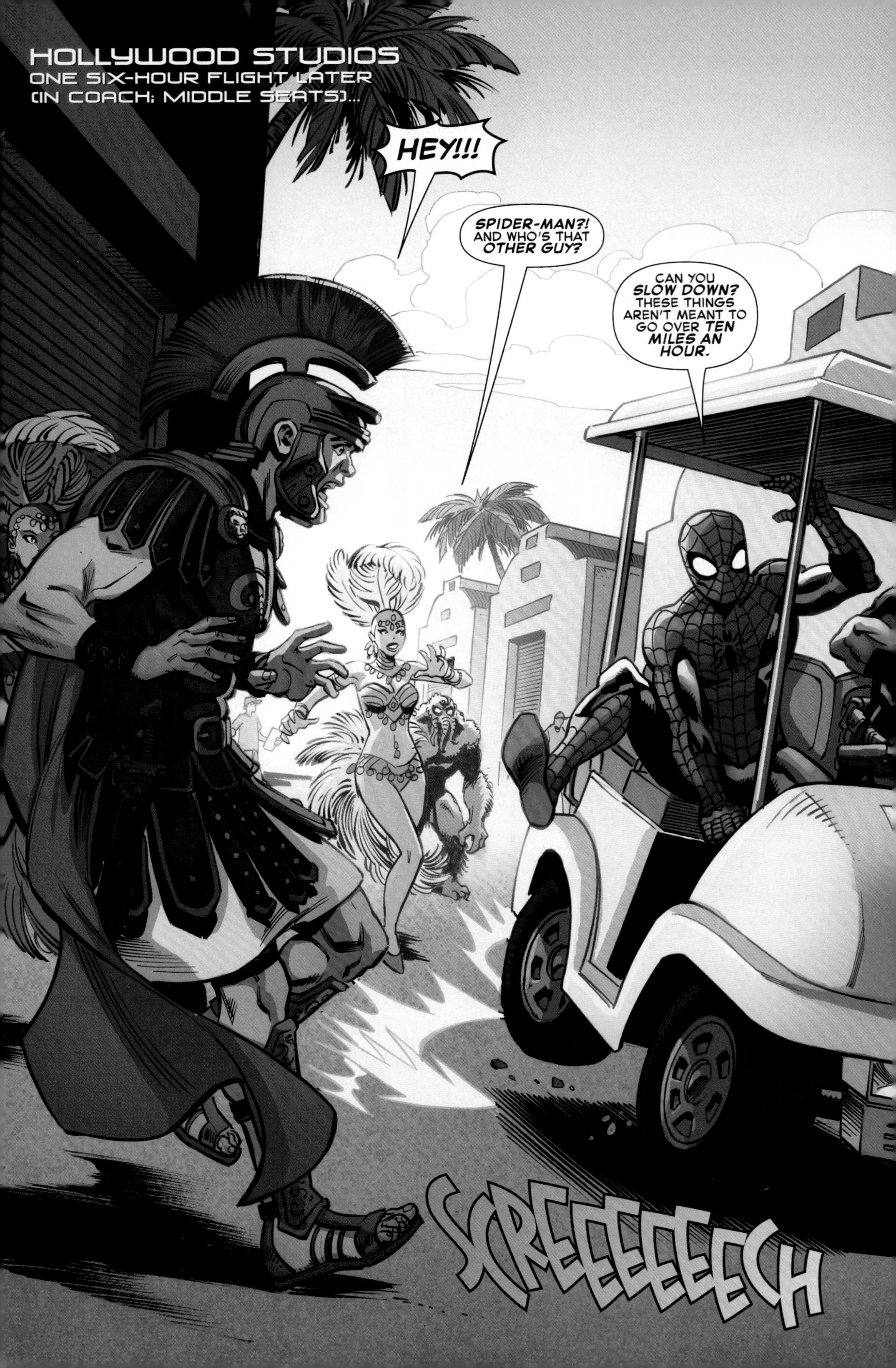
HOLLYWOOD STUDIOS
ONE SIX-HOUR FLIGHT LATER
(IN COACH; MIDDLE SEATS)...
HEY!!!
SPIDER-MAN?! AND WHO'S THAT OTHER GUY?
CAN YOU SLOW DOWN? THESE THINGS AREN'T MEANT TO GO OVER TEN MILES AN HOUR.
SCREEEEEEECH

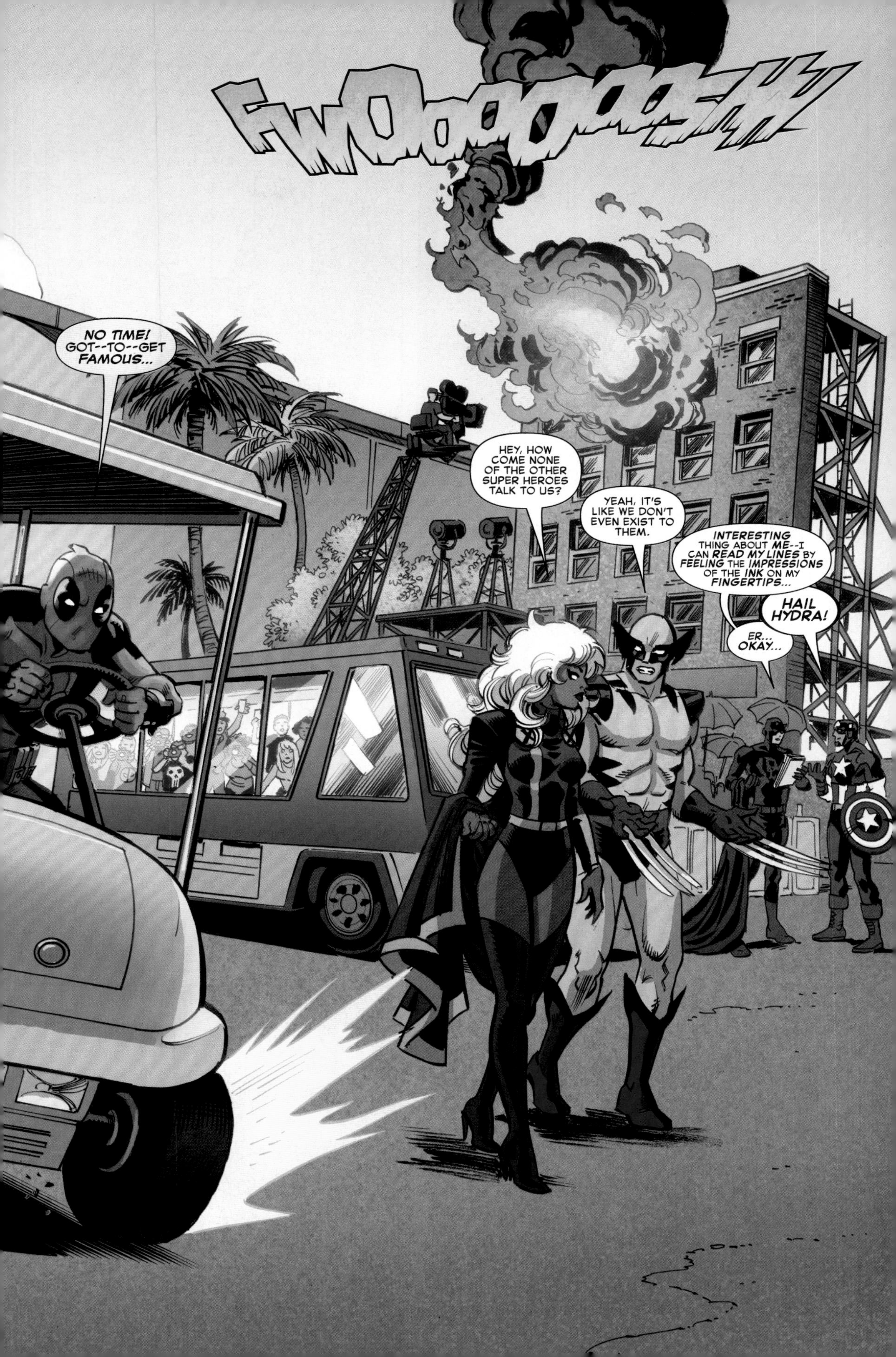
FWOOOOOOSH
NO TIME! GOT--TO--GET FAMOUS...
HEY, HOW COME NONE OF THE OTHER SUPER HEROES TALK TO US?
YEAH, IT'S LIKE WE DON'T EVEN EXIST TO THEM.
INTERESTING THING ABOUT ME--I CAN READ MY LINES BY FEELING THE IMPRESSIONS OF THE INK ON MY FINGERTIPS...
ER... OKAY...
HAIL HYDRA!

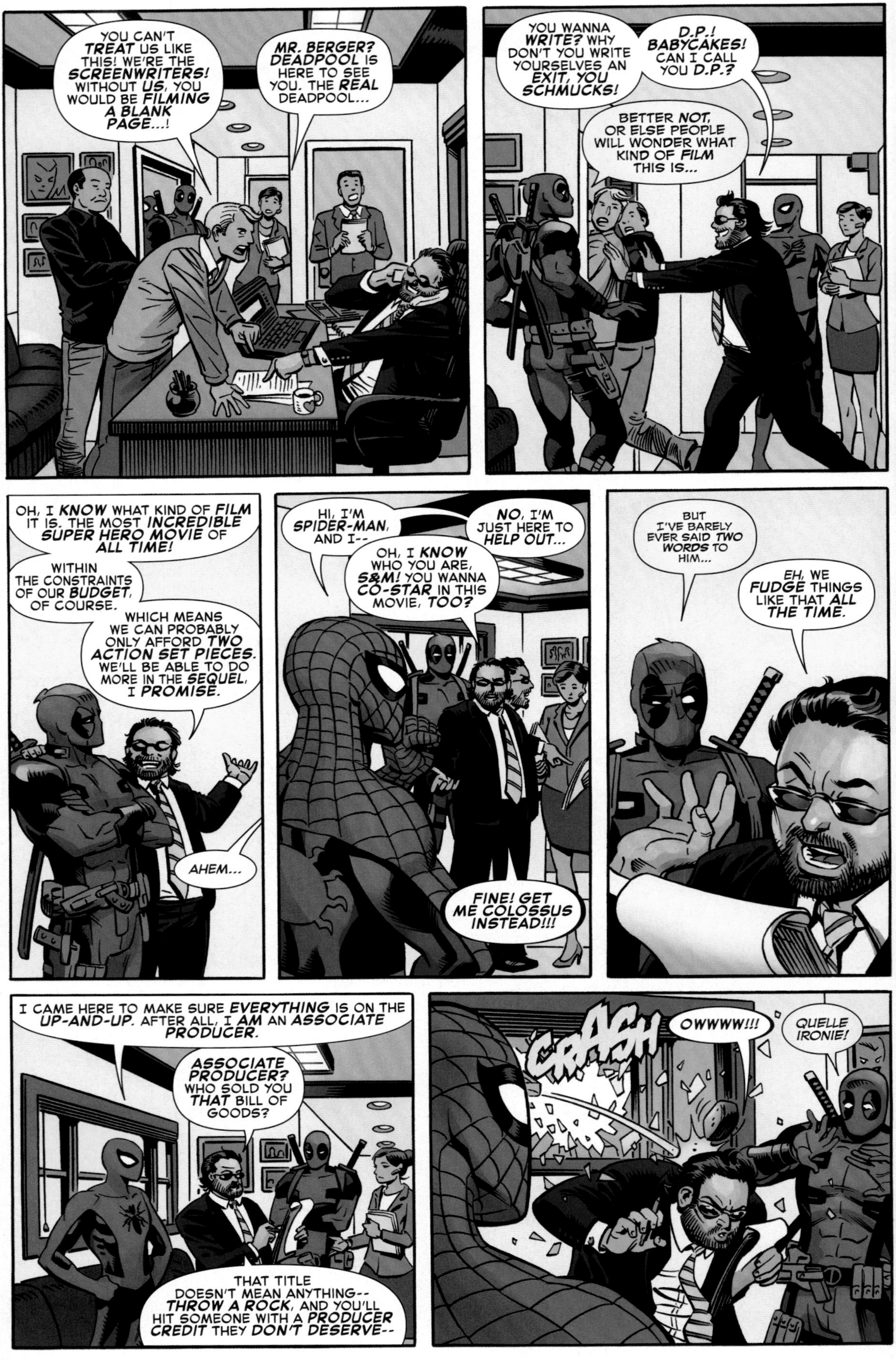

YOU CAN'T TREAT US LIKE THIS! WE'RE THE SCREENWRITERS! WITHOUT US, YOU WOULD BE FILMING A BLANK PAGE...!
MR. BERGER? DEADPOOL IS HERE TO SEE YOU. THE REAL DEADPOOL...
YOU WANNA WRITE? WHY DON'T YOU WRITE YOURSELVES AN EXIT, YOU SCHMUCKS!
D.P.! BABYCAKES! CAN I CALL YOU D.P.?
BETTER NOT, OR ELSE PEOPLE WILL WONDER WHAT KIND OF FILM THIS IS...
OH, I KNOW WHAT KIND OF FILM IT IS. THE MOST INCREDIBLE SUPER HERO MOVIE OF ALL TIME!
WITHIN THE CONSTRAINTS OF OUR BUDGET, OF COURSE.
WHICH MEANS WE CAN PROBABLY ONLY AFFORD TWO ACTION SET PIECES. WE'LL BE ABLE TO DO MORE IN THE SEQUEL, I PROMISE.
AHEM...
HI, I'M SPIDER-MAN, AND I--
OH, I KNOW WHO YOU ARE, S&M! YOU WANNA CO-STAR IN THIS MOVIE, TOO?
NO, I'M JUST HERE TO HELP OUT...
FINE! GET ME COLOSSUS INSTEAD!!!
BUT I'VE BARELY EVER SAID TWO WORDS TO HIM...
EH, WE FUDGE THINGS LIKE THAT ALL THE TIME.
I CAME HERE TO MAKE SURE EVERYTHING IS ON THE UP-AND-UP. AFTER ALL, I AM AN ASSOCIATE PRODUCER.
ASSOCIATE PRODUCER? WHO SOLD YOU THAT BILL OF GOODS?
THAT TITLE DOESN'T MEAN ANYTHING-- THROW A ROCK, AND YOU'LL HIT SOMEONE WITH A PRODUCER CREDIT THEY DON'T DESERVE--
CRASH
OWWWW!!!
QUELLE IRONIE!

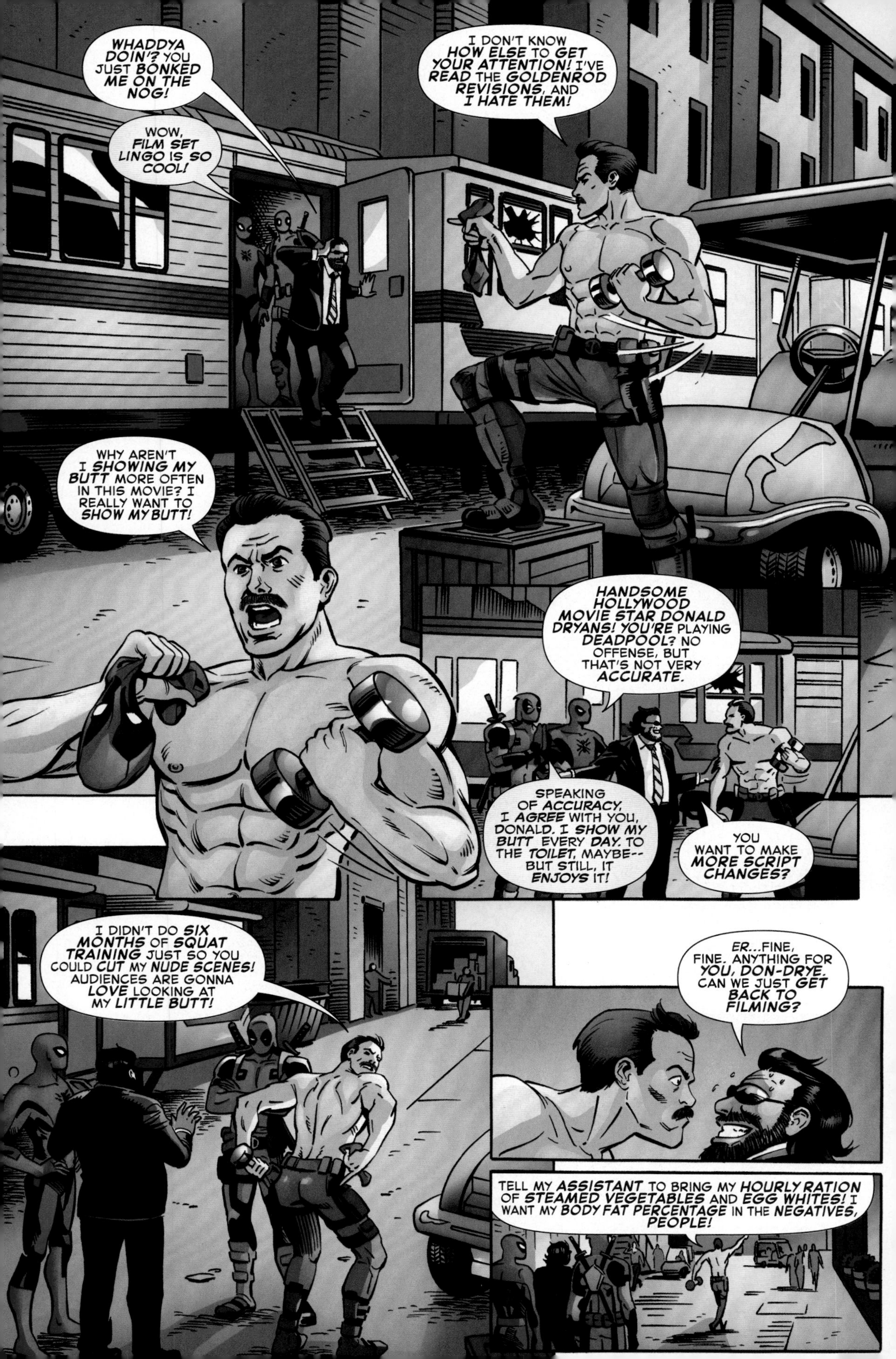
WHADDYA DOIN'? YOU JUST BONKED ME ON THE NOG!
WOW, FILM SET LINGO IS SO COOL!
I DON'T KNOW HOW ELSE TO GET YOUR ATTENTION! I'VE READ THE GOLDENROD REVISIONS, AND I HATE THEM!
WHY AREN'T I SHOWING MY BUTT MORE OFTEN IN THIS MOVIE? I REALLY WANT TO SHOW MY BUTT!
HANDSOME HOLLYWOOD MOVIE STAR DONALD DRYANS! YOU'RE PLAYING DEADPOOL? NO OFFENSE, BUT THAT'S NOT VERY ACCURATE.
SPEAKING OF ACCURACY, I AGREE WITH YOU, DONALD. I SHOW MY BUTT EVERY DAY. TO THE TOILET, MAYBE-- BUT STILL, IT ENJOYS IT!
YOU WANT TO MAKE MORE SCRIPT CHANGES?
I DIDN'T DO SIX MONTHS OF SQUAT TRAINING JUST SO YOU COULD CUT MY NUDE SCENES! AUDIENCES ARE GONNA LOVE LOOKING AT MY LITTLE BUTT!
ER...FINE, FINE. ANYTHING FOR YOU, DON-DRYE. CAN WE JUST GET BACK TO FILMING?
TELL MY ASSISTANT TO BRING MY HOURLY RATION OF STEAMED VEGETABLES AND EGG WHITES! I WANT MY BODY FAT PERCENTAGE IN THE NEGATIVES, PEOPLE!

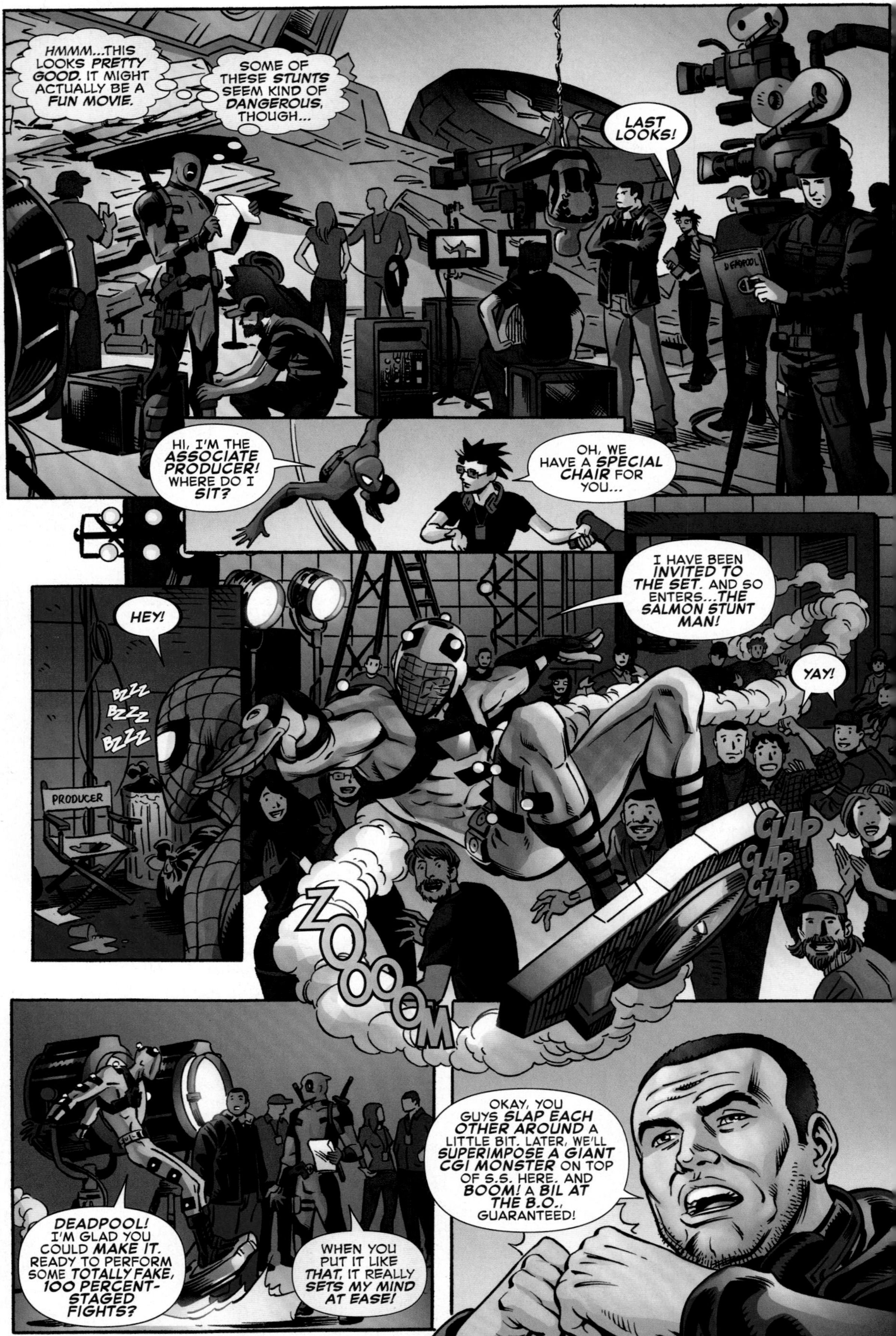

HMMM...THIS LOOKS PRETTY GOOD. IT MIGHT ACTUALLY BE A FUN MOVIE.
SOME OF THESE STUNTS SEEM KIND OF DANGEROUS, THOUGH...
LAST LOOKS!
DEADPOOL
HI, I'M THE ASSOCIATE PRODUCER! WHERE DO I SIT?
OH, WE HAVE A SPECIAL CHAIR FOR YOU...
HEY!
BZZZ BZZZ BZZZ
PRODUCER
I HAVE BEEN INVITED TO THE SET. AND SO ENTERS...THE SALMON STUNT MAN!
YAY!
CLAP CLAP CLAP
ZOOOOM
DEADPOOL! I'M GLAD YOU COULD MAKE IT. READY TO PERFORM SOME TOTALLY FAKE, 100 PERCENT-STAGED FIGHTS?
WHEN YOU PUT IT LIKE THAT, IT REALLY SETS MY MIND AT EASE!
OKAY, YOU GUYS SLAP EACH OTHER AROUND A LITTLE BIT. LATER, WE'LL SUPERIMPOSE A GIANT CGI MONSTER ON TOP OF S.S. HERE. AND BOOM! A BIL AT THE B.O., GUARANTEED!

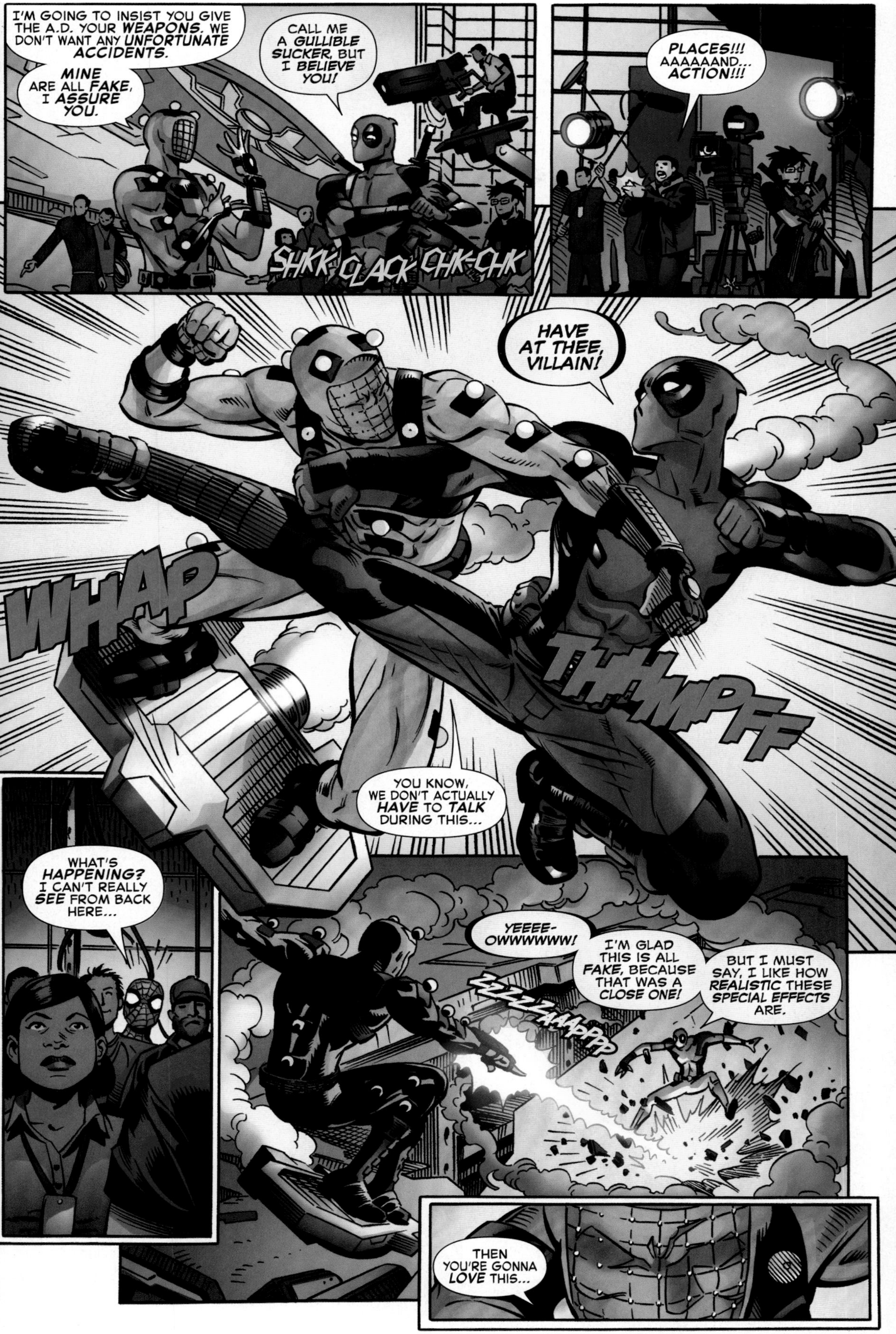
I'M GOING TO INSIST YOU GIVE THE A.D. YOUR WEAPONS. WE DON'T WANT ANY UNFORTUNATE ACCIDENTS.
MINE ARE ALL FAKE, I ASSURE YOU.
CALL ME A GULLIBLE SUCKER, BUT I BELIEVE YOU!
SHIKK CLACK CHK-CHK
PLACES!!! AAAAAAND... ACTION!!!
HAVE AT THEE, VILLAIN!
WHAP
THHMPFF
YOU KNOW, WE DON'T ACTUALLY HAVE TO TALK DURING THIS...
WHAT'S HAPPENING? I CAN'T REALLY SEE FROM BACK HERE...
YEEEE-OWWWWWW!
I'M GLAD THIS IS ALL FAKE, BECAUSE THAT WAS A CLOSE ONE!
BUT I MUST SAY, I LIKE HOW REALISTIC THESE SPECIAL EFFECTS ARE.
ZZZZZAAAPPPP
THEN YOU'RE GONNA LOVE THIS...

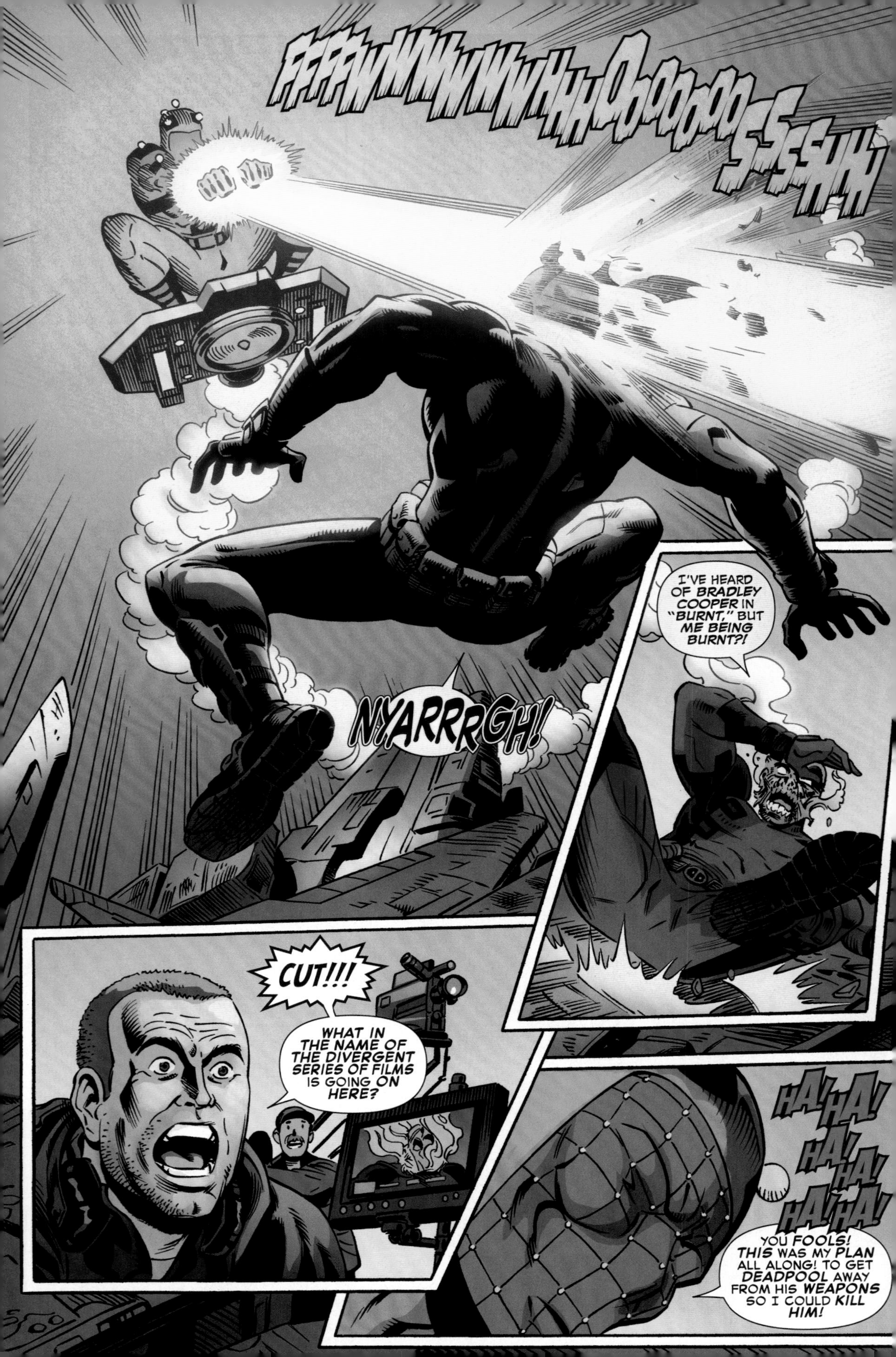
PFFFWWWWWWWWHHHOOOOOOOSSSHH
NYARRRGH!
I'VE HEARD OF BRADLEY COOPER IN "BURNT," BUT ME BEING BURNT?!
CUT!!!
WHAT IN THE NAME OF THE DIVERGENT SERIES OF FILMS IS GOING ON HERE?
HA HA! HA HA! HA HA!
YOU FOOLS! THIS WAS MY PLAN ALL ALONG! TO GET DEADPOOL AWAY FROM HIS WEAPONS SO I COULD KILL HIM!

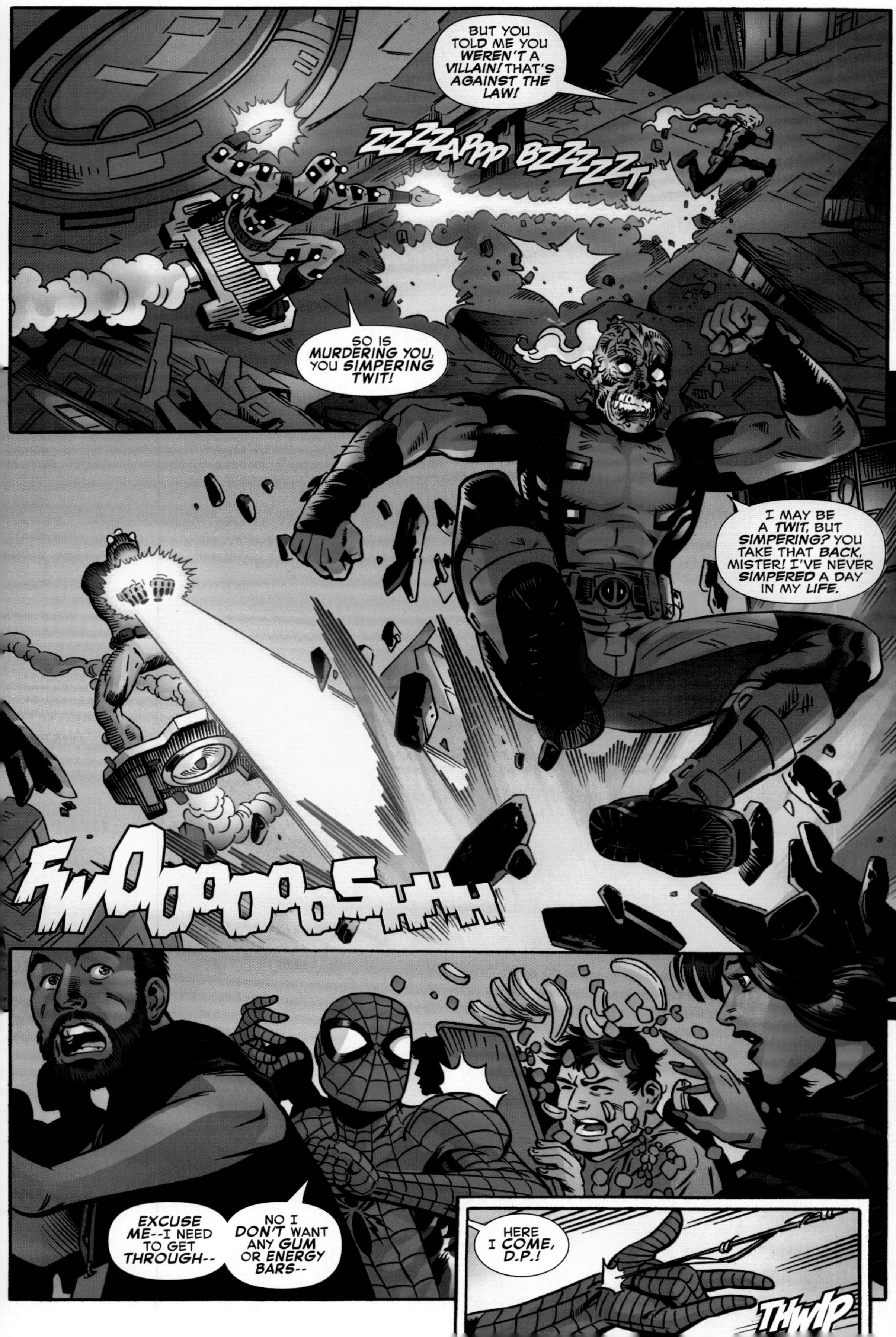
BUT YOU TOLD ME YOU WEREN'T A VILLAIN! THAT'S AGAINST THE LAW!
ZZZZAPPP BZZZZZT
SO IS MURDERING YOU, YOU SIMPERING TWIT!
I MAY BE A TWIT, BUT SIMPERING? YOU TAKE THAT BACK, MISTER! I'VE NEVER SIMPERED A DAY IN MY LIFE.
FWOOOOOOSHHH
EXCUSE ME--I NEED TO GET THROUGH--
NO I DON'T WANT ANY GUM OR ENERGY BARS--
HERE I COME, D.P.!
THWIP

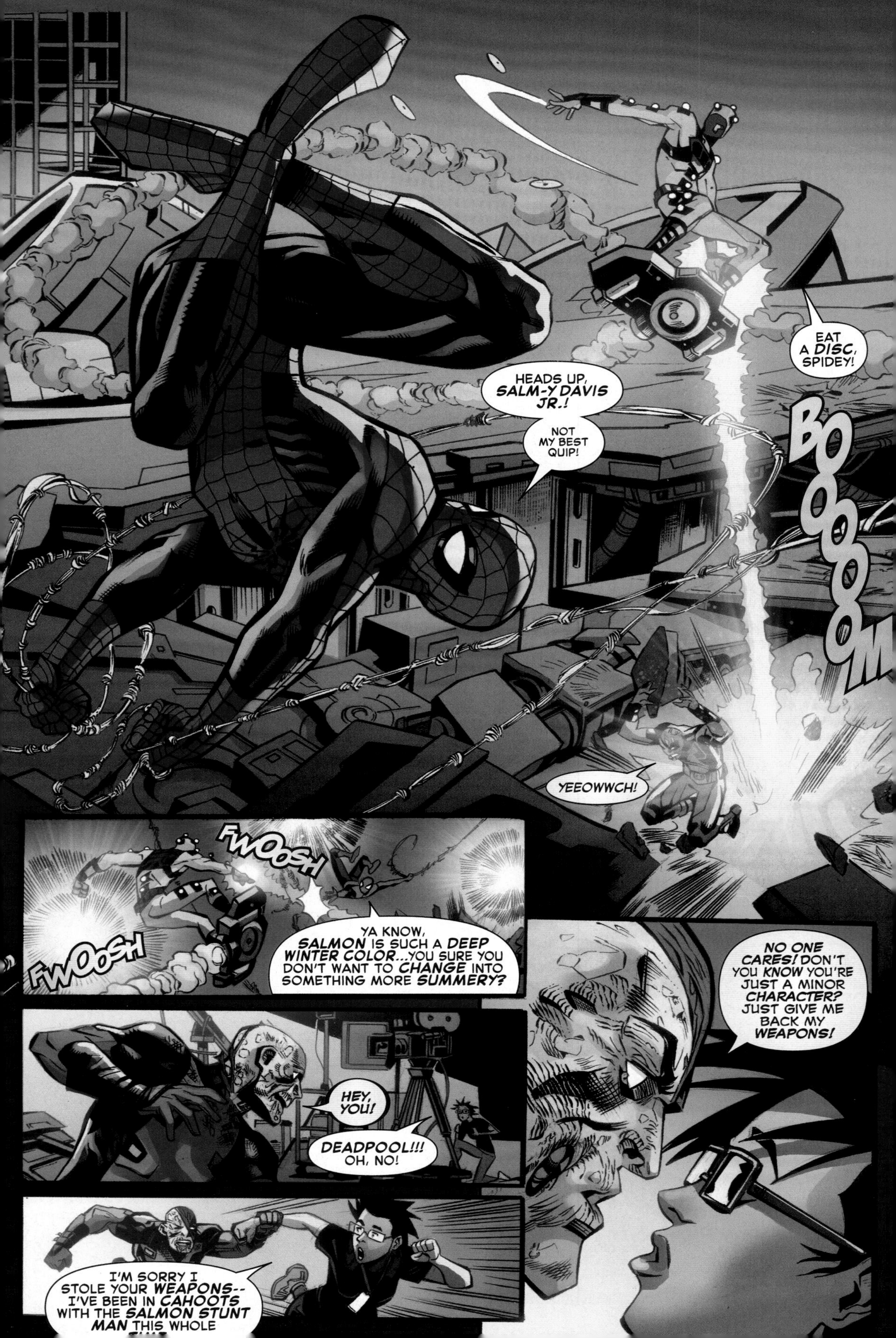
EAT A DISC, SPIDEY!
HEADS UP, SALM-Y DAVIS JR.!
NOT MY BEST QUIP!
BOOOOOOM
YEEOWWCH!
FWOOSH
FWOOSH
YA KNOW, SALMON IS SUCH A DEEP WINTER COLOR...YOU SURE YOU DON'T WANT TO CHANGE INTO SOMETHING MORE SUMMERY?
NO ONE CARES! DON'T YOU KNOW YOU'RE JUST A MINOR CHARACTER? JUST GIVE ME BACK MY WEAPONS!
HEY, YOU!
DEADPOOL!!! OH, NO!
I'M SORRY I STOLE YOUR WEAPONS-- I'VE BEEN IN CAHOOTS WITH THE SALMON STUNT MAN THIS WHOLE

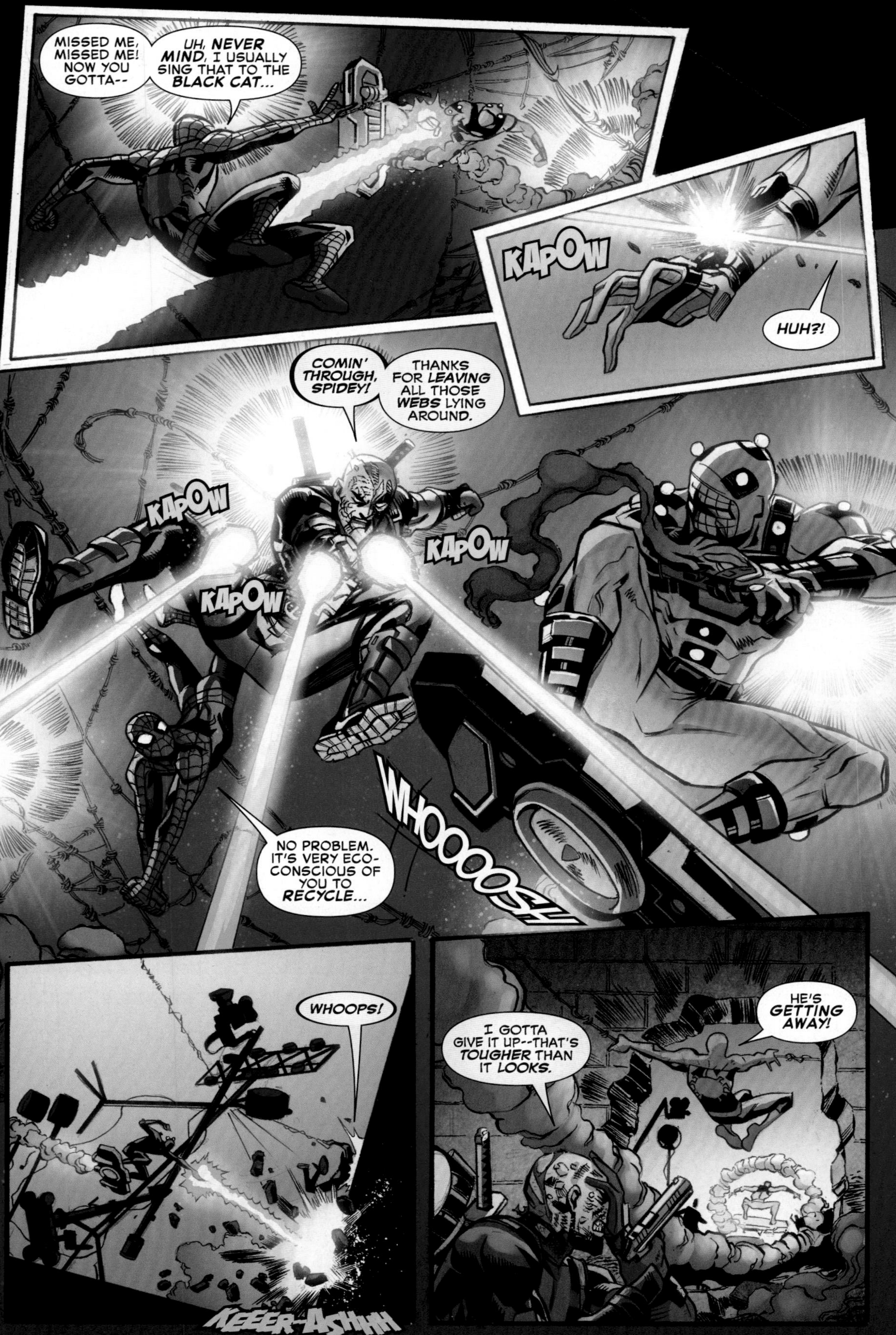
MISSED ME, MISSED ME! NOW YOU GOTTA--
UH, NEVER MIND, I USUALLY SING THAT TO THE BLACK CAT...
KAPOW
HUH?!
COMIN' THROUGH, SPIDEY!
THANKS FOR LEAVING ALL THOSE WEBS LYING AROUND.
KAPOW
KAPOW
KAPOW
NO PROBLEM. IT'S VERY ECO-CONSCIOUS OF YOU TO RECYCLE...
WHOOOOOSH
WHOOPS!
KEEER-ASHHH
HE'S GETTING AWAY!
I GOTTA GIVE IT UP--THAT'S TOUGHER THAN IT LOOKS.

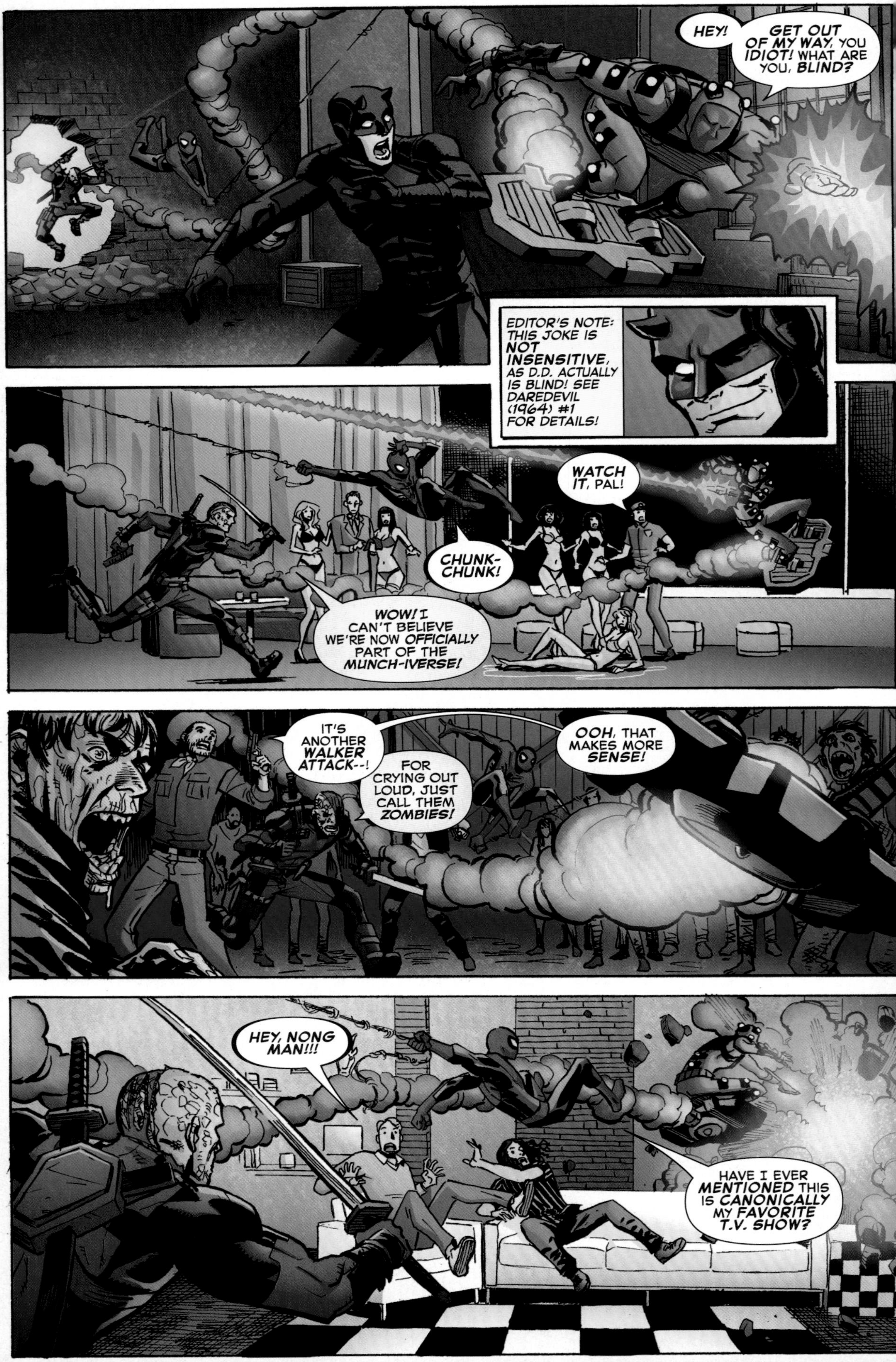
HEY!
GET OUT OF MY WAY, YOU IDIOT! WHAT ARE YOU, BLIND?
EDITOR'S NOTE: THIS JOKE IS NOT INSENSITIVE, AS D.D. ACTUALLY IS BLIND! SEE DAREDEVIL (1964) #1 FOR DETAILS!
WATCH IT, PAL!
CHUNK-CHUNK!
WOW! I CAN'T BELIEVE WE'RE NOW OFFICIALLY PART OF THE MUNCH-IVERSE!
IT'S ANOTHER WALKER ATTACK--!
OOH, THAT MAKES MORE SENSE!
FOR CRYING OUT LOUD, JUST CALL THEM ZOMBIES!
HEY, NONG MAN!!!
HAVE I EVER MENTIONED THIS IS CANONICALLY MY FAVORITE T.V. SHOW?

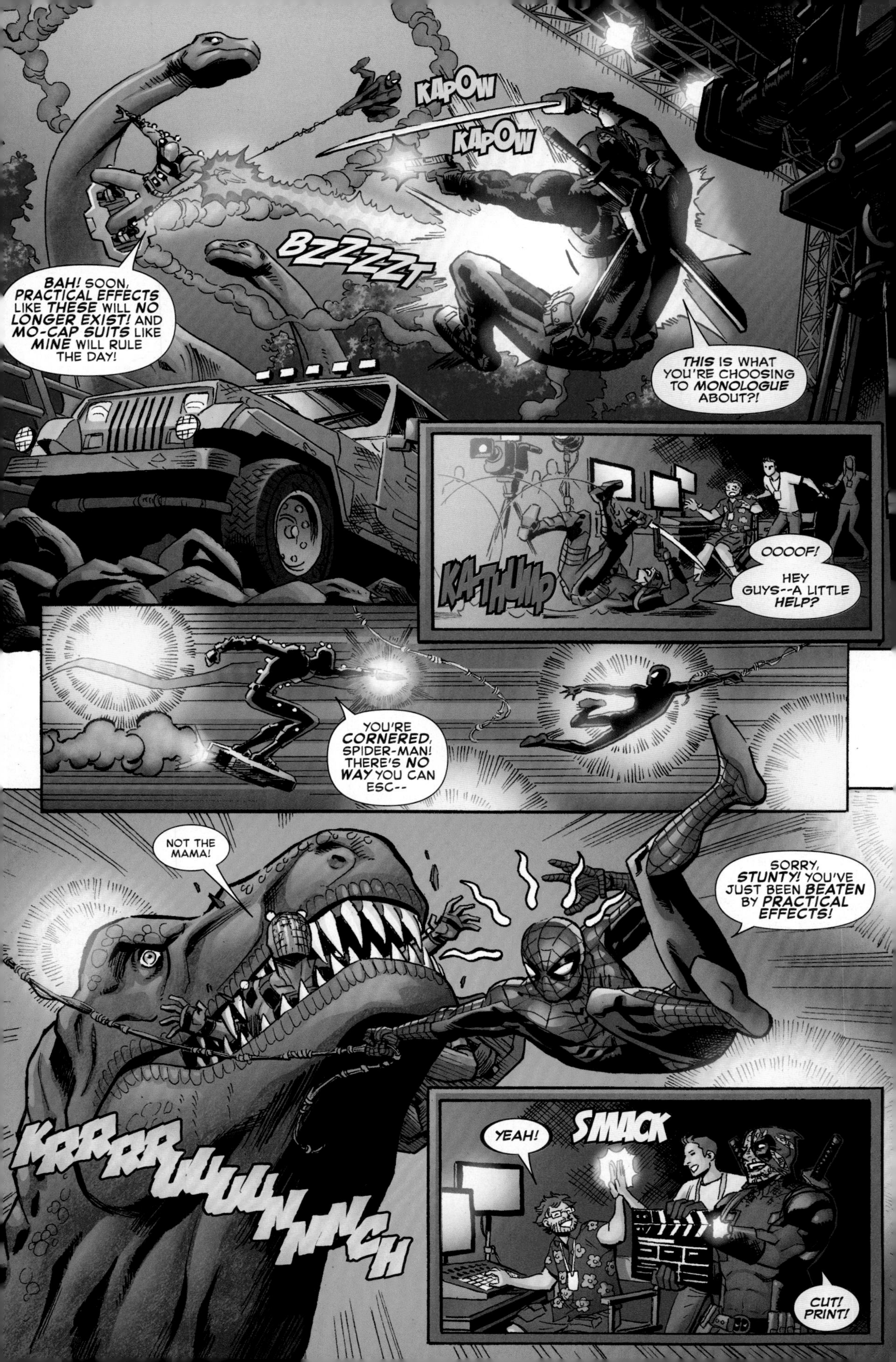
KAPOW
KAPOW
BZZZZZT
BAH! SOON, PRACTICAL EFFECTS LIKE THESE WILL NO LONGER EXIST! AND MO-CAP SUITS LIKE MINE WILL RULE THE DAY!
THIS IS WHAT YOU'RE CHOOSING TO MONOLOGUE ABOUT?!
KA-THUMP
OOOOF!
HEY GUYS--A LITTLE HELP?
YOU'RE CORNERED, SPIDER-MAN! THERE'S NO WAY YOU CAN ESC--
NOT THE MAMA!
SORRY, STUNTY! YOU'VE JUST BEEN BEATEN BY PRACTICAL EFFECTS!
KRRRRUUUNNNCH
YEAH!
SMACK
CUT! PRINT!

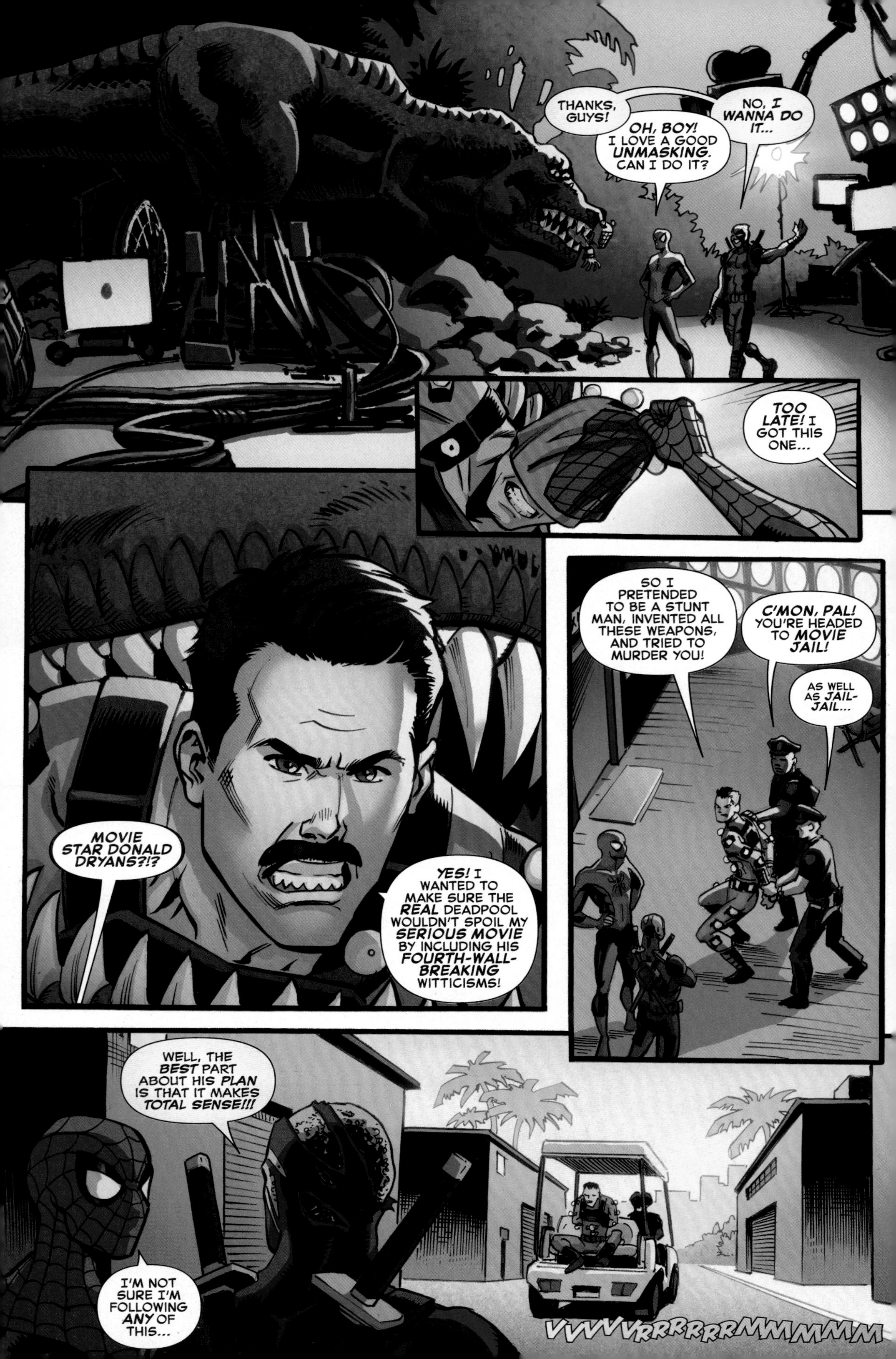
THANKS, GUYS!
OH, BOY! I LOVE A GOOD UNMASKING. CAN I DO IT?
NO, I WANNA DO IT...
TOO LATE! I GOT THIS ONE...
MOVIE STAR DONALD DRYANS?!?
YES! I WANTED TO MAKE SURE THE REAL DEADPOOL WOULDN'T SPOIL MY SERIOUS MOVIE BY INCLUDING HIS FOURTH-WALL-BREAKING WITTICISMS!
SO I PRETENDED TO BE A STUNT MAN, INVENTED ALL THESE WEAPONS, AND TRIED TO MURDER YOU!
C'MON, PAL! YOU'RE HEADED TO MOVIE JAIL!
AS WELL AS JAIL-JAIL...
WELL, THE BEST PART ABOUT HIS PLAN IS THAT IT MAKES TOTAL SENSE!!!
I'M NOT SURE I'M FOLLOWING ANY OF THIS...
VVVVVRRRRRRRMMMMMMM

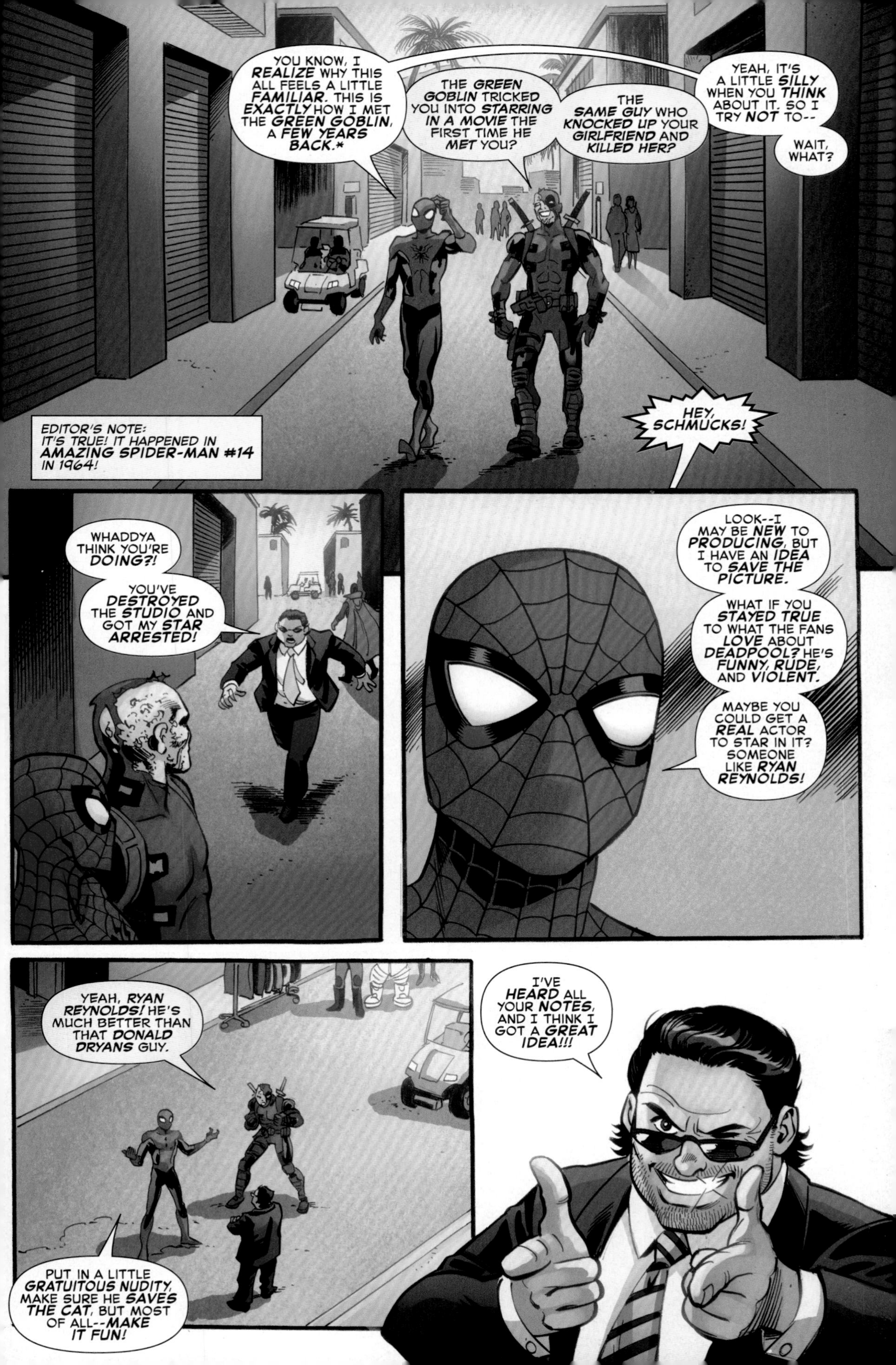

YOU KNOW, I REALIZE WHY THIS ALL FEELS A LITTLE FAMILIAR. THIS IS EXACTLY HOW I MET THE GREEN GOBLIN, A FEW YEARS BACK.*
THE GREEN GOBLIN TRICKED YOU INTO STARRING IN A MOVIE THE FIRST TIME HE MET YOU?
THE SAME GUY WHO KNOCKED UP YOUR GIRLFRIEND AND KILLED HER?
YEAH, IT'S A LITTLE SILLY WHEN YOU THINK ABOUT IT. SO I TRY NOT TO--
WAIT, WHAT?
EDITOR'S NOTE: IT'S TRUE! IT HAPPENED IN AMAZING SPIDER-MAN #14 IN 1964!
HEY, SCHMUCKS!
WHADDYA THINK YOU'RE DOING?!
YOU'VE DESTROYED THE STUDIO AND GOT MY STAR ARRESTED!
LOOK--I MAY BE NEW TO PRODUCING, BUT I HAVE AN IDEA TO SAVE THE PICTURE.
WHAT IF YOU STAYED TRUE TO WHAT THE FANS LOVE ABOUT DEADPOOL? HE'S FUNNY, RUDE, AND VIOLENT.
MAYBE YOU COULD GET A REAL ACTOR TO STAR IN IT? SOMEONE LIKE RYAN REYNOLDS!
YEAH, RYAN REYNOLDS! HE'S MUCH BETTER THAN THAT DONALD DRYANS GUY.
PUT IN A LITTLE GRATUITOUS NUDITY, MAKE SURE HE SAVES THE CAT, BUT MOST OF ALL--MAKE IT FUN!
I'VE HEARD ALL YOUR NOTES, AND I THINK I GOT A GREAT IDEA!!!

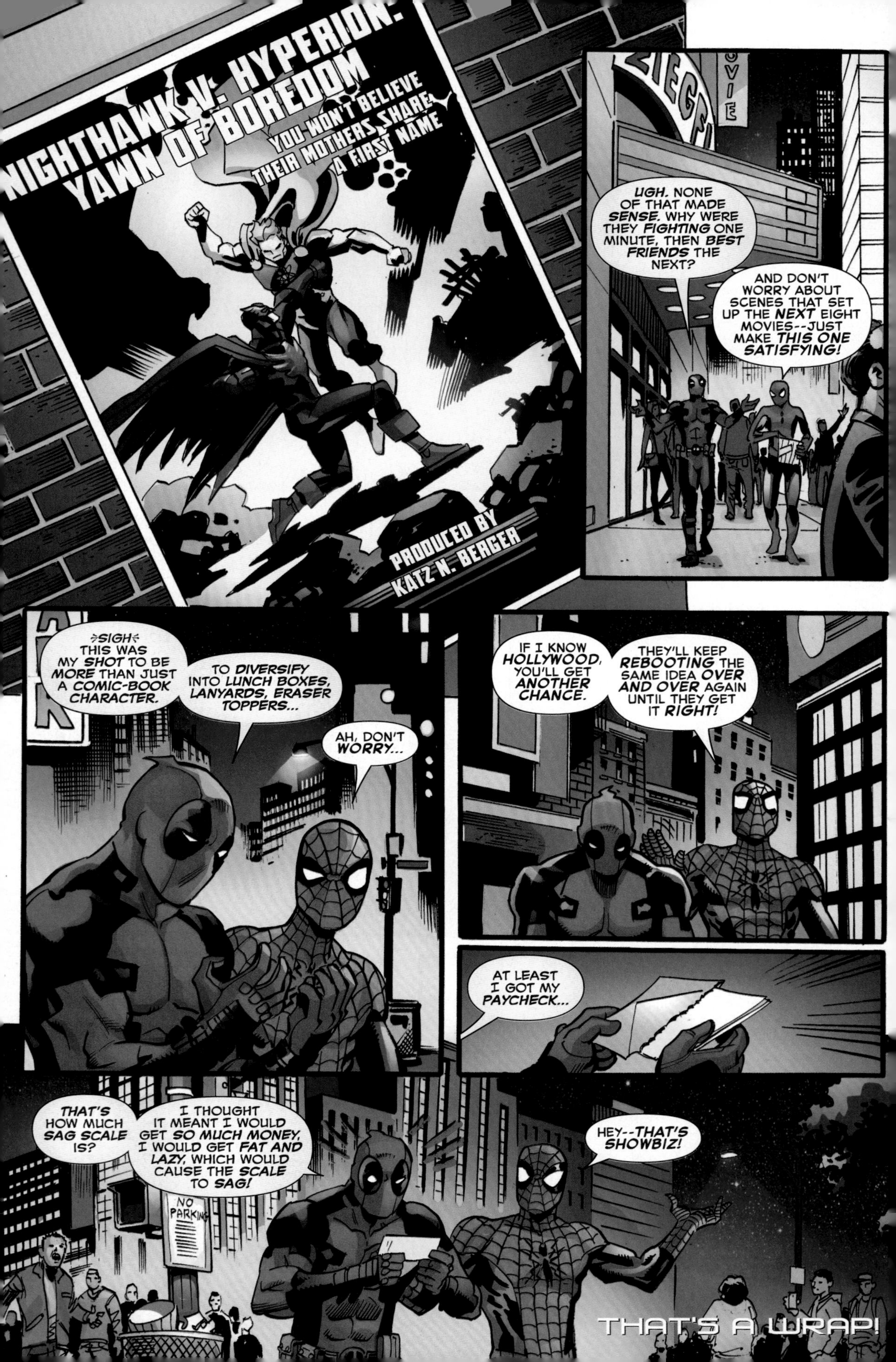
NIGHTHAWK V. HYPERION: YAWN OF BOREDOM
YOU WON'T BELIEVE THEIR MOTHERS SHARE A FIRST NAME
PRODUCED BY KATZ N. BERGER
ZIEGF
MOVIE
UGH. NONE OF THAT MADE SENSE. WHY WERE THEY FIGHTING ONE MINUTE, THEN BEST FRIENDS THE NEXT?
AND DON'T WORRY ABOUT SCENES THAT SET UP THE NEXT EIGHT MOVIES--JUST MAKE THIS ONE SATISFYING!
SIGH THIS WAS MY SHOT TO BE MORE THAN JUST A COMIC-BOOK CHARACTER.
TO DIVERSIFY INTO LUNCH BOXES, LANYARDS, ERASER TOPPERS...
AH, DON'T WORRY...
IF I KNOW HOLLYWOOD, YOU'LL GET ANOTHER CHANCE.
THEY'LL KEEP REBOOTING THE SAME IDEA OVER AND OVER AGAIN UNTIL THEY GET IT RIGHT!
AT LEAST I GOT MY PAYCHECK...
THAT'S HOW MUCH SAG SCALE IS?
I THOUGHT IT MEANT I WOULD GET SO MUCH MONEY, I WOULD GET FAT AND LAZY, WHICH WOULD CAUSE THE SCALE TO SAG!
HEY--THAT'S SHOWBIZ!
NO PARKING
THAT'S A WRAP!

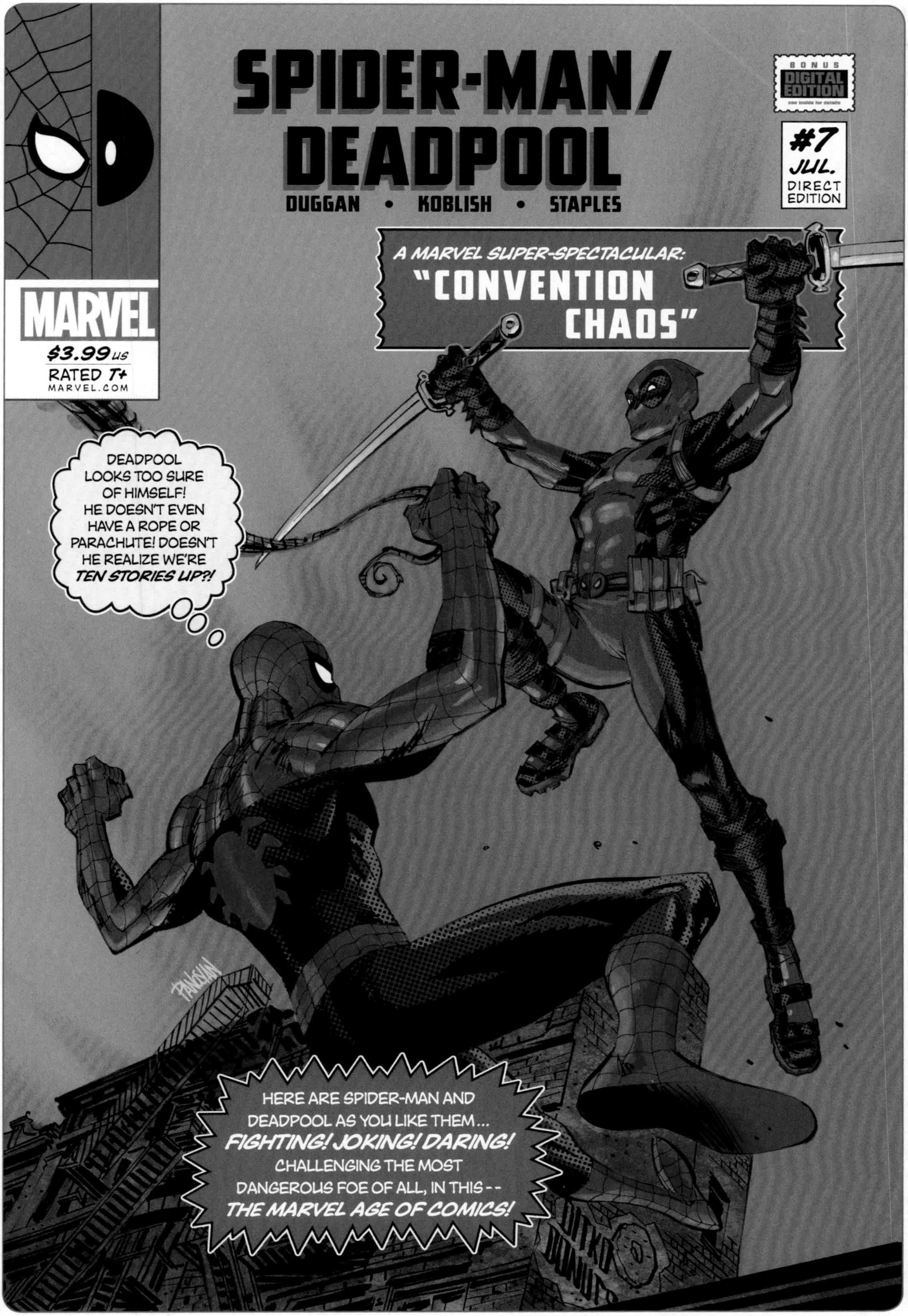
SPIDER-MAN/
DEADPOOL
DUGGAN • KOBLISH • STAPLES
BONUS
DIGITAL EDITION
#7
JUL.
DIRECT EDITION
A MARVEL SUPER-SPECTACULAR:
"CONVENTION CHAOS"
MARVEL
$3.99 US
RATED T+
MARVEL.COM
DEADPOOL LOOKS TOO SURE OF HIMSELF! HE DOESN'T EVEN HAVE A ROPE OR PARACHUTE! DOESN'T HE REALIZE WE'RE TEN STORIES UP?!
HERE ARE SPIDER-MAN AND DEADPOOL AS YOU LIKE THEM... FIGHTING! JOKING! DARING! CHALLENGING THE MOST DANGEROUS FOE OF ALL, IN THIS -- THE MARVEL AGE OF COMICS!

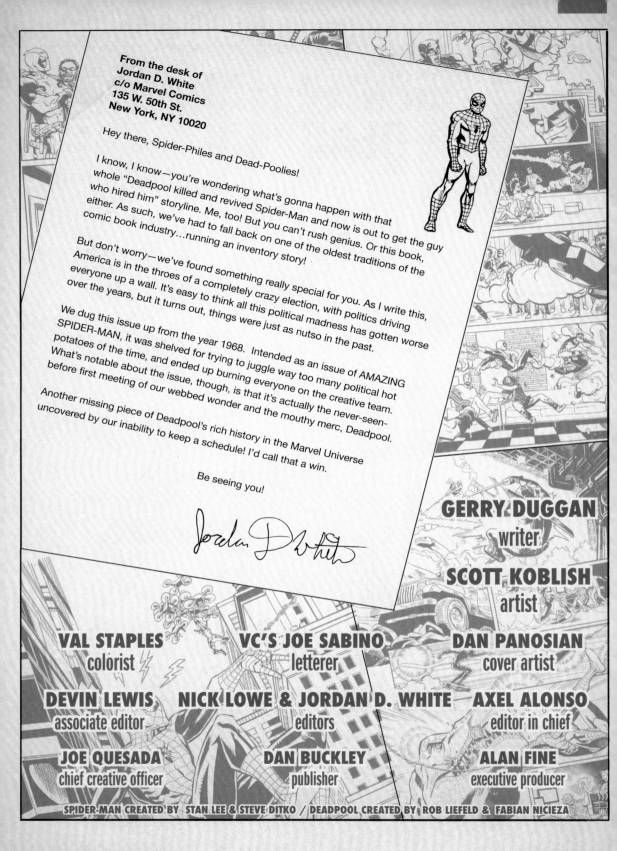

From the desk of
Jordan D. White
c/o Marvel Comics
135 W. 50th St.
New York, NY 10020

Hey there, Spider-Philes and Dead-Poolies!

I know, I know—you're wondering what's gonna happen with that whole "Deadpool killed and revived Spider-Man and now is out to get the guy who hired him" storyline. Me, too! But you can't rush genius. Or this book, either. As such, we've had to fall back on one of the oldest traditions of the comic book industry…running an inventory story!

But don't worry—we've found something really special for you. As I write this, America is in the throes of a completely crazy election, with politics driving everyone up a wall. It's easy to think all this political madness has gotten worse over the years, but it turns out, things were just as nutso in the past.

We dug this issue up from the year 1968. Intended as an issue of AMAZING SPIDER-MAN, it was shelved for trying to juggle way too many political hot potatoes of the time, and ended up burning everyone on the creative team. What's notable about the issue, though, is that it's actually the never-seen-before first meeting of our webbed wonder and the mouthy merc, Deadpool.

Another missing piece of Deadpool's rich history in the Marvel Universe uncovered by our inability to keep a schedule! I'd call that a win.

Be seeing you!

Jordan D. White

GERRY DUGGAN
writer

SCOTT KOBLISH
artist

VAL STAPLES
colorist

VC'S JOE SABINO
letterer

DAN PANOSIAN
cover artist

DEVIN LEWIS
associate editor

NICK LOWE & JORDAN D. WHITE
editors

AXEL ALONSO
editor in chief

JOE QUESADA
chief creative officer

DAN BUCKLEY
publisher

ALAN FINE
executive producer

SPIDER-MAN CREATED BY STAN LEE & STEVE DITKO / DEADPOOL CREATED BY ROB LIEFELD & FABIAN NICIEZA

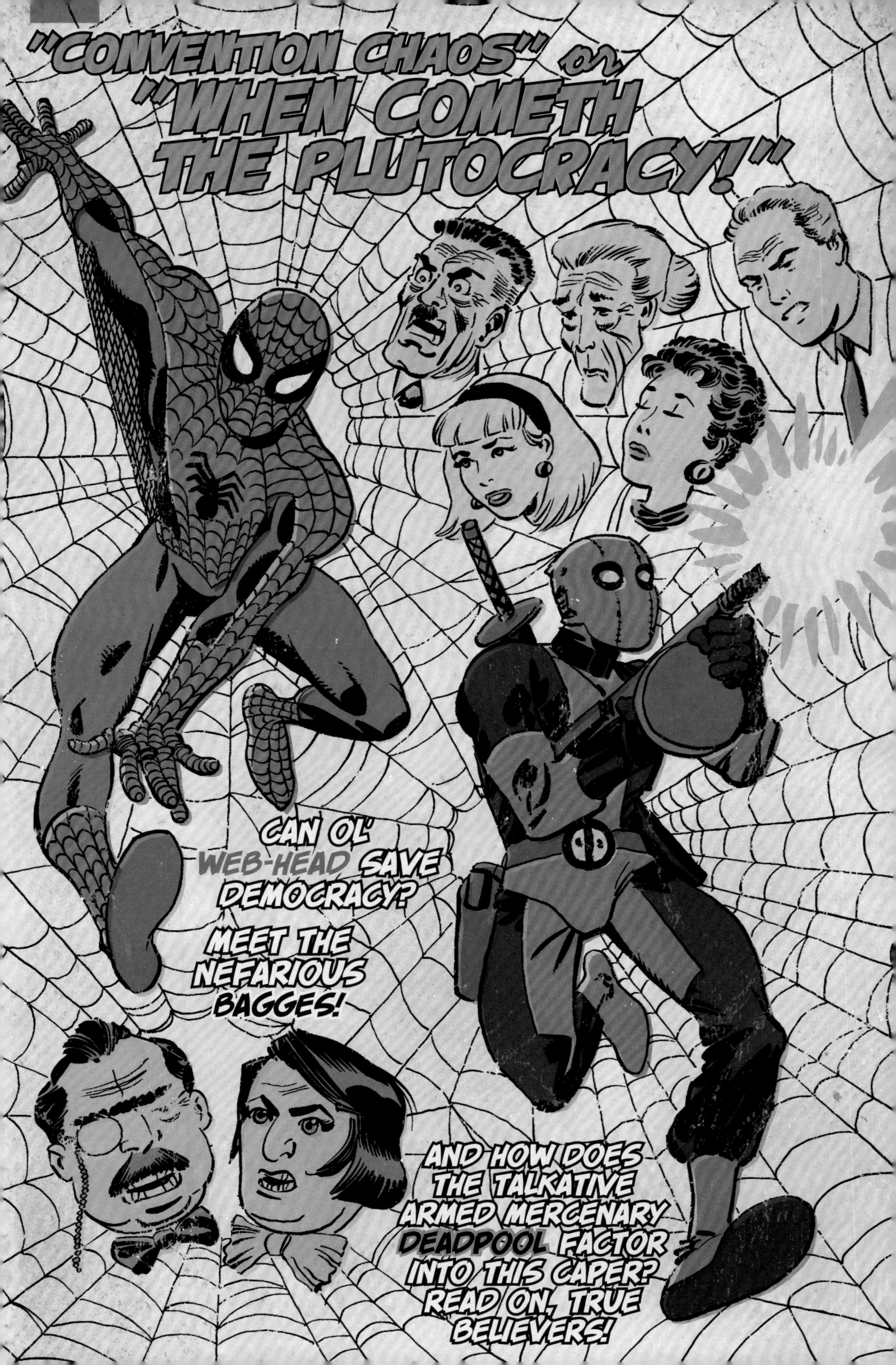
"CONVENTION CHAOS" or "WHEN COMETH THE PLUTOCRACY!"
CAN OL' WEB-HEAD SAVE DEMOCRACY?
MEET THE NEFARIOUS BAGGES!
AND HOW DOES THE TALKATIVE ARMED MERCENARY DEADPOOL FACTOR INTO THIS CAPER? READ ON, TRUE BELIEVERS!

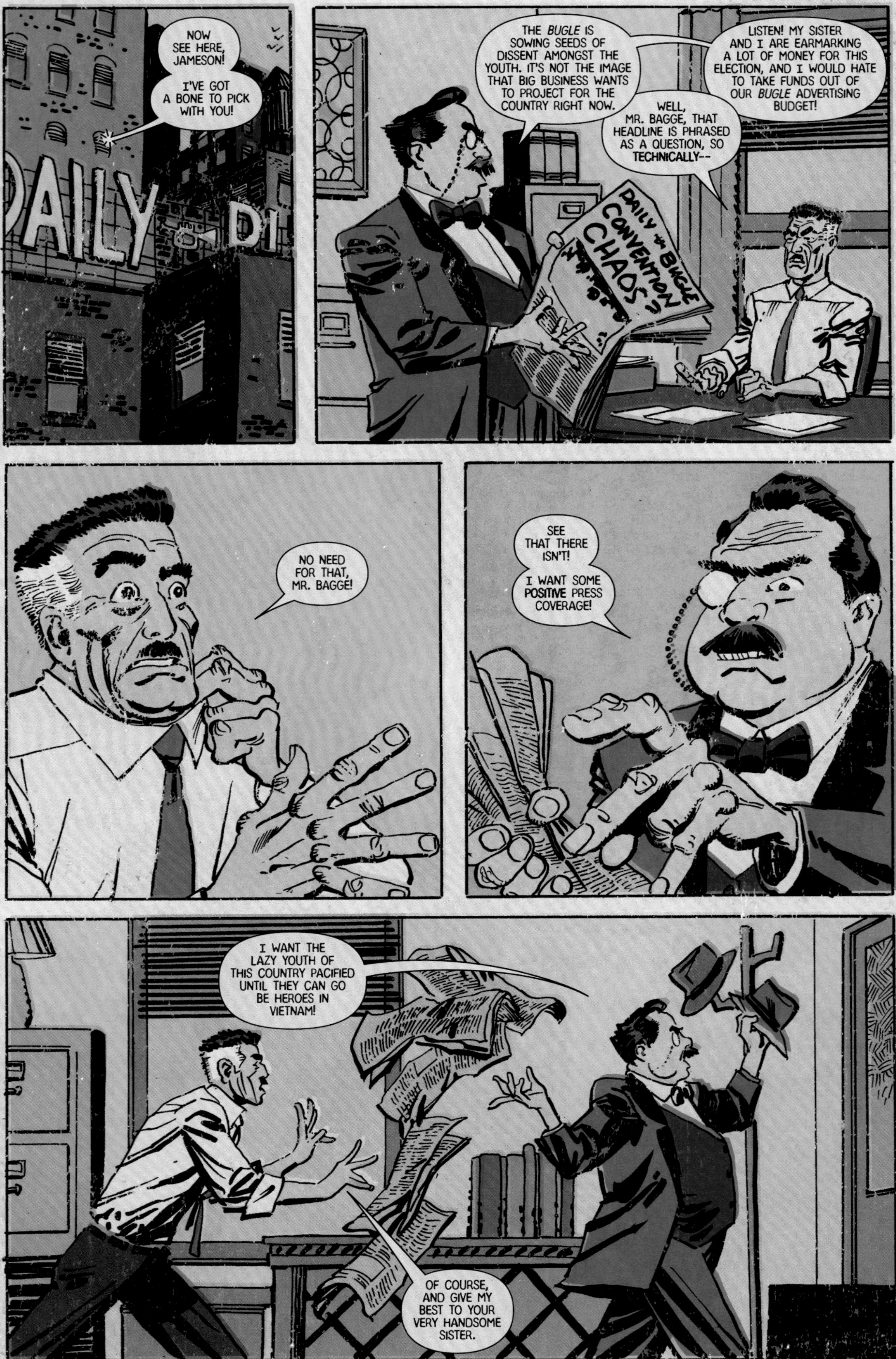
NOW SEE HERE, JAMESON!
I'VE GOT A BONE TO PICK WITH YOU!
DAILY BUGLE
THE BUGLE IS SOWING SEEDS OF DISSENT AMONGST THE YOUTH. IT'S NOT THE IMAGE THAT BIG BUSINESS WANTS TO PROJECT FOR THE COUNTRY RIGHT NOW.
DAILY BUGLE CONVENTION CHAOS?
WELL, MR. BAGGE, THAT HEADLINE IS PHRASED AS A QUESTION, SO TECHNICALLY--
LISTEN! MY SISTER AND I ARE EARMARKING A LOT OF MONEY FOR THIS ELECTION, AND I WOULD HATE TO TAKE FUNDS OUT OF OUR BUGLE ADVERTISING BUDGET!
NO NEED FOR THAT, MR. BAGGE!
SEE THAT THERE ISN'T!
I WANT SOME POSITIVE PRESS COVERAGE!
I WANT THE LAZY YOUTH OF THIS COUNTRY PACIFIED UNTIL THEY CAN GO BE HEROES IN VIETNAM!
OF COURSE, AND GIVE MY BEST TO YOUR VERY HANDSOME SISTER.

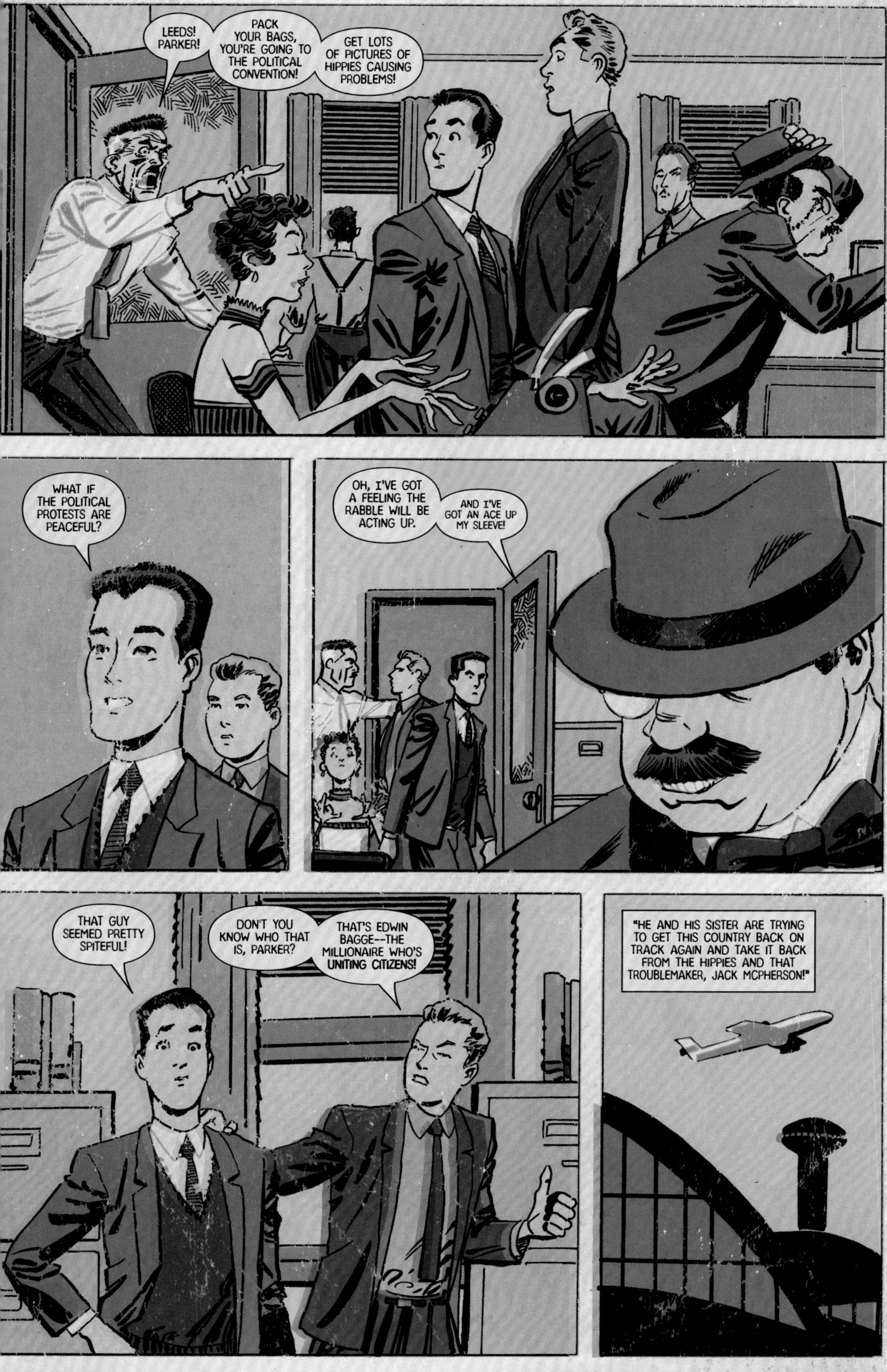
LEEDS! PARKER!
PACK YOUR BAGS, YOU'RE GOING TO THE POLITICAL CONVENTION!
GET LOTS OF PICTURES OF HIPPIES CAUSING PROBLEMS!
WHAT IF THE POLITICAL PROTESTS ARE PEACEFUL?
OH, I'VE GOT A FEELING THE RABBLE WILL BE ACTING UP.
AND I'VE GOT AN ACE UP MY SLEEVE!
THAT GUY SEEMED PRETTY SPITEFUL!
DON'T YOU KNOW WHO THAT IS, PARKER?
THAT'S EDWIN BAGGE--THE MILLIONAIRE WHO'S UNITING CITIZENS!
"HE AND HIS SISTER ARE TRYING TO GET THIS COUNTRY BACK ON TRACK AGAIN AND TAKE IT BACK FROM THE HIPPIES AND THAT TROUBLEMAKER, JACK MCPHERSON!"

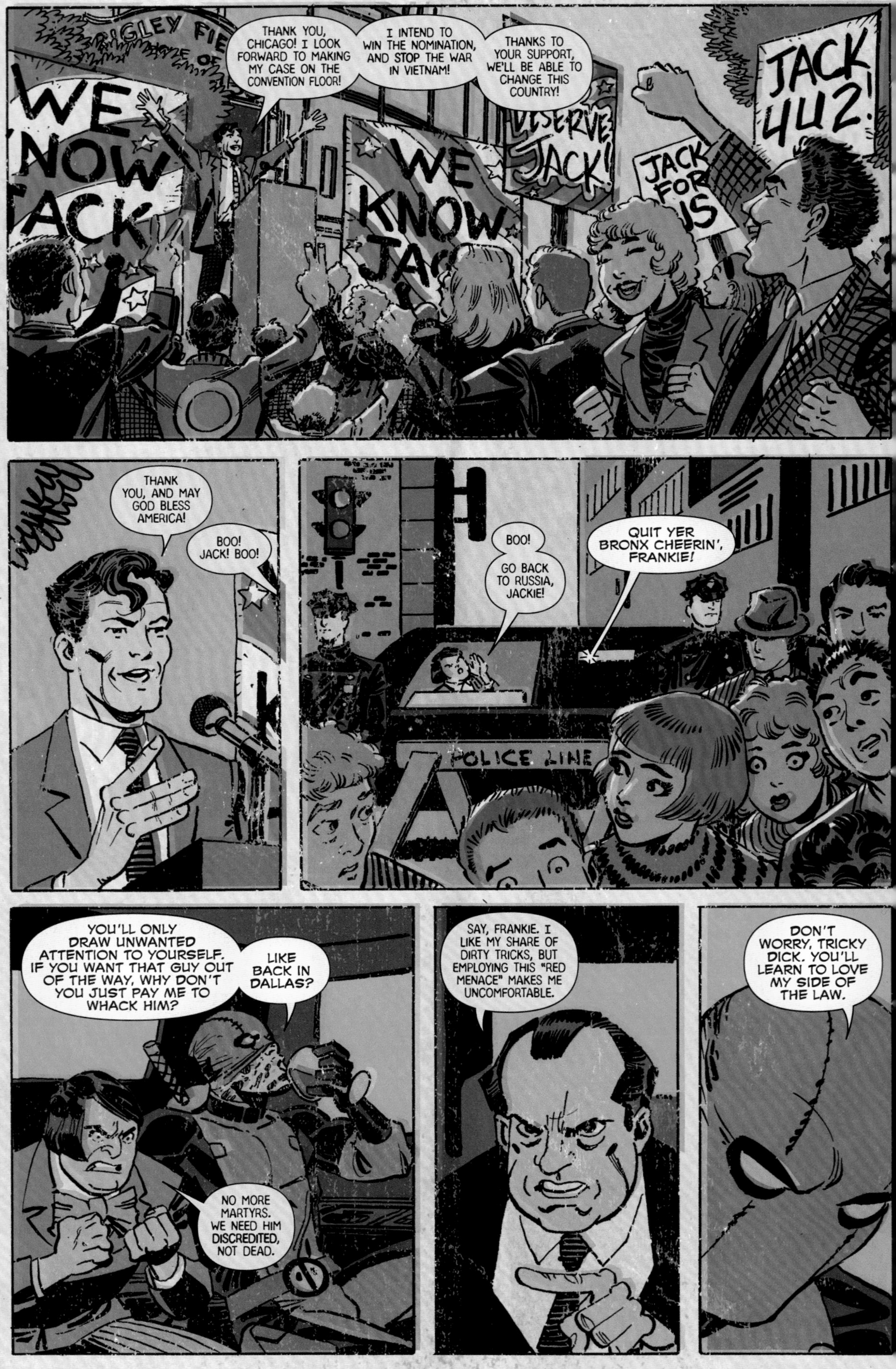
WRIGLEY FIE
HOME OF
WE KNOW JACK
THANK YOU, CHICAGO! I LOOK FORWARD TO MAKING MY CASE ON THE CONVENTION FLOOR!
I INTEND TO WIN THE NOMINATION, AND STOP THE WAR IN VIETNAM!
THANKS TO YOUR SUPPORT, WE'LL BE ABLE TO CHANGE THIS COUNTRY!
DESERVE JACK!
WE KNOW JAC
JACK FOR US
JACK 4 U2!
THANK YOU, AND MAY GOD BLESS AMERICA!
BOO! JACK! BOO!
BOO!
GO BACK TO RUSSIA, JACKIE!
QUIT YER BRONX CHEERIN', FRANKIE!
POLICE LINE
YOU'LL ONLY DRAW UNWANTED ATTENTION TO YOURSELF. IF YOU WANT THAT GUY OUT OF THE WAY, WHY DON'T YOU JUST PAY ME TO WHACK HIM?
LIKE BACK IN DALLAS?
NO MORE MARTYRS. WE NEED HIM DISCREDITED, NOT DEAD.
SAY, FRANKIE. I LIKE MY SHARE OF DIRTY TRICKS, BUT EMPLOYING THIS "RED MENACE" MAKES ME UNCOMFORTABLE.
DON'T WORRY, TRICKY DICK. YOU'LL LEARN TO LOVE MY SIDE OF THE LAW.

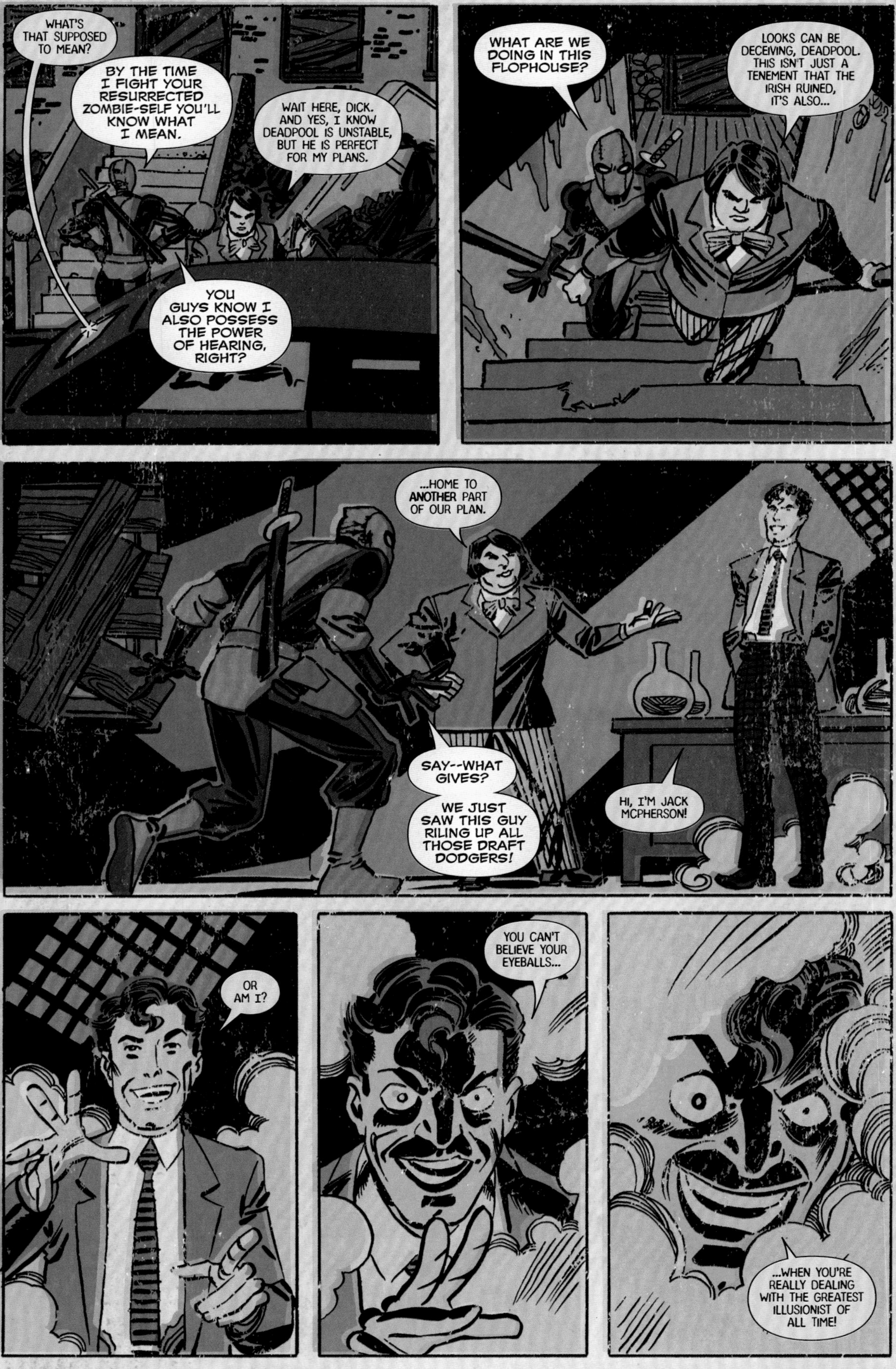
WHAT'S THAT SUPPOSED TO MEAN?
BY THE TIME I FIGHT YOUR RESURRECTED ZOMBIE-SELF YOU'LL KNOW WHAT I MEAN.
WAIT HERE, DICK. AND YES, I KNOW DEADPOOL IS UNSTABLE, BUT HE IS PERFECT FOR MY PLANS.
YOU GUYS KNOW I ALSO POSSESS THE POWER OF HEARING, RIGHT?
WHAT ARE WE DOING IN THIS FLOPHOUSE?
LOOKS CAN BE DECEIVING, DEADPOOL. THIS ISN'T JUST A TENEMENT THAT THE IRISH RUINED, IT'S ALSO...
...HOME TO ANOTHER PART OF OUR PLAN.
SAY--WHAT GIVES?
WE JUST SAW THIS GUY RILING UP ALL THOSE DRAFT DODGERS!
HI, I'M JACK MCPHERSON!
OR AM I?
YOU CAN'T BELIEVE YOUR EYEBALLS...
...WHEN YOU'RE REALLY DEALING WITH THE GREATEST ILLUSIONIST OF ALL TIME!

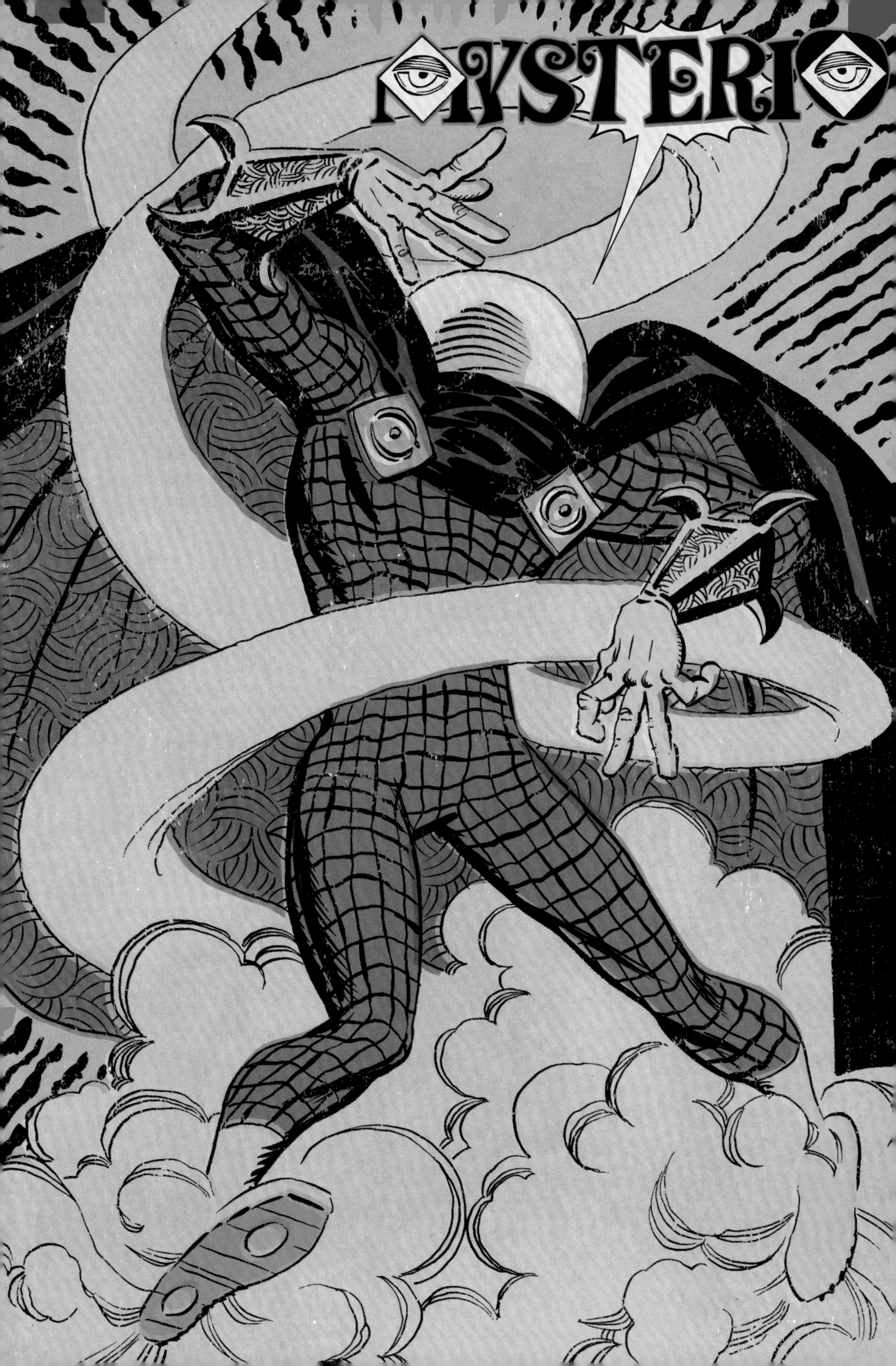
MYSTERIO

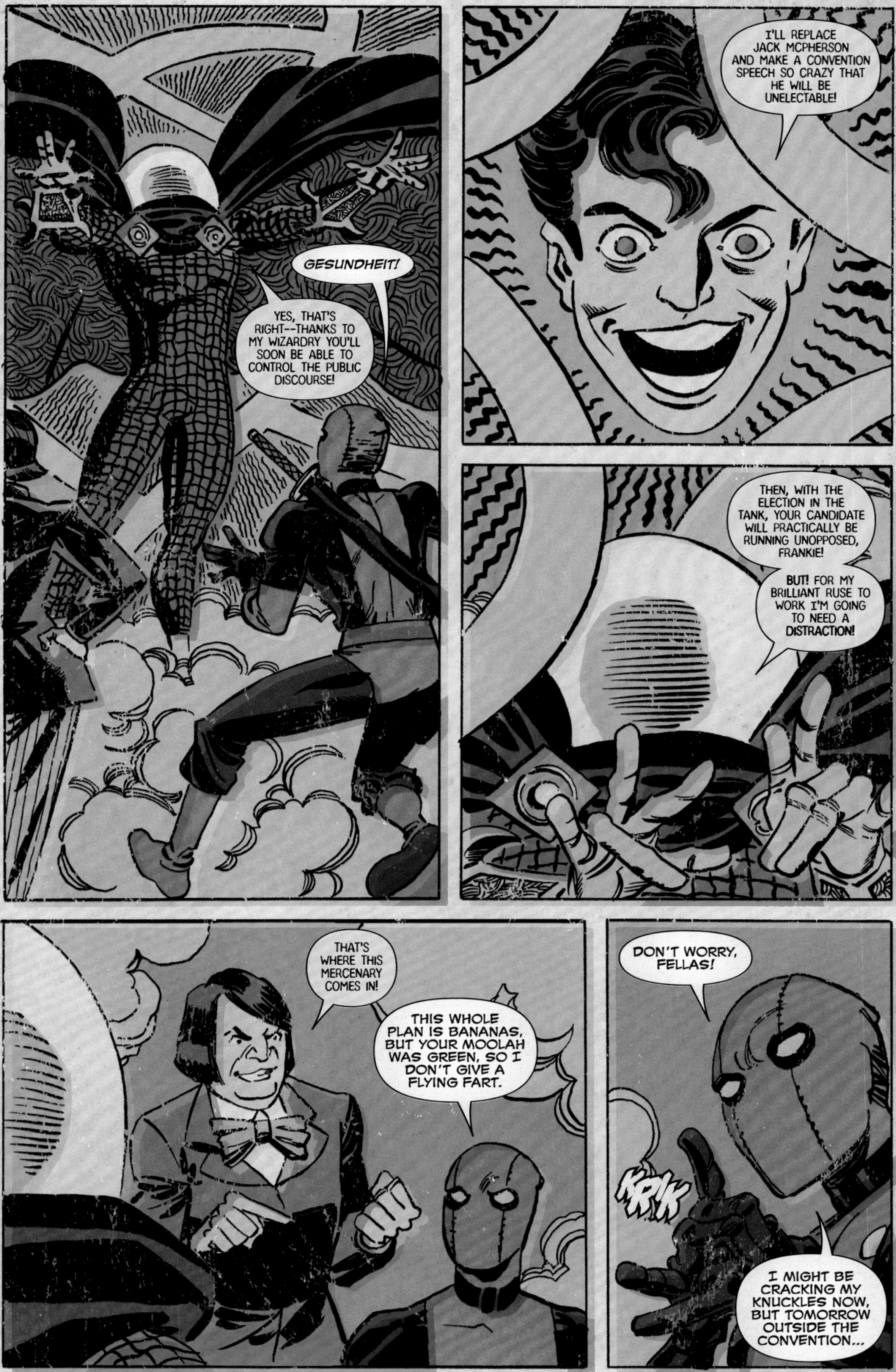
GESUNDHEIT!
YES, THAT'S RIGHT--THANKS TO MY WIZARDRY YOU'LL SOON BE ABLE TO CONTROL THE PUBLIC DISCOURSE!
I'LL REPLACE JACK MCPHERSON AND MAKE A CONVENTION SPEECH SO CRAZY THAT HE WILL BE UNELECTABLE!
THEN, WITH THE ELECTION IN THE TANK, YOUR CANDIDATE WILL PRACTICALLY BE RUNNING UNOPPOSED, FRANKIE!
BUT! FOR MY BRILLIANT RUSE TO WORK I'M GOING TO NEED A DISTRACTION!
THAT'S WHERE THIS MERCENARY COMES IN!
THIS WHOLE PLAN IS BANANAS, BUT YOUR MOOLAH WAS GREEN, SO I DON'T GIVE A FLYING FART.
DON'T WORRY, FELLAS!
KRIK
I MIGHT BE CRACKING MY KNUCKLES NOW, BUT TOMORROW OUTSIDE THE CONVENTION...

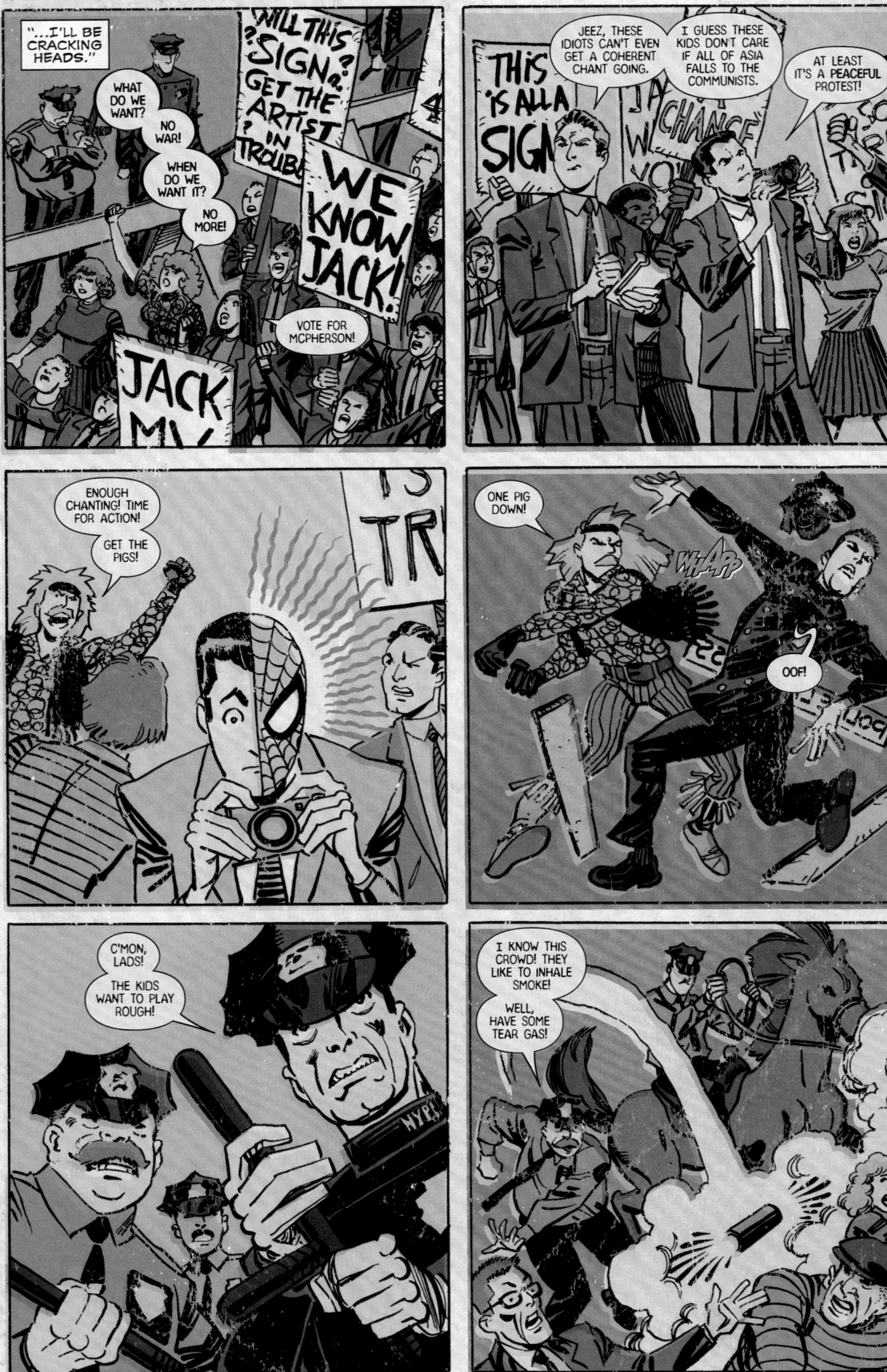
"...I'LL BE CRACKING HEADS."
WHAT DO WE WANT?
NO WAR!
WHEN DO WE WANT IT?
NO MORE!
?WILL THIS SIGN?? GET THE ARTIST IN TROUB
WE KNOW JACK!
JACK
VOTE FOR MCPHERSON!
JEEZ, THESE IDIOTS CAN'T EVEN GET A COHERENT CHANT GOING.
I GUESS THESE KIDS DON'T CARE IF ALL OF ASIA FALLS TO THE COMMUNISTS.
AT LEAST IT'S A PEACEFUL PROTEST!
THIS IS ALL A SIG
CHANCE
ENOUGH CHANTING! TIME FOR ACTION!
GET THE PIGS!
ONE PIG DOWN!
WHAPP
OOF!
C'MON, LADS!
THE KIDS WANT TO PLAY ROUGH!
NYPD
I KNOW THIS CROWD! THEY LIKE TO INHALE SMOKE!
WELL, HAVE SOME TEAR GAS!

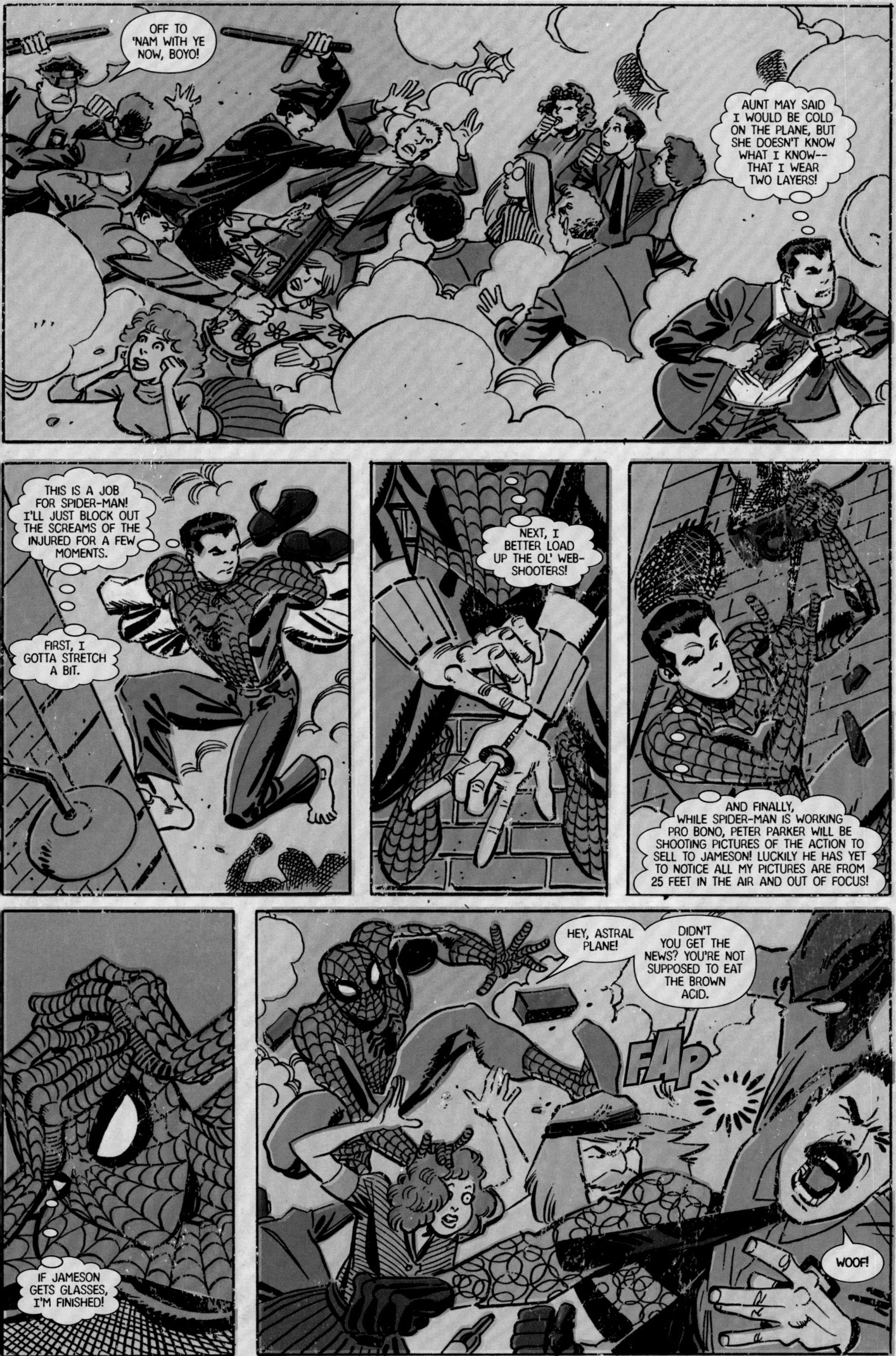
OFF TO 'NAM WITH YE NOW, BOYO!
AUNT MAY SAID I WOULD BE COLD ON THE PLANE, BUT SHE DOESN'T KNOW WHAT I KNOW-- THAT I WEAR TWO LAYERS!
THIS IS A JOB FOR SPIDER-MAN! I'LL JUST BLOCK OUT THE SCREAMS OF THE INJURED FOR A FEW MOMENTS.
FIRST, I GOTTA STRETCH A BIT.
NEXT, I BETTER LOAD UP THE OL' WEB-SHOOTERS!
AND FINALLY, WHILE SPIDER-MAN IS WORKING PRO BONO, PETER PARKER WILL BE SHOOTING PICTURES OF THE ACTION TO SELL TO JAMESON! LUCKILY HE HAS YET TO NOTICE ALL MY PICTURES ARE FROM 25 FEET IN THE AIR AND OUT OF FOCUS!
IF JAMESON GETS GLASSES, I'M FINISHED!
HEY, ASTRAL PLANE!
DIDN'T YOU GET THE NEWS? YOU'RE NOT SUPPOSED TO EAT THE BROWN ACID.
FAP
WOOF!

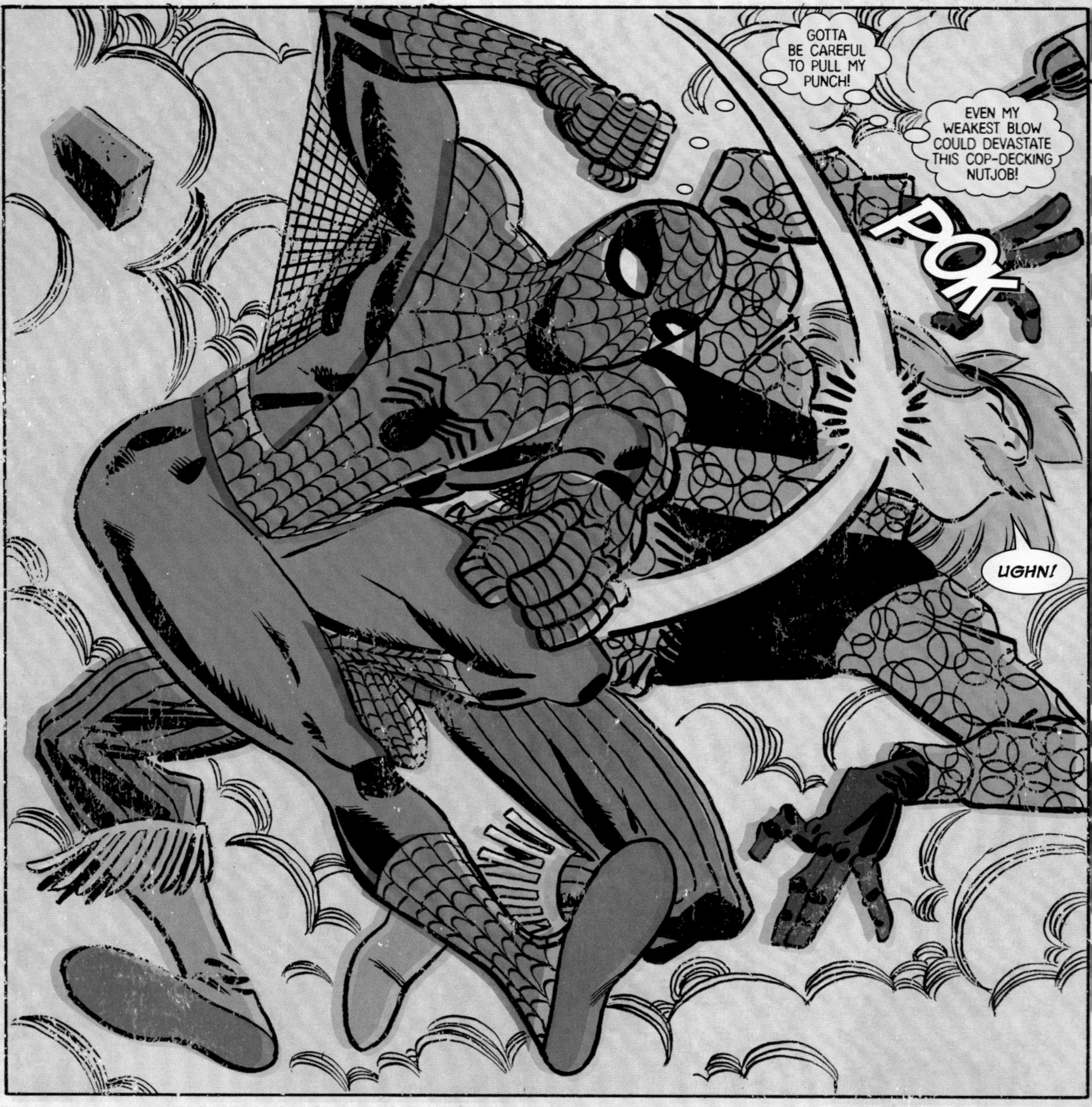
GOTTA BE CAREFUL TO PULL MY PUNCH!
EVEN MY WEAKEST BLOW COULD DEVASTATE THIS COP-DECKING NUTJOB!
POK
UGHN!

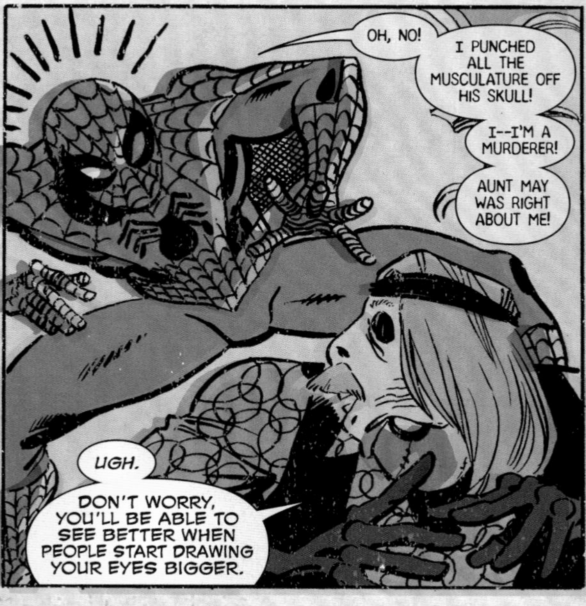
OH, NO!
I PUNCHED ALL THE MUSCULATURE OFF HIS SKULL!
I--I'M A MURDERER!
AUNT MAY WAS RIGHT ABOUT ME!
UGH.
DON'T WORRY, YOU'LL BE ABLE TO SEE BETTER WHEN PEOPLE START DRAWING YOUR EYES BIGGER.

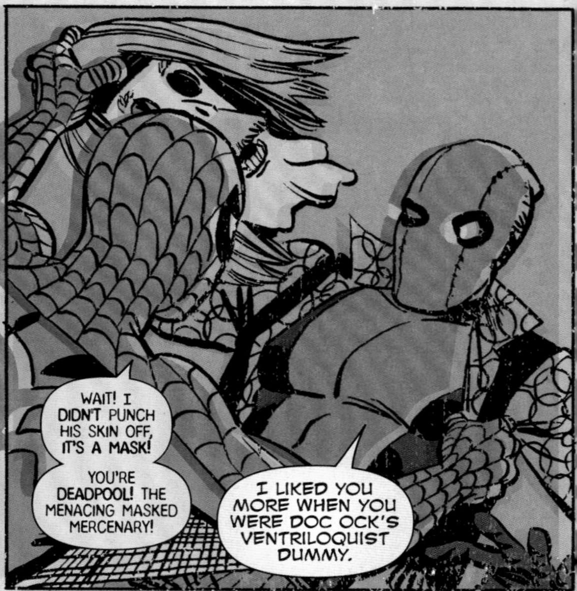
WAIT! I DIDN'T PUNCH HIS SKIN OFF, IT'S A MASK!
YOU'RE DEADPOOL! THE MENACING MASKED MERCENARY!
I LIKED YOU MORE WHEN YOU WERE DOC OCK'S VENTRILOQUIST DUMMY.

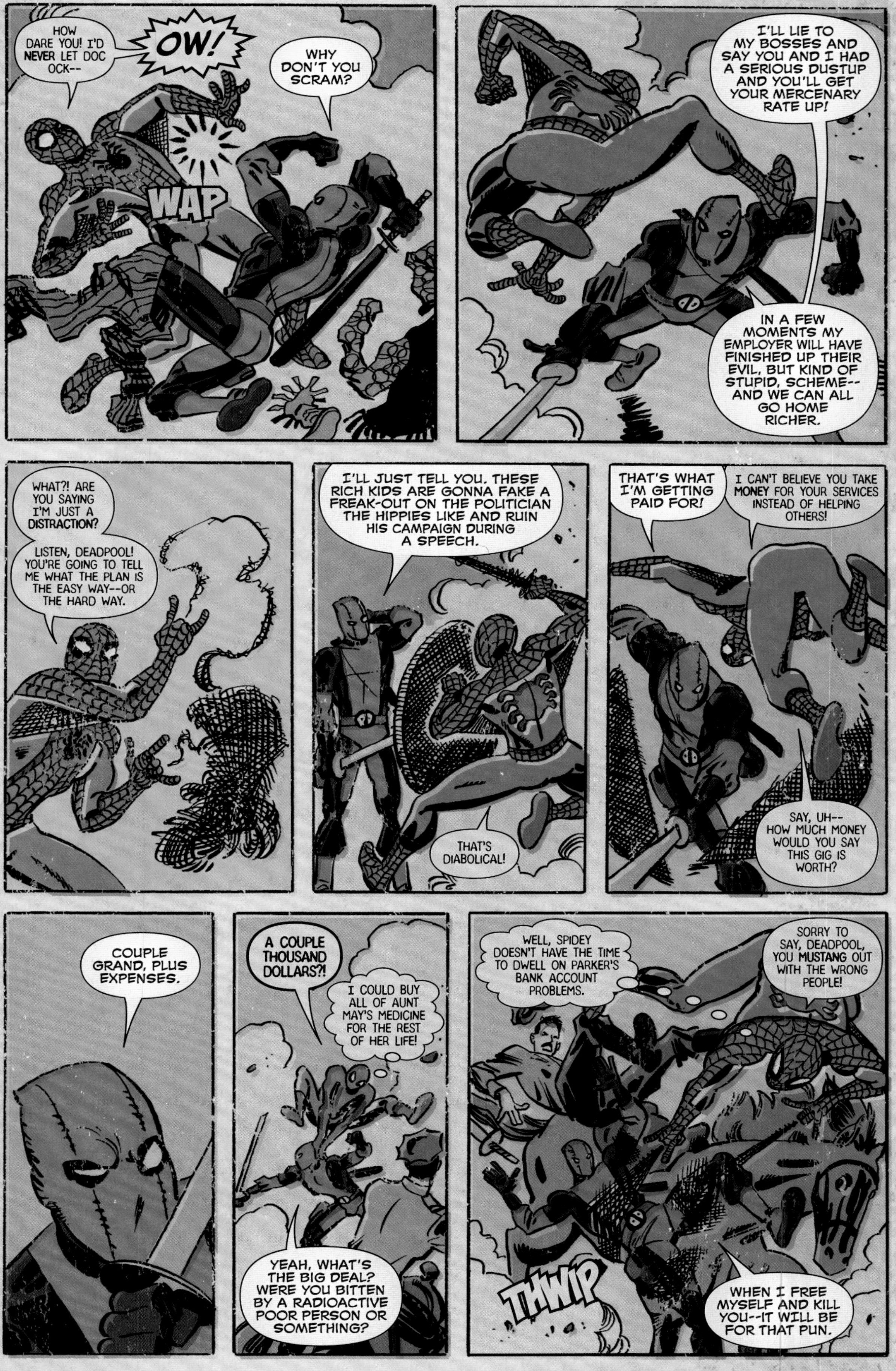
HOW DARE YOU! I'D NEVER LET DOC OCK--
OW!
WHY DON'T YOU SCRAM?
WAP
I'LL LIE TO MY BOSSES AND SAY YOU AND I HAD A SERIOUS DUSTUP AND YOU'LL GET YOUR MERCENARY RATE UP!
IN A FEW MOMENTS MY EMPLOYER WILL HAVE FINISHED UP THEIR EVIL, BUT KIND OF STUPID, SCHEME-- AND WE CAN ALL GO HOME RICHER.
WHAT?! ARE YOU SAYING I'M JUST A DISTRACTION?
LISTEN, DEADPOOL! YOU'RE GOING TO TELL ME WHAT THE PLAN IS THE EASY WAY--OR THE HARD WAY.
I'LL JUST TELL YOU. THESE RICH KIDS ARE GONNA FAKE A FREAK-OUT ON THE POLITICIAN THE HIPPIES LIKE AND RUIN HIS CAMPAIGN DURING A SPEECH.
THAT'S DIABOLICAL!
THAT'S WHAT I'M GETTING PAID FOR!
I CAN'T BELIEVE YOU TAKE MONEY FOR YOUR SERVICES INSTEAD OF HELPING OTHERS!
SAY, UH-- HOW MUCH MONEY WOULD YOU SAY THIS GIG IS WORTH?
COUPLE GRAND, PLUS EXPENSES.
A COUPLE THOUSAND DOLLARS?!
I COULD BUY ALL OF AUNT MAY'S MEDICINE FOR THE REST OF HER LIFE!
YEAH, WHAT'S THE BIG DEAL? WERE YOU BITTEN BY A RADIOACTIVE POOR PERSON OR SOMETHING?
WELL, SPIDEY DOESN'T HAVE THE TIME TO DWELL ON PARKER'S BANK ACCOUNT PROBLEMS.
SORRY TO SAY, DEADPOOL, YOU MUSTANG OUT WITH THE WRONG PEOPLE!
THWIP
WHEN I FREE MYSELF AND KILL YOU--IT WILL BE FOR THAT PUN.

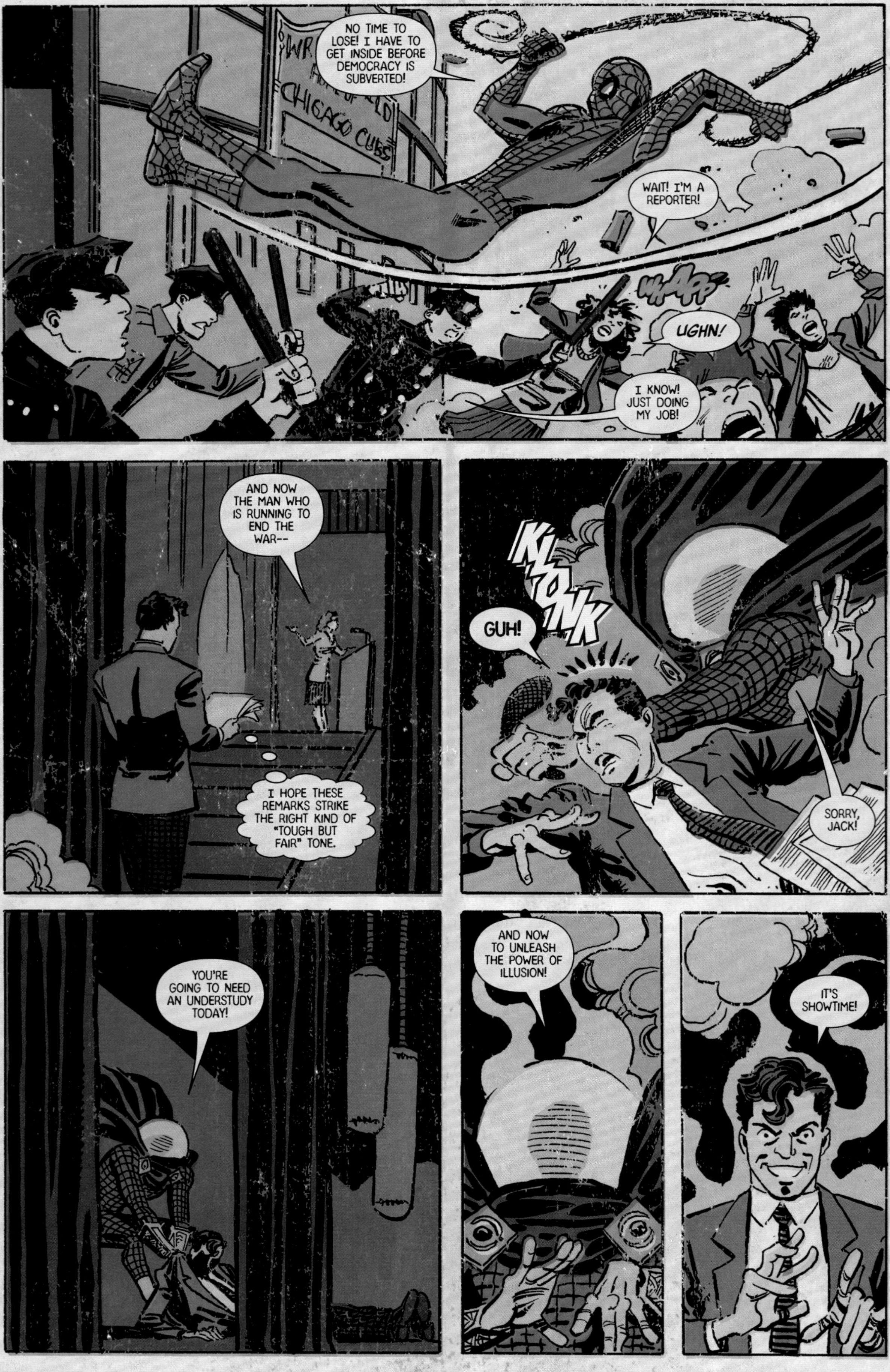
WR
CHICAGO CUBS
NO TIME TO LOSE! I HAVE TO GET INSIDE BEFORE DEMOCRACY IS SUBVERTED!
WAIT! I'M A REPORTER!
WHAPP
UGHN!
I KNOW! JUST DOING MY JOB!
AND NOW THE MAN WHO IS RUNNING TO END THE WAR--
I HOPE THESE REMARKS STRIKE THE RIGHT KIND OF "TOUGH BUT FAIR" TONE.
KLONK
GUH!
SORRY, JACK!
YOU'RE GOING TO NEED AN UNDERSTUDY TODAY!
AND NOW TO UNLEASH THE POWER OF ILLUSION!
IT'S SHOWTIME!

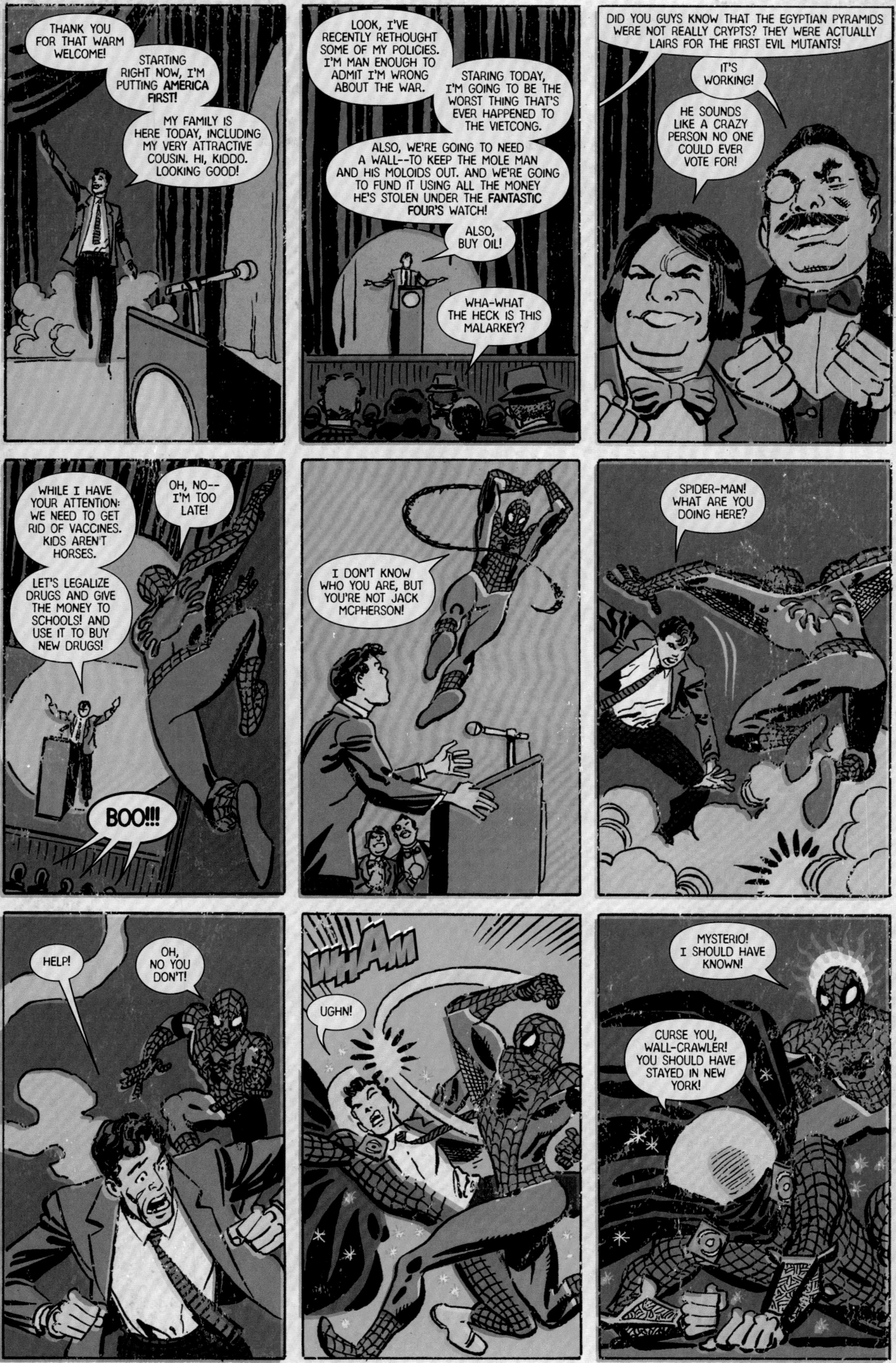
THANK YOU FOR THAT WARM WELCOME!
STARTING RIGHT NOW, I'M PUTTING **AMERICA FIRST!**
MY FAMILY IS HERE TODAY, INCLUDING MY VERY ATTRACTIVE COUSIN. HI, KIDDO. LOOKING GOOD!
LOOK, I'VE RECENTLY RETHOUGHT SOME OF MY POLICIES. I'M MAN ENOUGH TO ADMIT I'M WRONG ABOUT THE WAR.
STARING TODAY, I'M GOING TO BE THE WORST THING THAT'S EVER HAPPENED TO THE VIETCONG.
ALSO, WE'RE GOING TO NEED A WALL--TO KEEP THE MOLE MAN AND HIS MOLOIDS OUT. AND WE'RE GOING TO FUND IT USING ALL THE MONEY HE'S STOLEN UNDER THE **FANTASTIC FOUR'S** WATCH!
ALSO, BUY OIL!
WHA-WHAT THE HECK IS THIS MALARKEY?
DID YOU GUYS KNOW THAT THE EGYPTIAN PYRAMIDS WERE NOT REALLY CRYPTS? THEY WERE ACTUALLY LAIRS FOR THE FIRST EVIL MUTANTS!
IT'S WORKING!
HE SOUNDS LIKE A CRAZY PERSON NO ONE COULD EVER VOTE FOR!
WHILE I HAVE YOUR ATTENTION: WE NEED TO GET RID OF VACCINES. KIDS AREN'T HORSES.
LET'S LEGALIZE DRUGS AND GIVE THE MONEY TO SCHOOLS! AND USE IT TO BUY NEW DRUGS!
OH, NO-- I'M TOO LATE!
BOO!!!
I DON'T KNOW WHO YOU ARE, BUT YOU'RE NOT JACK MCPHERSON!
SPIDER-MAN! WHAT ARE YOU DOING HERE?
HELP!
OH, NO YOU DON'T!
WHAM
UGHN!
MYSTERIO! I SHOULD HAVE KNOWN!
CURSE YOU, WALL-CRAWLER! YOU SHOULD HAVE STAYED IN NEW YORK!

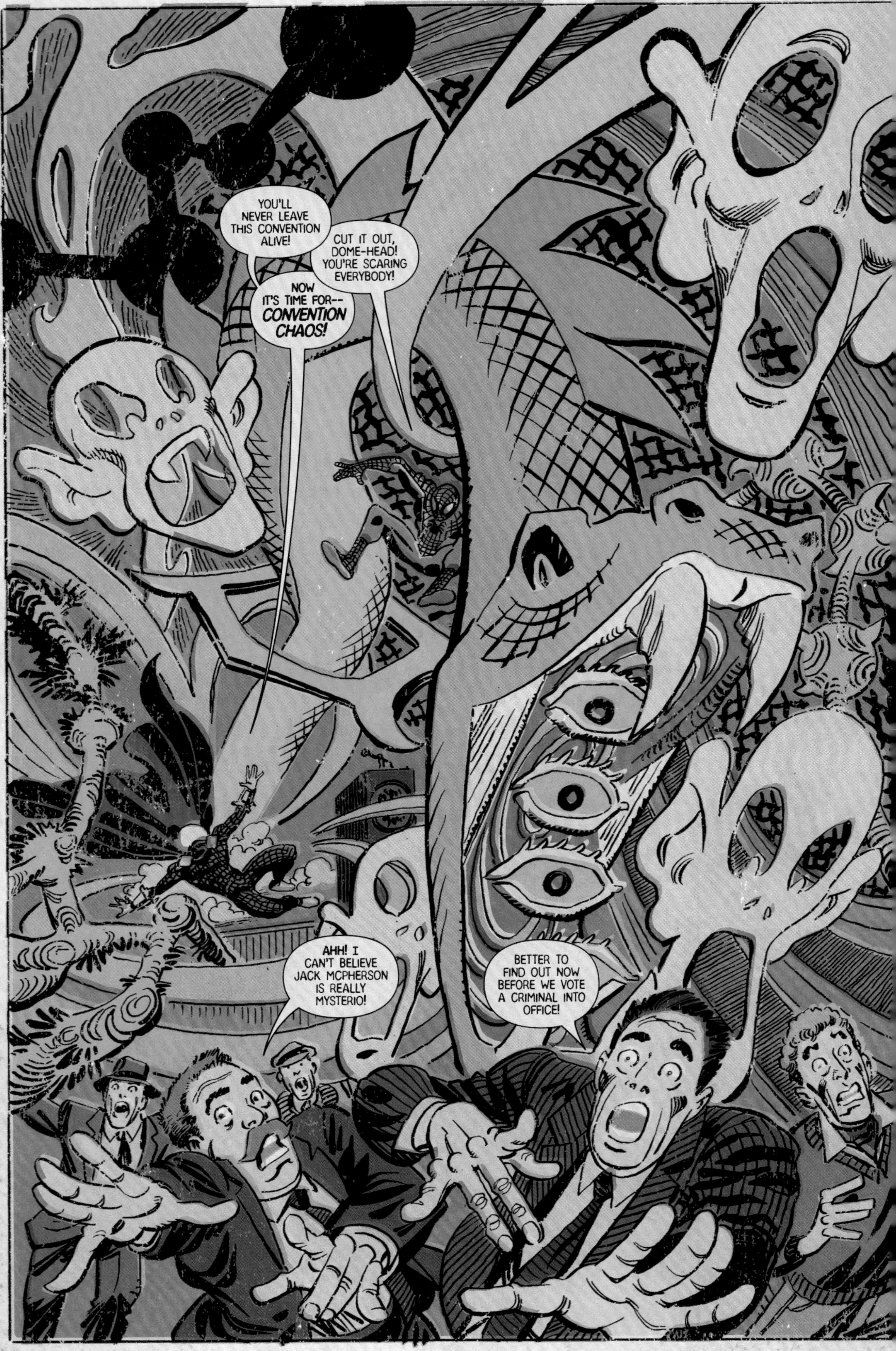
YOU'LL NEVER LEAVE THIS CONVENTION ALIVE!
NOW IT'S TIME FOR-- CONVENTION CHAOS!
CUT IT OUT, DOME-HEAD! YOU'RE SCARING EVERYBODY!
AHH! I CAN'T BELIEVE JACK MCPHERSON IS REALLY MYSTERIO!
BETTER TO FIND OUT NOW BEFORE WE VOTE A CRIMINAL INTO OFFICE!

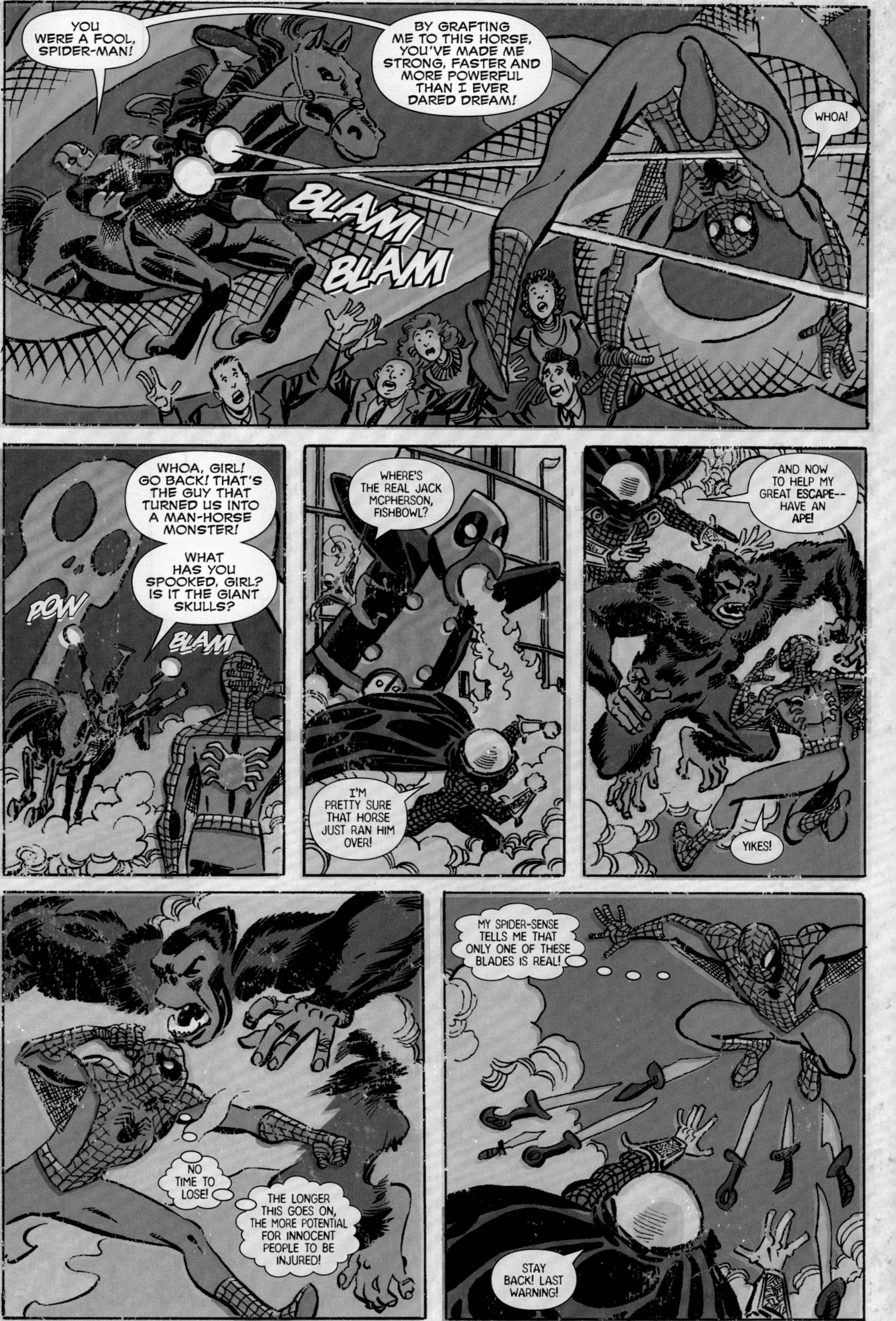
YOU WERE A FOOL, SPIDER-MAN!
BY GRAFTING ME TO THIS HORSE, YOU'VE MADE ME STRONG, FASTER AND MORE POWERFUL THAN I EVER DARED DREAM!
WHOA!
BLAM
BLAM
WHOA, GIRL! GO BACK! THAT'S THE GUY THAT TURNED US INTO A MAN-HORSE MONSTER!
WHAT HAS YOU SPOOKED, GIRL? IS IT THE GIANT SKULLS?
POW
BLAM
WHERE'S THE REAL JACK MCPHERSON, FISHBOWL?
I'M PRETTY SURE THAT HORSE JUST RAN HIM OVER!
AND NOW TO HELP MY GREAT ESCAPE-- HAVE AN APE!
YIKES!
NO TIME TO LOSE!
THE LONGER THIS GOES ON, THE MORE POTENTIAL FOR INNOCENT PEOPLE TO BE INJURED!
MY SPIDER-SENSE TELLS ME THAT ONLY ONE OF THESE BLADES IS REAL!
STAY BACK! LAST WARNING!

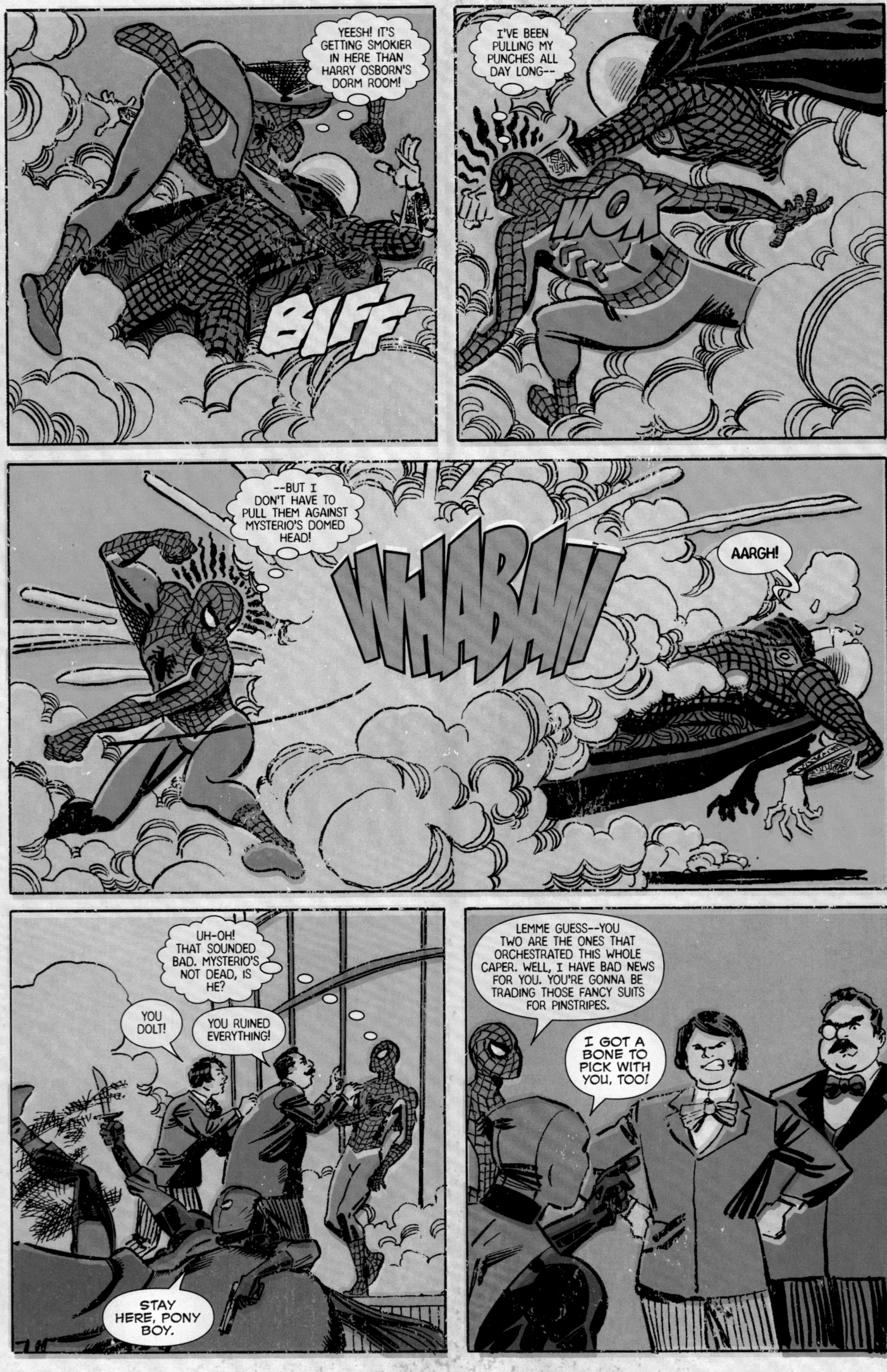
YEESH! IT'S GETTING SMOKIER IN HERE THAN HARRY OSBORN'S DORM ROOM!
BIFF
I'VE BEEN PULLING MY PUNCHES ALL DAY LONG--
WOK
--BUT I DON'T HAVE TO PULL THEM AGAINST MYSTERIO'S DOMED HEAD!
WHABAM
AARGH!
UH-OH! THAT SOUNDED BAD. MYSTERIO'S NOT DEAD, IS HE?
YOU DOLT!
YOU RUINED EVERYTHING!
STAY HERE, PONY BOY.
LEMME GUESS--YOU TWO ARE THE ONES THAT ORCHESTRATED THIS WHOLE CAPER. WELL, I HAVE BAD NEWS FOR YOU. YOU'RE GONNA BE TRADING THOSE FANCY SUITS FOR PINSTRIPES.
I GOT A BONE TO PICK WITH YOU, TOO!

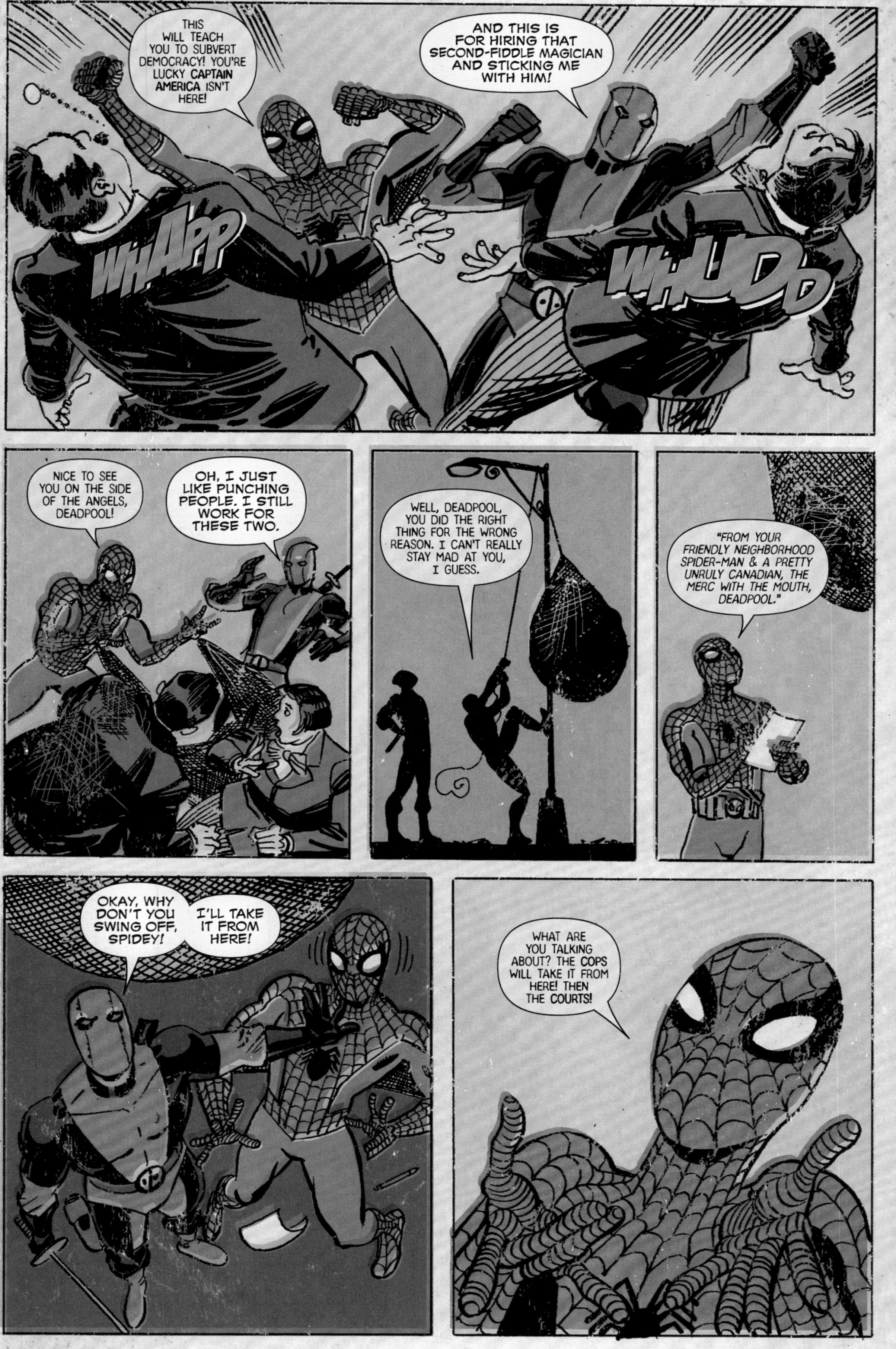
THIS WILL TEACH YOU TO SUBVERT DEMOCRACY! YOU'RE LUCKY CAPTAIN AMERICA ISN'T HERE!
AND THIS IS FOR HIRING THAT SECOND-FIDDLE MAGICIAN AND STICKING ME WITH HIM!
WHAPP
WHUDD
NICE TO SEE YOU ON THE SIDE OF THE ANGELS, DEADPOOL!
OH, I JUST LIKE PUNCHING PEOPLE. I STILL WORK FOR THESE TWO.
WELL, DEADPOOL, YOU DID THE RIGHT THING FOR THE WRONG REASON. I CAN'T REALLY STAY MAD AT YOU, I GUESS.
"FROM YOUR FRIENDLY NEIGHBORHOOD SPIDER-MAN & A PRETTY UNRULY CANADIAN, THE MERC WITH THE MOUTH, DEADPOOL."
OKAY, WHY DON'T YOU SWING OFF, SPIDEY!
I'LL TAKE IT FROM HERE!
WHAT ARE YOU TALKING ABOUT? THE COPS WILL TAKE IT FROM HERE! THEN THE COURTS!

HA-HA! YOU'RE REALLY A RUBE, SPIDER-MAN. THESE TWO ARE MUCH TOO RICH TO FACE JUSTICE.

WHOA!

THERE'S NO PROOF WE WERE INVOLVED IN THIS FRACAS!

OH, WHO CARES. YOU WANT TO RULE THE WORLD? JUST BE SMART ABOUT IT.

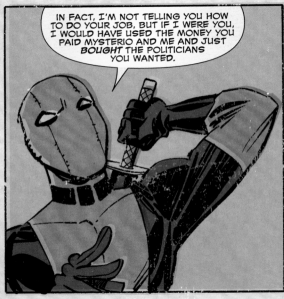

IN FACT, I'M NOT TELLING YOU HOW TO DO YOUR JOB, BUT IF I WERE YOU, I WOULD HAVE USED THE MONEY YOU PAID MYSTERIO AND ME AND JUST *BOUGHT* THE POLITICIANS YOU WANTED.

HYPOTHETICALLY, HOW WOULD THAT WORK?

WAIT--YOU'RE SAYING JUST TREAT THE POLITICIANS LIKE ONE OUR HENCHMEN?

HYPOTHETICAL HENCHMEN!

YOU DISGUST ME, DEADPOOL!

I LEARNED THE HARD WAY THAT WITH GREAT POWER COMES GREAT RESPONSIBILITY, BUT--

BUT I KNOW THAT'S JUST A FORTUNE COOKIE THAT ONLY A SUCKER WOULD FALL FOR.

THE TRUTH IS: *WITH GREAT WEALTH COMES GREAT POWER!*

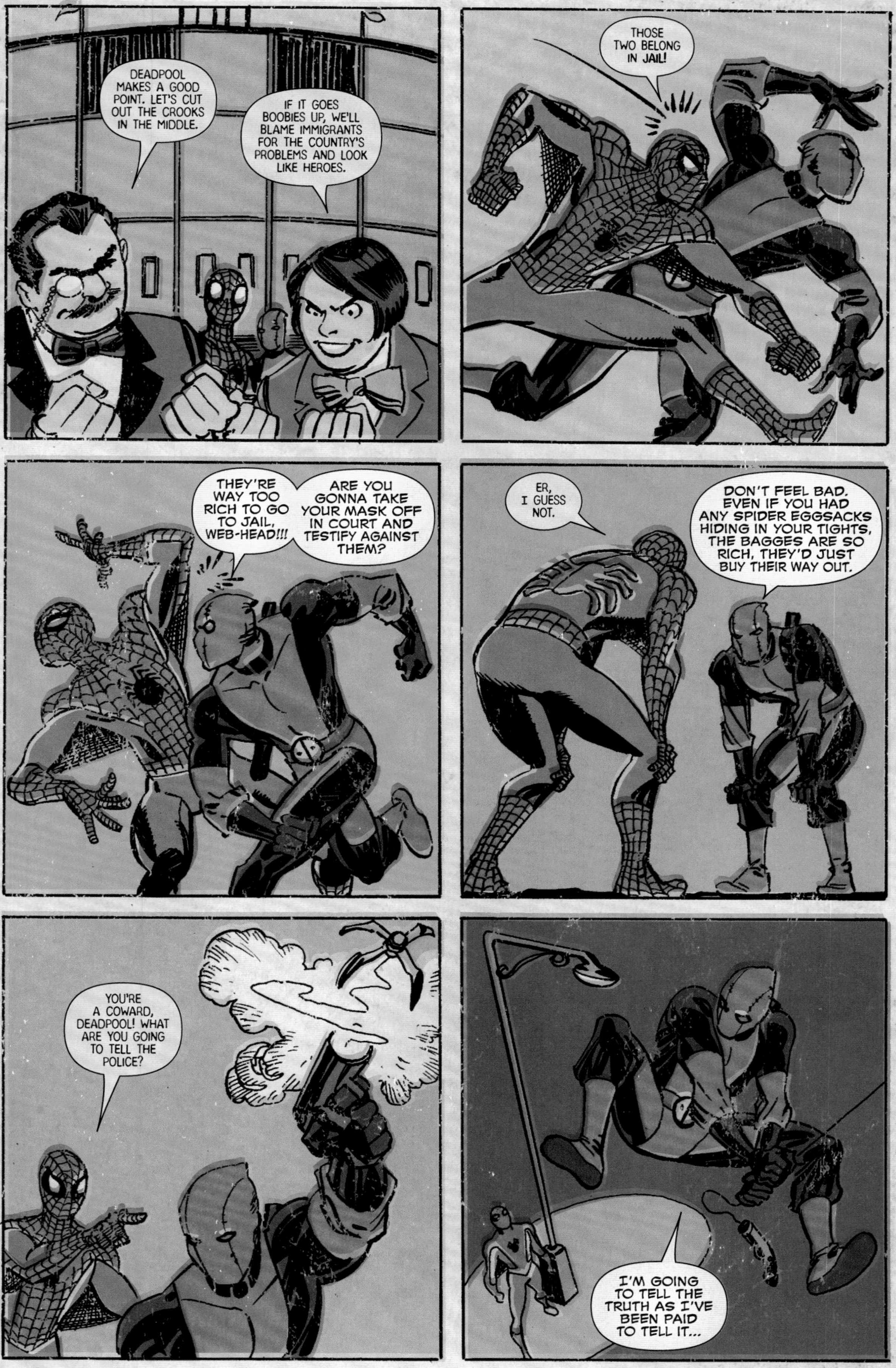
DEADPOOL MAKES A GOOD POINT. LET'S CUT OUT THE CROOKS IN THE MIDDLE.
IF IT GOES BOOBIES UP, WE'LL BLAME IMMIGRANTS FOR THE COUNTRY'S PROBLEMS AND LOOK LIKE HEROES.
THOSE TWO BELONG IN JAIL!
THEY'RE WAY TOO RICH TO GO TO JAIL, WEB-HEAD!!!
ARE YOU GONNA TAKE YOUR MASK OFF IN COURT AND TESTIFY AGAINST THEM?
ER, I GUESS NOT.
DON'T FEEL BAD. EVEN IF YOU HAD ANY SPIDER EGGSACKS HIDING IN YOUR TIGHTS, THE BAGGES ARE SO RICH, THEY'D JUST BUY THEIR WAY OUT.
YOU'RE A COWARD, DEADPOOL! WHAT ARE YOU GOING TO TELL THE POLICE?
I'M GOING TO TELL THE TRUTH AS I'VE BEEN PAID TO TELL IT...

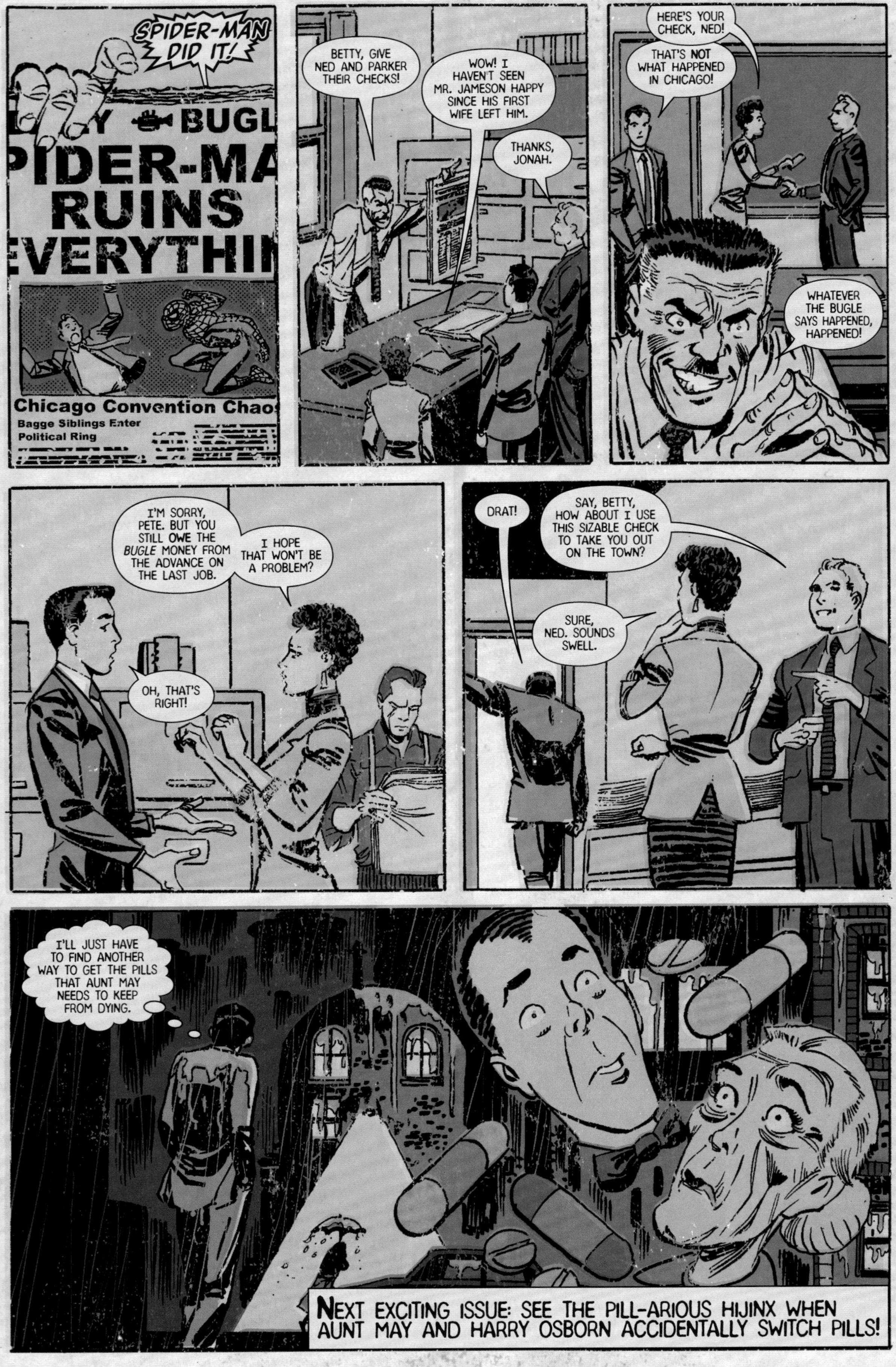
SPIDER-MAN DID IT!
BUGL
PIDER-MA
RUINS
EVERYTHI
Chicago Convention Chao
Bagge Siblings Enter
Political Ring
BETTY, GIVE NED AND PARKER THEIR CHECKS!
WOW! I HAVEN'T SEEN MR. JAMESON HAPPY SINCE HIS FIRST WIFE LEFT HIM.
THANKS, JONAH.
HERE'S YOUR CHECK, NED!
THAT'S NOT WHAT HAPPENED IN CHICAGO!
WHATEVER THE BUGLE SAYS HAPPENED, HAPPENED!
I'M SORRY, PETE. BUT YOU STILL OWE THE BUGLE MONEY FROM THE ADVANCE ON THE LAST JOB.
I HOPE THAT WON'T BE A PROBLEM?
OH, THAT'S RIGHT!
DRAT!
SAY, BETTY, HOW ABOUT I USE THIS SIZABLE CHECK TO TAKE YOU OUT ON THE TOWN?
SURE, NED. SOUNDS SWELL.
I'LL JUST HAVE TO FIND ANOTHER WAY TO GET THE PILLS THAT AUNT MAY NEEDS TO KEEP FROM DYING.
NEXT EXCITING ISSUE: SEE THE PILL-ARIOUS HIJINX WHEN AUNT MAY AND HARRY OSBORN ACCIDENTALLY SWITCH PILLS!

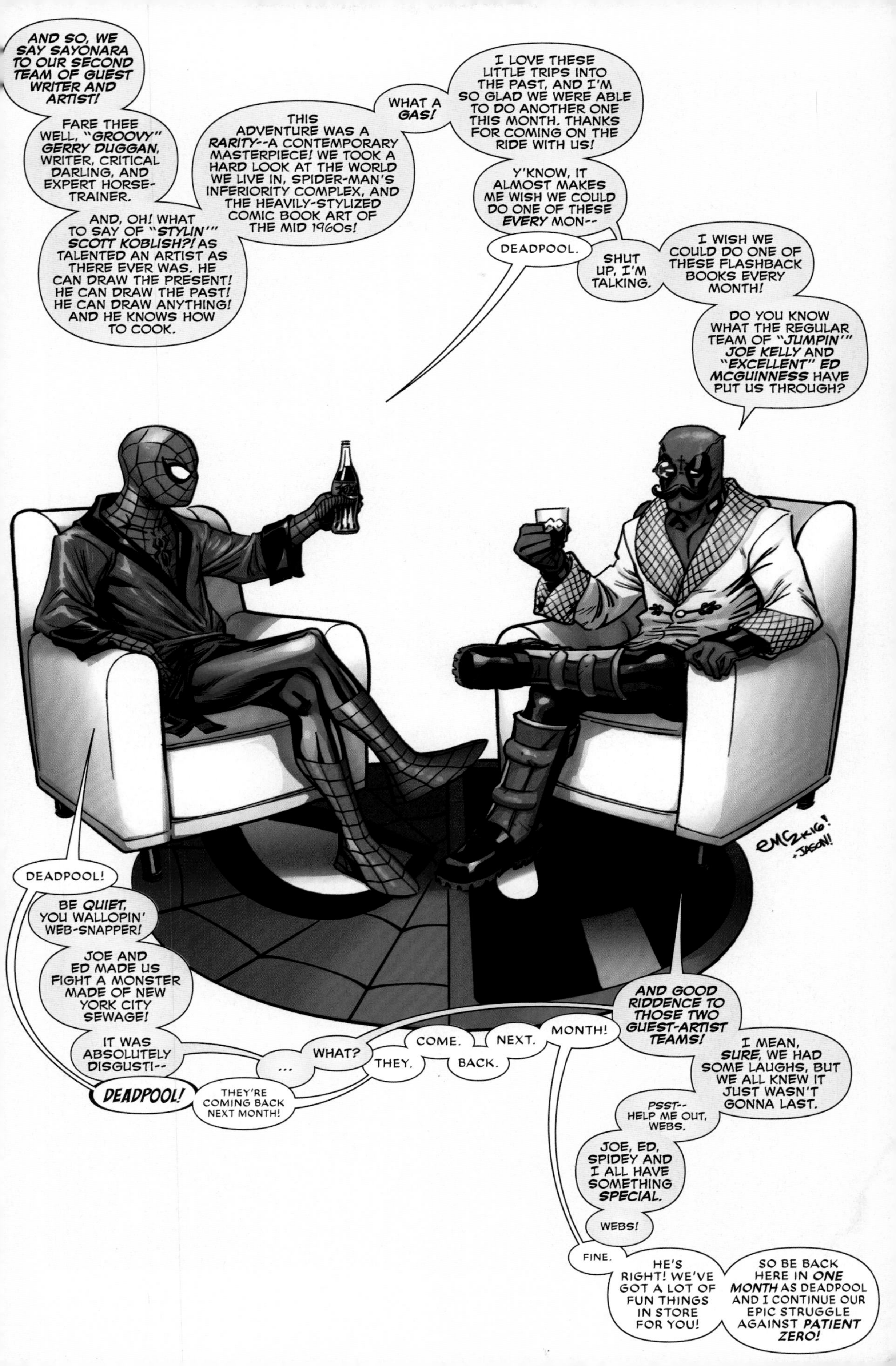
AND SO, WE SAY SAYONARA TO OUR SECOND TEAM OF GUEST WRITER AND ARTIST!
FARE THEE WELL, "GROOVY" GERRY DUGGAN, WRITER, CRITICAL DARLING, AND EXPERT HORSE-TRAINER.
AND, OH! WHAT TO SAY OF "STYLIN'" SCOTT KOBLISH?! AS TALENTED AN ARTIST AS THERE EVER WAS. HE CAN DRAW THE PRESENT! HE CAN DRAW THE PAST! HE CAN DRAW ANYTHING! AND HE KNOWS HOW TO COOK.
THIS ADVENTURE WAS A RARITY--A CONTEMPORARY MASTERPIECE! WE TOOK A HARD LOOK AT THE WORLD WE LIVE IN, SPIDER-MAN'S INFERIORITY COMPLEX, AND THE HEAVILY-STYLIZED COMIC BOOK ART OF THE MID 1960s!
WHAT A GAS!
I LOVE THESE LITTLE TRIPS INTO THE PAST, AND I'M SO GLAD WE WERE ABLE TO DO ANOTHER ONE THIS MONTH. THANKS FOR COMING ON THE RIDE WITH US!
Y'KNOW, IT ALMOST MAKES ME WISH WE COULD DO ONE OF THESE EVERY MON--
DEADPOOL.
SHUT UP, I'M TALKING.
I WISH WE COULD DO ONE OF THESE FLASHBACK BOOKS EVERY MONTH!
DO YOU KNOW WHAT THE REGULAR TEAM OF "JUMPIN'" JOE KELLY AND "EXCELLENT" ED MCGUINNESS HAVE PUT US THROUGH?
DEADPOOL!
BE QUIET, YOU WALLOPIN' WEB-SNAPPER!
JOE AND ED MADE US FIGHT A MONSTER MADE OF NEW YORK CITY SEWAGE!
IT WAS ABSOLUTELY DISGUSTI--
DEADPOOL!
THEY'RE COMING BACK NEXT MONTH!
...
WHAT?
THEY.
COME.
BACK.
NEXT.
MONTH!
AND GOOD RIDDENCE TO THOSE TWO GUEST-ARTIST TEAMS!
I MEAN, SURE, WE HAD SOME LAUGHS, BUT WE ALL KNEW IT JUST WASN'T GONNA LAST.
PSST-- HELP ME OUT, WEBS.
JOE, ED, SPIDEY AND I ALL HAVE SOMETHING SPECIAL.
WEBS!
FINE.
HE'S RIGHT! WE'VE GOT A LOT OF FUN THINGS IN STORE FOR YOU!
SO BE BACK HERE IN ONE MONTH AS DEADPOOL AND I CONTINUE OUR EPIC STRUGGLE AGAINST PATIENT ZERO!

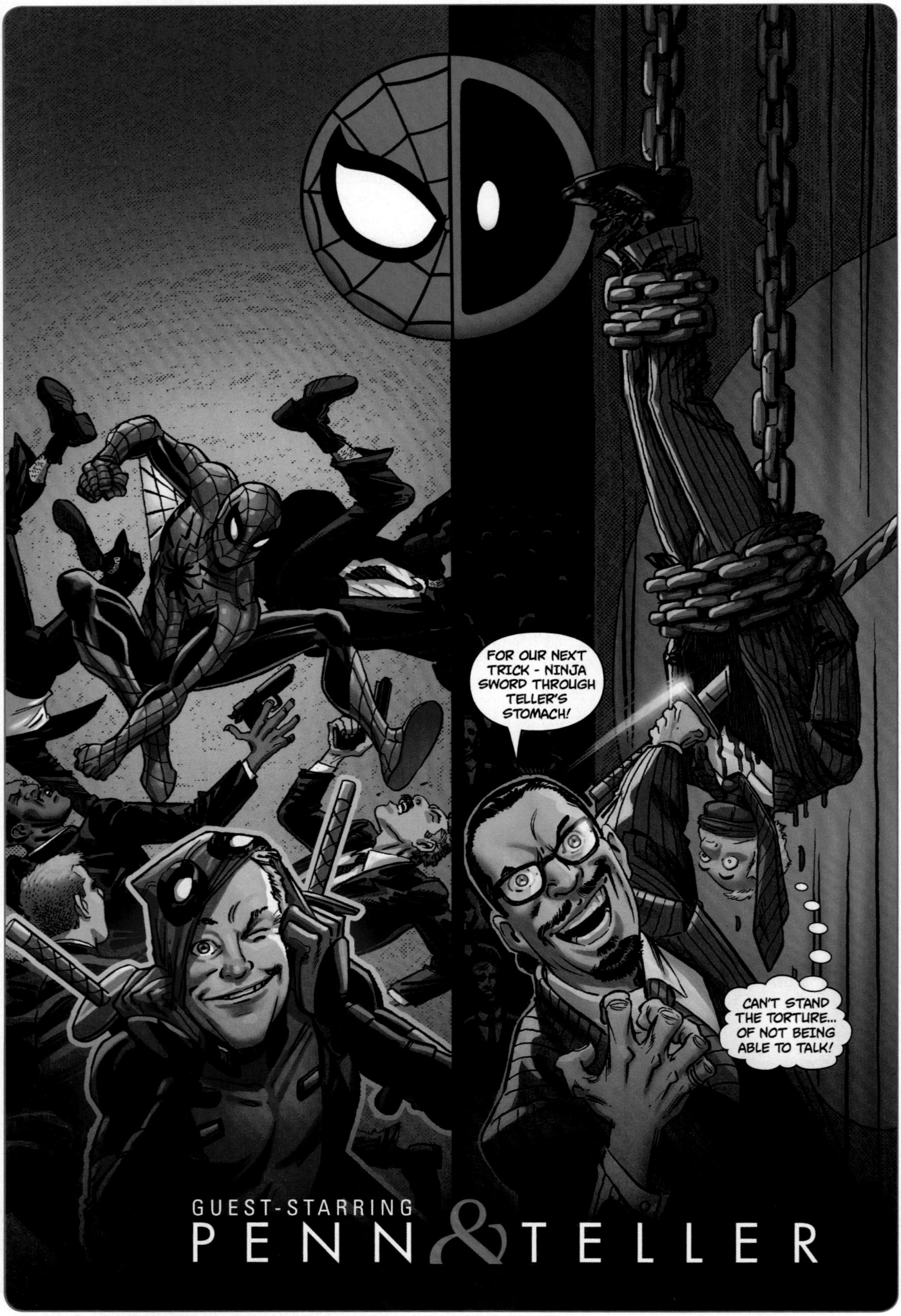
FOR OUR NEXT TRICK - NINJA SWORD THROUGH TELLER'S STOMACH!
CAN'T STAND THE TORTURE... OF NOT BEING ABLE TO TALK!
GUEST-STARRING
PENN & TELLER

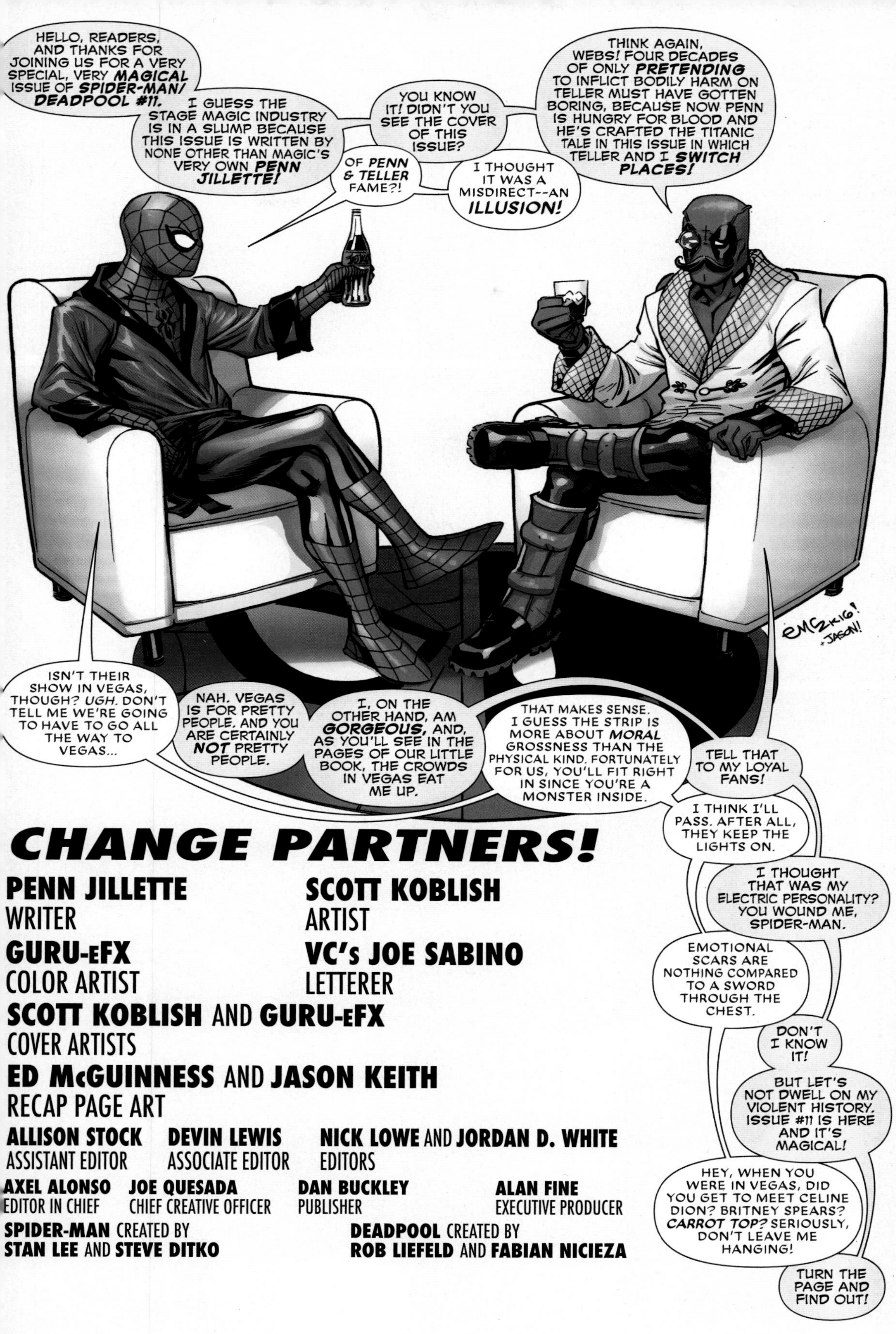
HELLO, READERS, AND THANKS FOR JOINING US FOR A VERY SPECIAL, VERY MAGICAL ISSUE OF SPIDER-MAN/ DEADPOOL #11.
I GUESS THE STAGE MAGIC INDUSTRY IS IN A SLUMP BECAUSE THIS ISSUE IS WRITTEN BY NONE OTHER THAN MAGIC'S VERY OWN PENN JILLETTE!
YOU KNOW IT! DIDN'T YOU SEE THE COVER OF THIS ISSUE?
OF PENN & TELLER FAME?!
I THOUGHT IT WAS A MISDIRECT--AN ILLUSION!
THINK AGAIN, WEBS! FOUR DECADES OF ONLY PRETENDING TO INFLICT BODILY HARM ON TELLER MUST HAVE GOTTEN BORING, BECAUSE NOW PENN IS HUNGRY FOR BLOOD AND HE'S CRAFTED THE TITANIC TALE IN THIS ISSUE IN WHICH TELLER AND I SWITCH PLACES!
ISN'T THEIR SHOW IN VEGAS, THOUGH? UGH. DON'T TELL ME WE'RE GOING TO HAVE TO GO ALL THE WAY TO VEGAS...
NAH. VEGAS IS FOR PRETTY PEOPLE. AND YOU ARE CERTAINLY NOT PRETTY PEOPLE.
I, ON THE OTHER HAND, AM GORGEOUS, AND, AS YOU'LL SEE IN THE PAGES OF OUR LITTLE BOOK, THE CROWDS IN VEGAS EAT ME UP.
THAT MAKES SENSE. I GUESS THE STRIP IS MORE ABOUT MORAL GROSSNESS THAN THE PHYSICAL KIND. FORTUNATELY FOR US, YOU'LL FIT RIGHT IN SINCE YOU'RE A MONSTER INSIDE.
TELL THAT TO MY LOYAL FANS!
I THINK I'LL PASS. AFTER ALL, THEY KEEP THE LIGHTS ON.
I THOUGHT THAT WAS MY ELECTRIC PERSONALITY? YOU WOUND ME, SPIDER-MAN.
EMOTIONAL SCARS ARE NOTHING COMPARED TO A SWORD THROUGH THE CHEST.
DON'T I KNOW IT!
BUT LET'S NOT DWELL ON MY VIOLENT HISTORY. ISSUE #11 IS HERE AND IT'S MAGICAL!
HEY, WHEN YOU WERE IN VEGAS, DID YOU GET TO MEET CELINE DION? BRITNEY SPEARS? CARROT TOP? SERIOUSLY, DON'T LEAVE ME HANGING!
TURN THE PAGE AND FIND OUT!

CHANGE PARTNERS!

PENN JILLETTE
WRITER

SCOTT KOBLISH
ARTIST

GURU-eFX
COLOR ARTIST

VC's JOE SABINO
LETTERER

SCOTT KOBLISH AND **GURU-eFX**
COVER ARTISTS

ED McGUINNESS AND **JASON KEITH**
RECAP PAGE ART

ALLISON STOCK
ASSISTANT EDITOR

DEVIN LEWIS
ASSOCIATE EDITOR

NICK LOWE AND **JORDAN D. WHITE**
EDITORS

AXEL ALONSO
EDITOR IN CHIEF

JOE QUESADA
CHIEF CREATIVE OFFICER

DAN BUCKLEY
PUBLISHER

ALAN FINE
EXECUTIVE PRODUCER

SPIDER-MAN CREATED BY
STAN LEE AND **STEVE DITKO**

DEADPOOL CREATED BY
ROB LIEFELD AND **FABIAN NICIEZA**

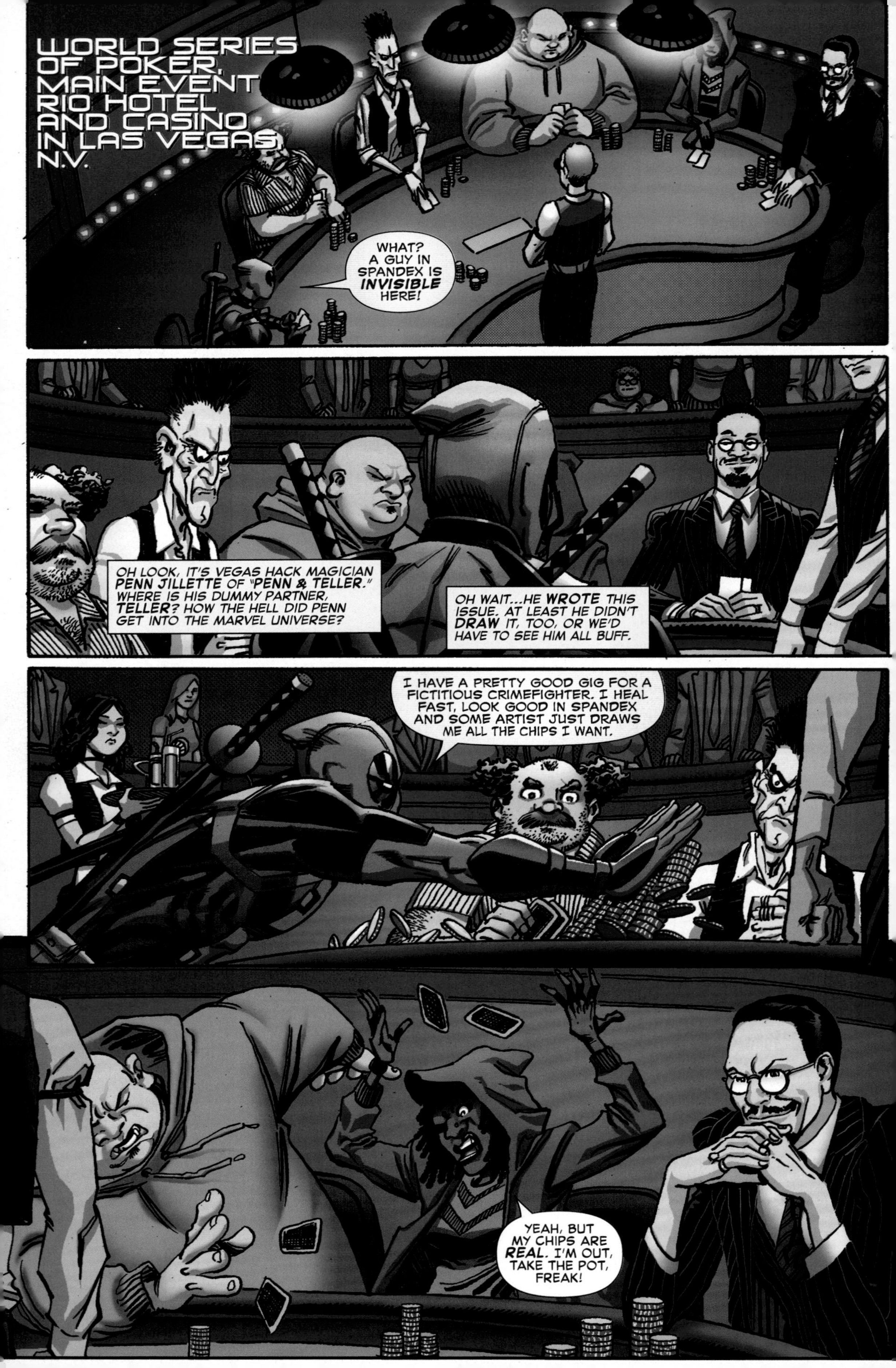
WORLD SERIES OF POKER, MAIN EVENT RIO HOTEL AND CASINO IN LAS VEGAS N.V.
WHAT? A GUY IN SPANDEX IS INVISIBLE HERE!
OH LOOK, IT'S VEGAS HACK MAGICIAN PENN JILLETTE OF "PENN & TELLER." WHERE IS HIS DUMMY PARTNER, TELLER? HOW THE HELL DID PENN GET INTO THE MARVEL UNIVERSE?
OH WAIT...HE WROTE THIS ISSUE. AT LEAST HE DIDN'T DRAW IT, TOO, OR WE'D HAVE TO SEE HIM ALL BUFF.
I HAVE A PRETTY GOOD GIG FOR A FICTITIOUS CRIMEFIGHTER. I HEAL FAST, LOOK GOOD IN SPANDEX AND SOME ARTIST JUST DRAWS ME ALL THE CHIPS I WANT.
YEAH, BUT MY CHIPS ARE REAL. I'M OUT, TAKE THE POT, FREAK!

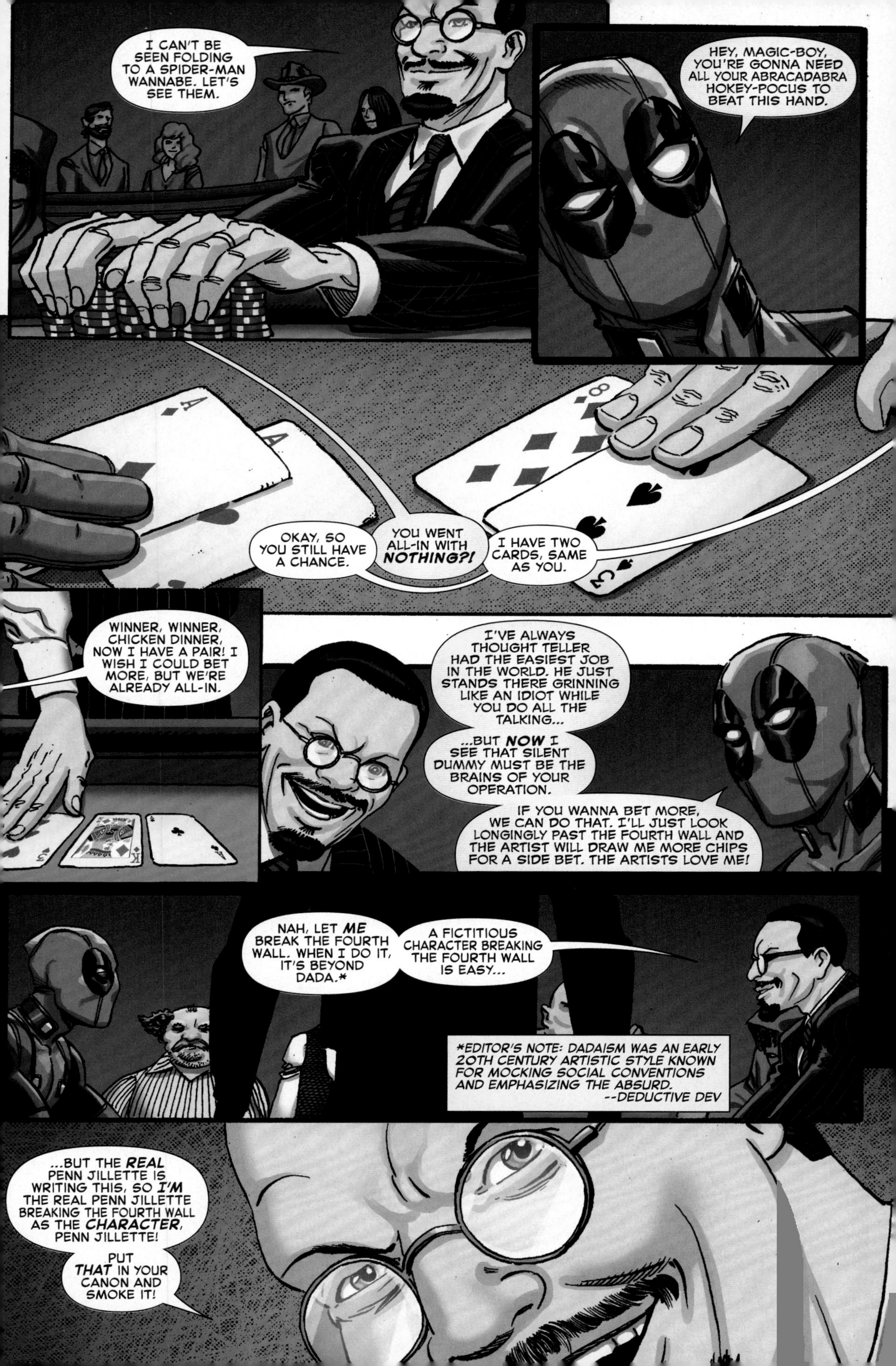
I CAN'T BE SEEN FOLDING TO A SPIDER-MAN WANNABE. LET'S SEE THEM.
HEY, MAGIC-BOY, YOU'RE GONNA NEED ALL YOUR ABRACADABRA HOKEY-POCUS TO BEAT THIS HAND.
I HAVE TWO CARDS, SAME AS YOU.
YOU WENT ALL-IN WITH NOTHING?!
OKAY, SO YOU STILL HAVE A CHANCE.
WINNER, WINNER, CHICKEN DINNER, NOW I HAVE A PAIR! I WISH I COULD BET MORE, BUT WE'RE ALREADY ALL-IN.
I'VE ALWAYS THOUGHT TELLER HAD THE EASIEST JOB IN THE WORLD. HE JUST STANDS THERE GRINNING LIKE AN IDIOT WHILE YOU DO ALL THE TALKING...
...BUT NOW I SEE THAT SILENT DUMMY MUST BE THE BRAINS OF YOUR OPERATION.
IF YOU WANNA BET MORE, WE CAN DO THAT. I'LL JUST LOOK LONGINGLY PAST THE FOURTH WALL AND THE ARTIST WILL DRAW ME MORE CHIPS FOR A SIDE BET. THE ARTISTS LOVE ME!
A FICTITIOUS CHARACTER BREAKING THE FOURTH WALL IS EASY...
NAH, LET ME BREAK THE FOURTH WALL. WHEN I DO IT, IT'S BEYOND DADA.*
*EDITOR'S NOTE: DADAISM WAS AN EARLY 20TH CENTURY ARTISTIC STYLE KNOWN FOR MOCKING SOCIAL CONVENTIONS AND EMPHASIZING THE ABSURD. --DEDUCTIVE DEV
...BUT THE REAL PENN JILLETTE IS WRITING THIS, SO I'M THE REAL PENN JILLETTE BREAKING THE FOURTH WALL AS THE CHARACTER, PENN JILLETTE!
PUT THAT IN YOUR CANON AND SMOKE IT!

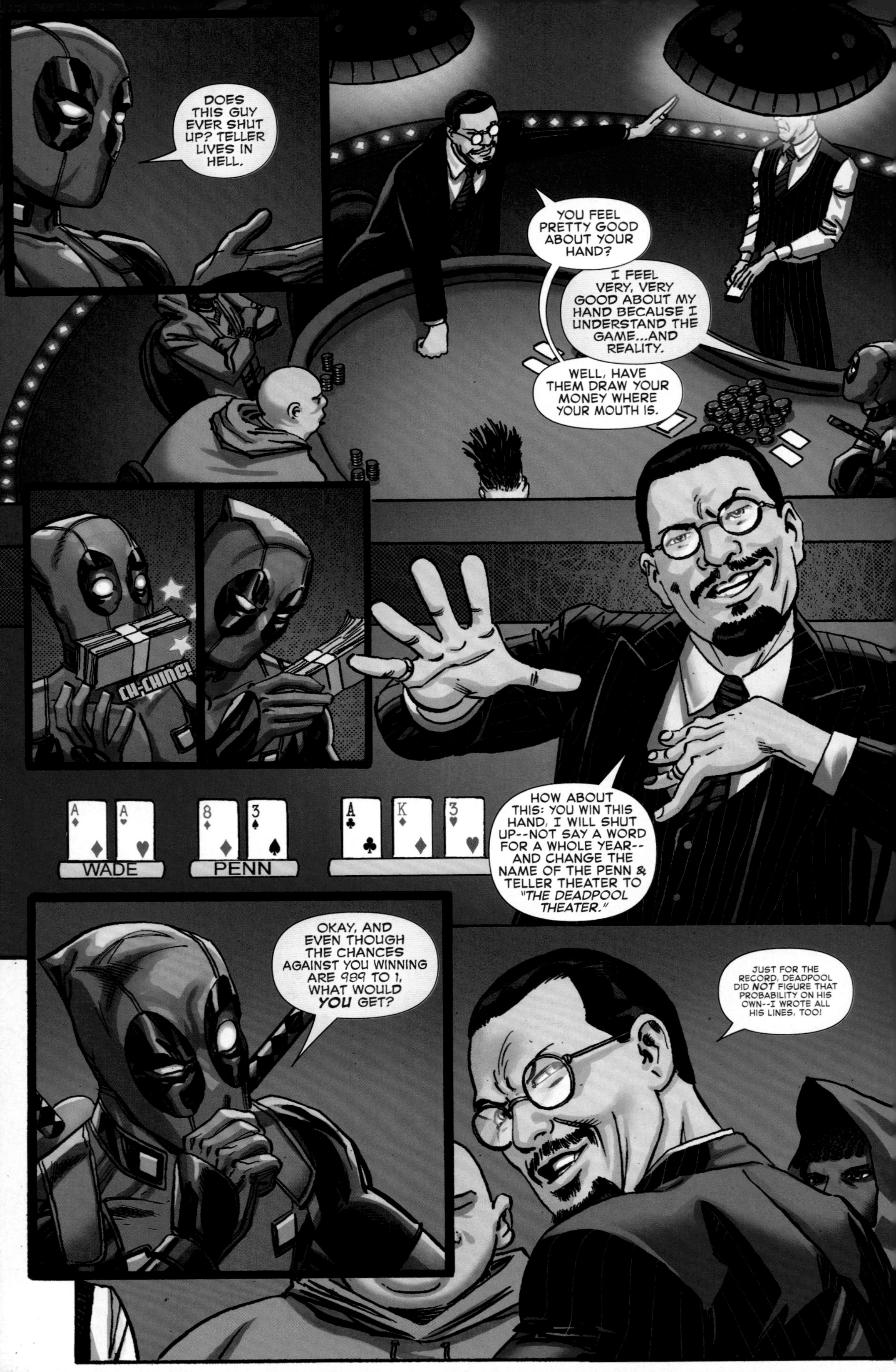

DOES THIS GUY EVER SHUT UP? TELLER LIVES IN HELL.
YOU FEEL PRETTY GOOD ABOUT YOUR HAND?
I FEEL VERY, VERY GOOD ABOUT MY HAND BECAUSE I UNDERSTAND THE GAME...AND REALITY.
WELL, HAVE THEM DRAW YOUR MONEY WHERE YOUR MOUTH IS.
CH-CHING!
A A 8 3 A K 3
WADE
PENN
HOW ABOUT THIS: YOU WIN THIS HAND, I WILL SHUT UP--NOT SAY A WORD FOR A WHOLE YEAR--AND CHANGE THE NAME OF THE PENN & TELLER THEATER TO "THE DEADPOOL THEATER."
OKAY, AND EVEN THOUGH THE CHANCES AGAINST YOU WINNING ARE 989 TO 1, WHAT WOULD YOU GET?
JUST FOR THE RECORD, DEADPOOL DID NOT FIGURE THAT PROBABILITY ON HIS OWN--I WROTE ALL HIS LINES, TOO!

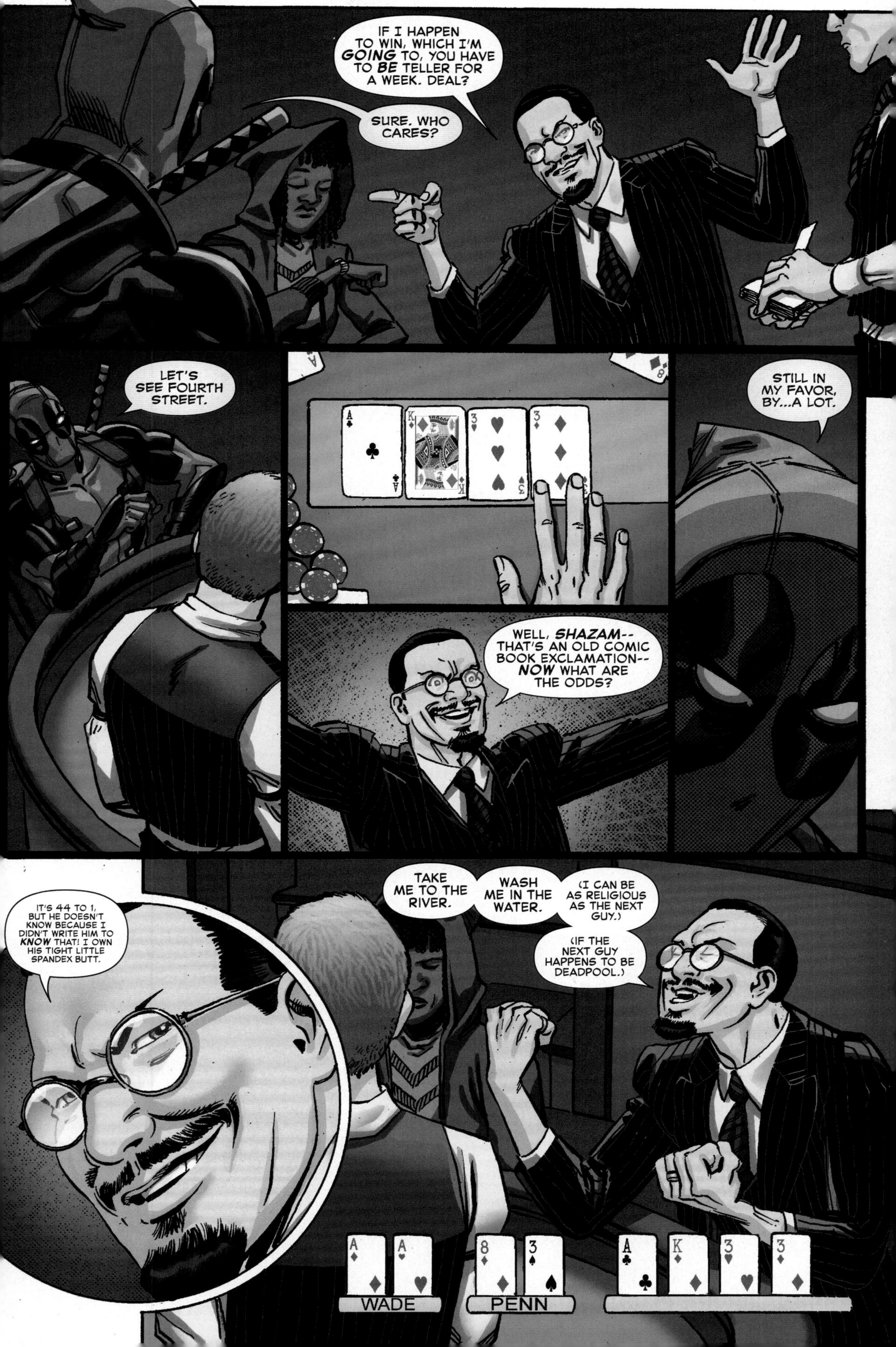

IF I HAPPEN TO WIN, WHICH I'M GOING TO, YOU HAVE TO BE TELLER FOR A WEEK. DEAL?
SURE. WHO CARES?
LET'S SEE FOURTH STREET.
STILL IN MY FAVOR, BY...A LOT.
WELL, SHAZAM-- THAT'S AN OLD COMIC BOOK EXCLAMATION-- NOW WHAT ARE THE ODDS?
IT'S 44 TO 1, BUT HE DOESN'T KNOW BECAUSE I DIDN'T WRITE HIM TO KNOW THAT! I OWN HIS TIGHT LITTLE SPANDEX BUTT.
TAKE ME TO THE RIVER.
WASH ME IN THE WATER.
(I CAN BE AS RELIGIOUS AS THE NEXT GUY.)
(IF THE NEXT GUY HAPPENS TO BE DEADPOOL.)
WADE
PENN

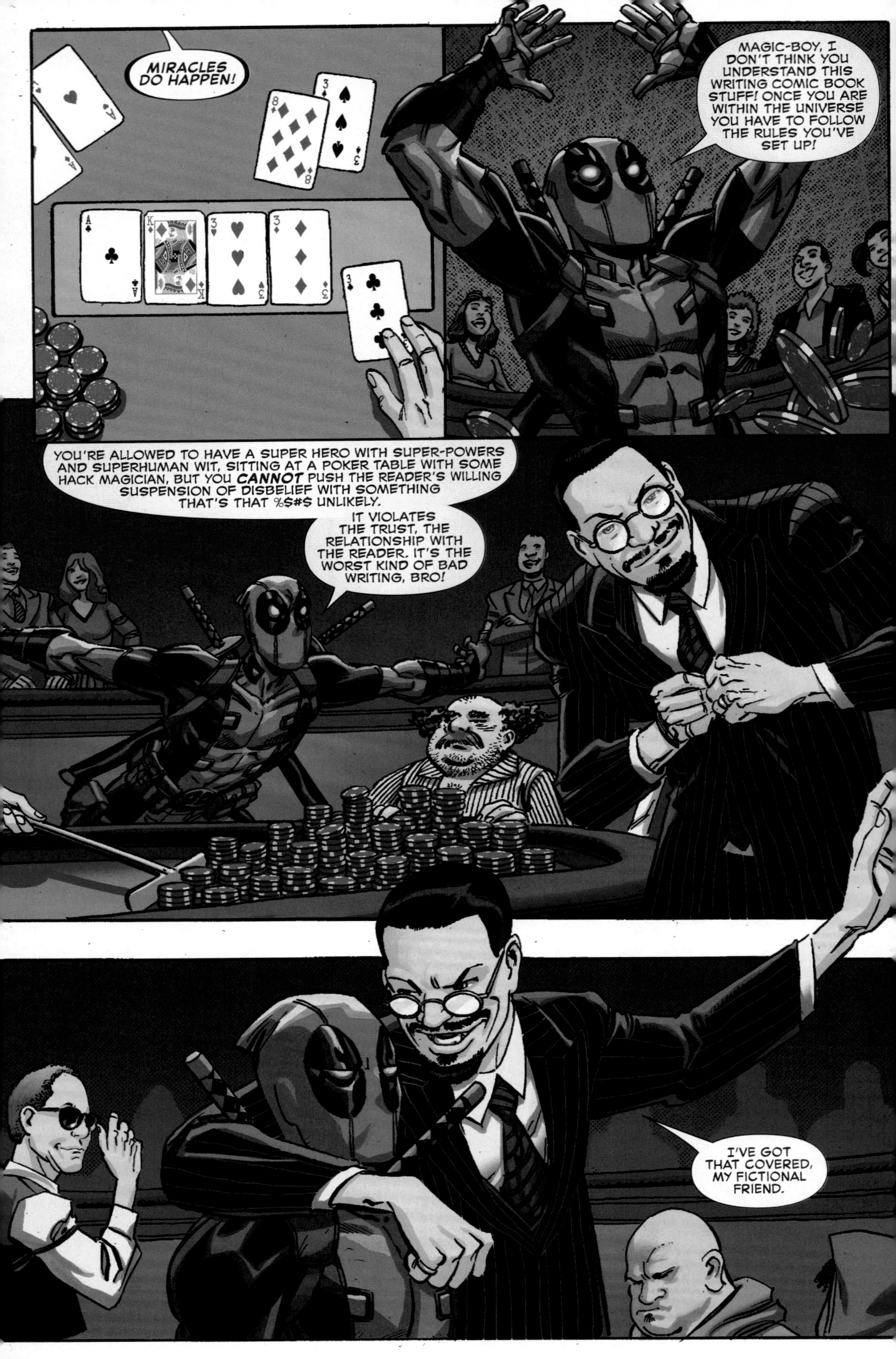
MIRACLES DO HAPPEN!
MAGIC-BOY, I DON'T THINK YOU UNDERSTAND THIS WRITING COMIC BOOK STUFF! ONCE YOU ARE WITHIN THE UNIVERSE YOU HAVE TO FOLLOW THE RULES YOU'VE SET UP!
YOU'RE ALLOWED TO HAVE A SUPER HERO WITH SUPER-POWERS AND SUPERHUMAN WIT, SITTING AT A POKER TABLE WITH SOME HACK MAGICIAN, BUT YOU CANNOT PUSH THE READER'S WILLING SUSPENSION OF DISBELIEF WITH SOMETHING THAT'S THAT %$#$ UNLIKELY.
IT VIOLATES THE TRUST, THE RELATIONSHIP WITH THE READER. IT'S THE WORST KIND OF BAD WRITING, BRO!
I'VE GOT THAT COVERED, MY FICTIONAL FRIEND.

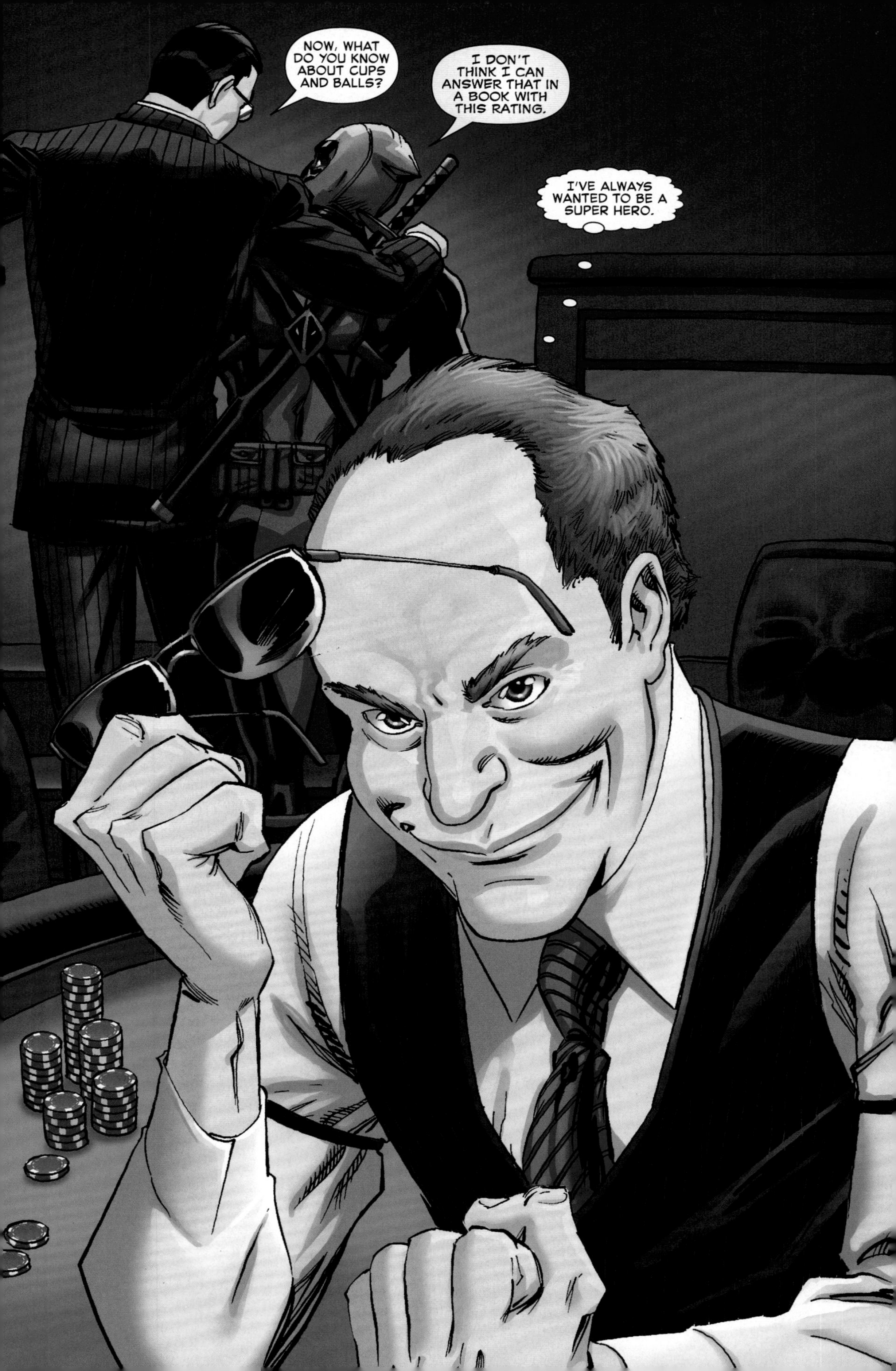
NOW, WHAT DO YOU KNOW ABOUT CUPS AND BALLS?
I DON'T THINK I CAN ANSWER THAT IN A BOOK WITH THIS RATING.
I'VE ALWAYS WANTED TO BE A SUPER HERO.

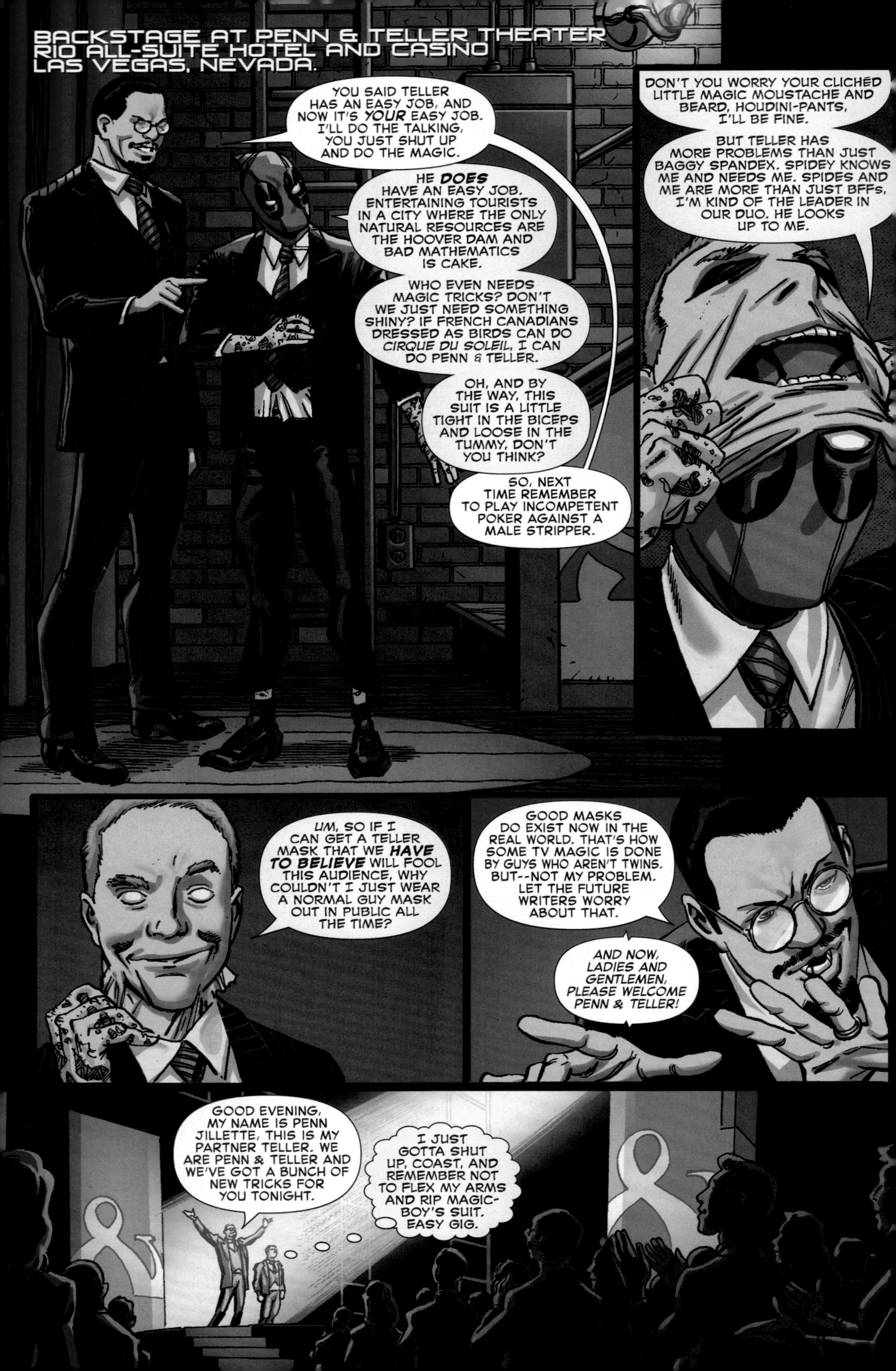
BACKSTAGE AT PENN & TELLER THEATER RIO ALL-SUITE HOTEL AND CASINO LAS VEGAS, NEVADA.
YOU SAID TELLER HAS AN EASY JOB, AND NOW IT'S YOUR EASY JOB. I'LL DO THE TALKING, YOU JUST SHUT UP AND DO THE MAGIC.
HE DOES HAVE AN EASY JOB. ENTERTAINING TOURISTS IN A CITY WHERE THE ONLY NATURAL RESOURCES ARE THE HOOVER DAM AND BAD MATHEMATICS IS CAKE.
WHO EVEN NEEDS MAGIC TRICKS? DON'T WE JUST NEED SOMETHING SHINY? IF FRENCH CANADIANS DRESSED AS BIRDS CAN DO CIRQUE DU SOLEIL, I CAN DO PENN & TELLER.
OH, AND BY THE WAY, THIS SUIT IS A LITTLE TIGHT IN THE BICEPS AND LOOSE IN THE TUMMY, DON'T YOU THINK?
SO, NEXT TIME REMEMBER TO PLAY INCOMPETENT POKER AGAINST A MALE STRIPPER.
DON'T YOU WORRY YOUR CLICHED LITTLE MAGIC MOUSTACHE AND BEARD, HOUDINI-PANTS, I'LL BE FINE.
BUT TELLER HAS MORE PROBLEMS THAN JUST BAGGY SPANDEX. SPIDEY KNOWS ME AND NEEDS ME. SPIDES AND ME ARE MORE THAN JUST BFFS, I'M KIND OF THE LEADER IN OUR DUO. HE LOOKS UP TO ME.
UM, SO IF I CAN GET A TELLER MASK THAT WE HAVE TO BELIEVE WILL FOOL THIS AUDIENCE, WHY COULDN'T I JUST WEAR A NORMAL GUY MASK OUT IN PUBLIC ALL THE TIME?
GOOD MASKS DO EXIST NOW IN THE REAL WORLD. THAT'S HOW SOME TV MAGIC IS DONE BY GUYS WHO AREN'T TWINS. BUT--NOT MY PROBLEM. LET THE FUTURE WRITERS WORRY ABOUT THAT.
AND NOW, LADIES AND GENTLEMEN, PLEASE WELCOME PENN & TELLER!
GOOD EVENING, MY NAME IS PENN JILLETTE, THIS IS MY PARTNER TELLER. WE ARE PENN & TELLER AND WE'VE GOT A BUNCH OF NEW TRICKS FOR YOU TONIGHT.
I JUST GOTTA SHUT UP, COAST, AND REMEMBER NOT TO FLEX MY ARMS AND RIP MAGIC-BOY'S SUIT. EASY GIG.

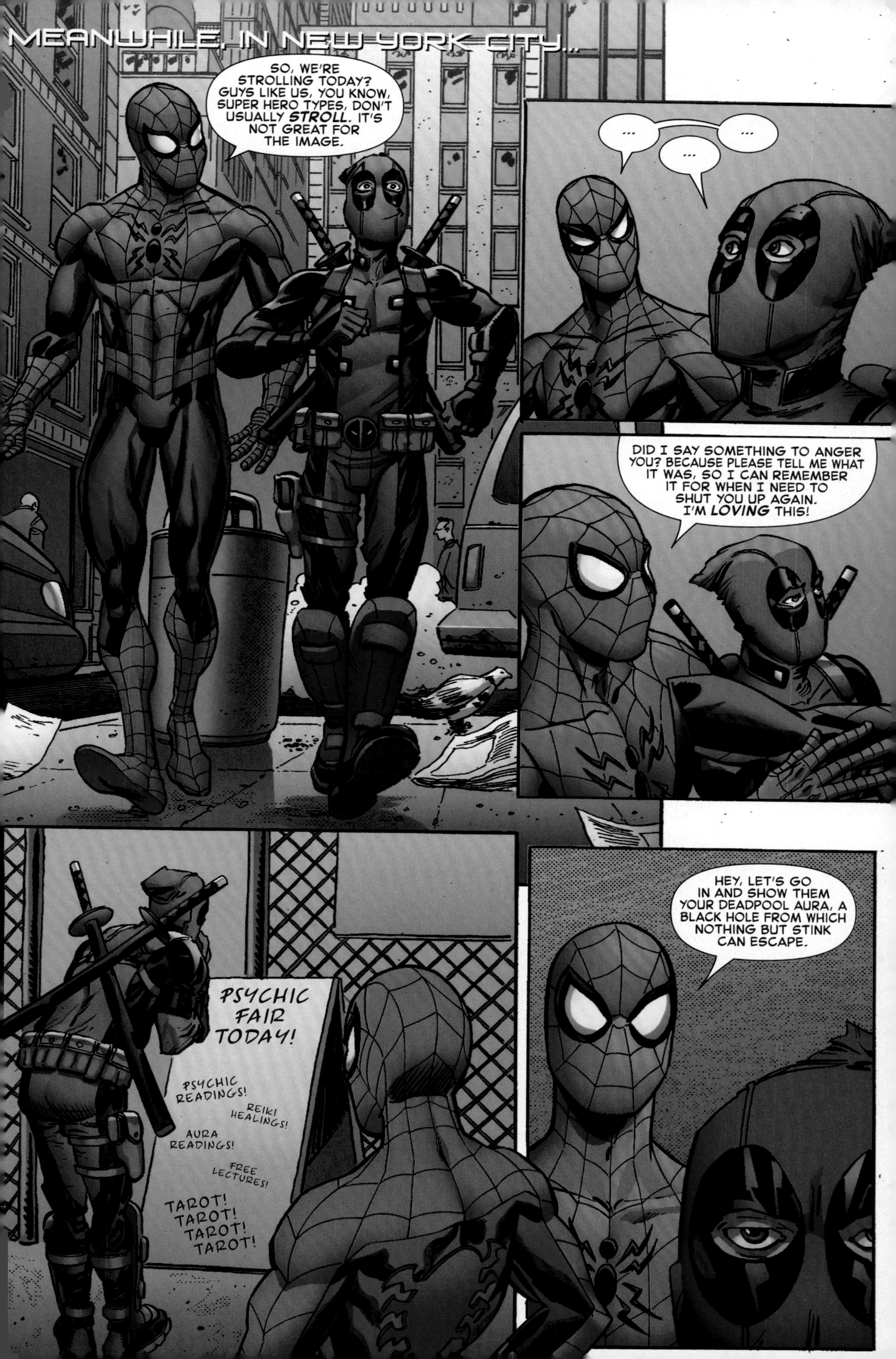
MEANWHILE, IN NEW YORK CITY...
SO, WE'RE STROLLING TODAY? GUYS LIKE US, YOU KNOW, SUPER HERO TYPES, DON'T USUALLY STROLL. IT'S NOT GREAT FOR THE IMAGE.
...
...
...
DID I SAY SOMETHING TO ANGER YOU? BECAUSE PLEASE TELL ME WHAT IT WAS, SO I CAN REMEMBER IT FOR WHEN I NEED TO SHUT YOU UP AGAIN. I'M LOVING THIS!
PSYCHIC FAIR TODAY!
PSYCHIC READINGS!
REIKI HEALINGS!
AURA READINGS!
FREE LECTURES!
TAROT! TAROT! TAROT! TAROT!
HEY, LET'S GO IN AND SHOW THEM YOUR DEADPOOL AURA, A BLACK HOLE FROM WHICH NOTHING BUT STINK CAN ESCAPE.

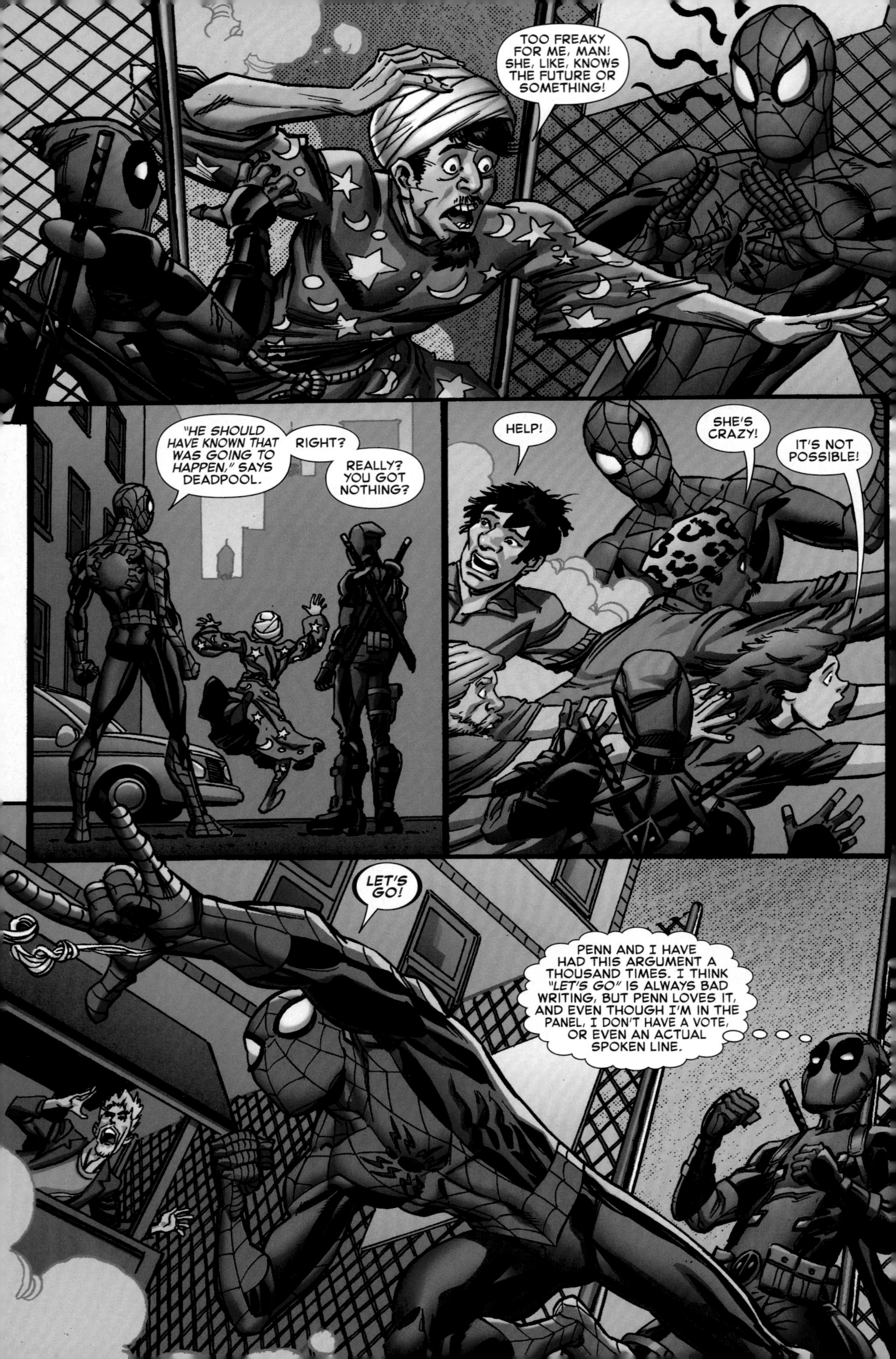
TOO FREAKY FOR ME, MAN! SHE, LIKE, KNOWS THE FUTURE OR SOMETHING!
"HE SHOULD HAVE KNOWN THAT WAS GOING TO HAPPEN," SAYS DEADPOOL.
RIGHT?
REALLY? YOU GOT NOTHING?
HELP!
SHE'S CRAZY!
IT'S NOT POSSIBLE!
LET'S GO!
PENN AND I HAVE HAD THIS ARGUMENT A THOUSAND TIMES. I THINK "LET'S GO" IS ALWAYS BAD WRITING, BUT PENN LOVES IT, AND EVEN THOUGH I'M IN THE PANEL, I DON'T HAVE A VOTE, OR EVEN AN ACTUAL SPOKEN LINE.

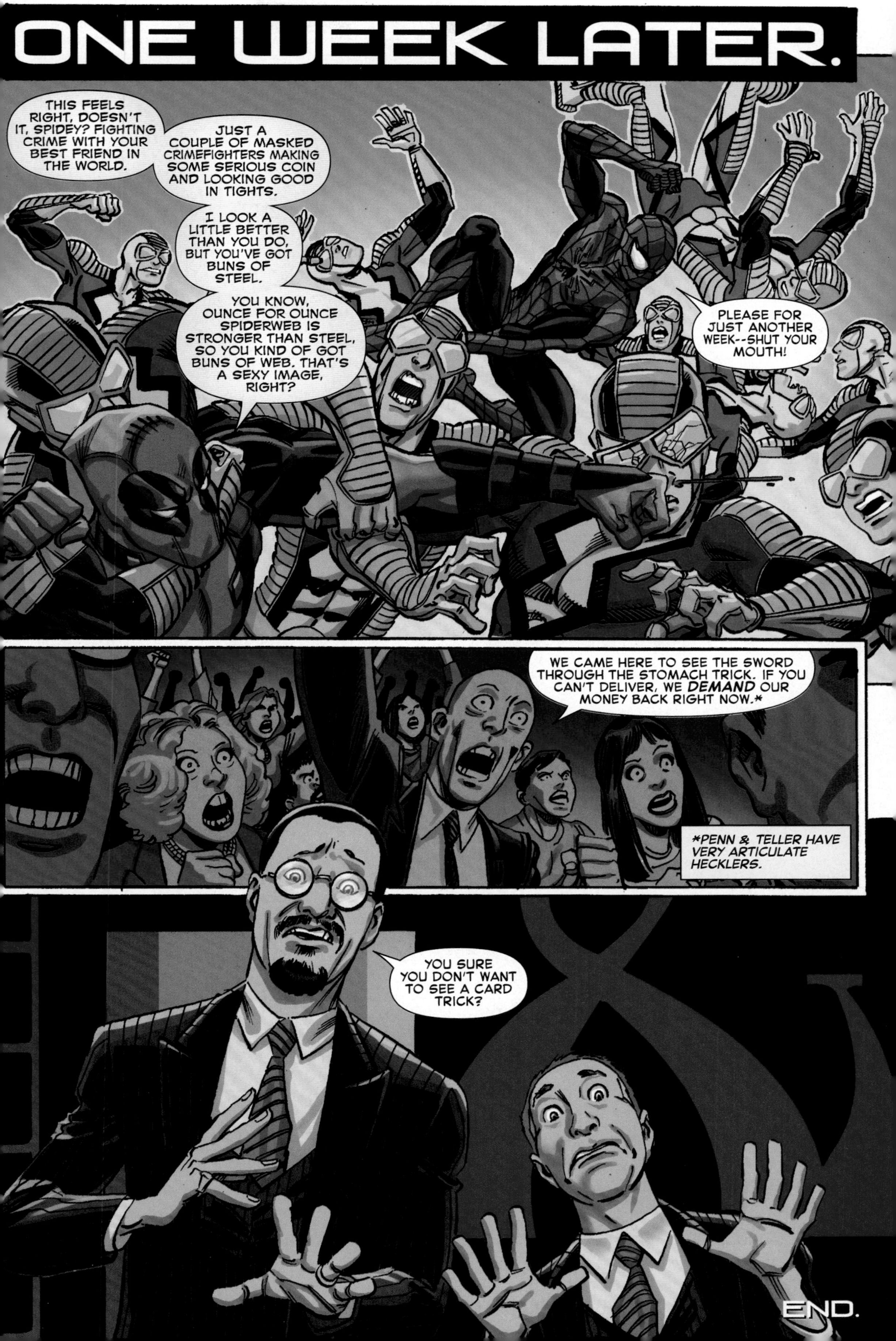

ONE WEEK LATER.
THIS FEELS RIGHT, DOESN'T IT, SPIDEY? FIGHTING CRIME WITH YOUR BEST FRIEND IN THE WORLD.
JUST A COUPLE OF MASKED CRIMEFIGHTERS MAKING SOME SERIOUS COIN AND LOOKING GOOD IN TIGHTS.
I LOOK A LITTLE BETTER THAN YOU DO, BUT YOU'VE GOT BUNS OF STEEL.
YOU KNOW, OUNCE FOR OUNCE SPIDERWEB IS STRONGER THAN STEEL, SO YOU KIND OF GOT BUNS OF WEB. THAT'S A SEXY IMAGE, RIGHT?
PLEASE FOR JUST ANOTHER WEEK--SHUT YOUR MOUTH!
WE CAME HERE TO SEE THE SWORD THROUGH THE STOMACH TRICK. IF YOU CAN'T DELIVER, WE DEMAND OUR MONEY BACK RIGHT NOW.*
*PENN & TELLER HAVE VERY ARTICULATE HECKLERS.
YOU SURE YOU DON'T WANT TO SEE A CARD TRICK?
END.

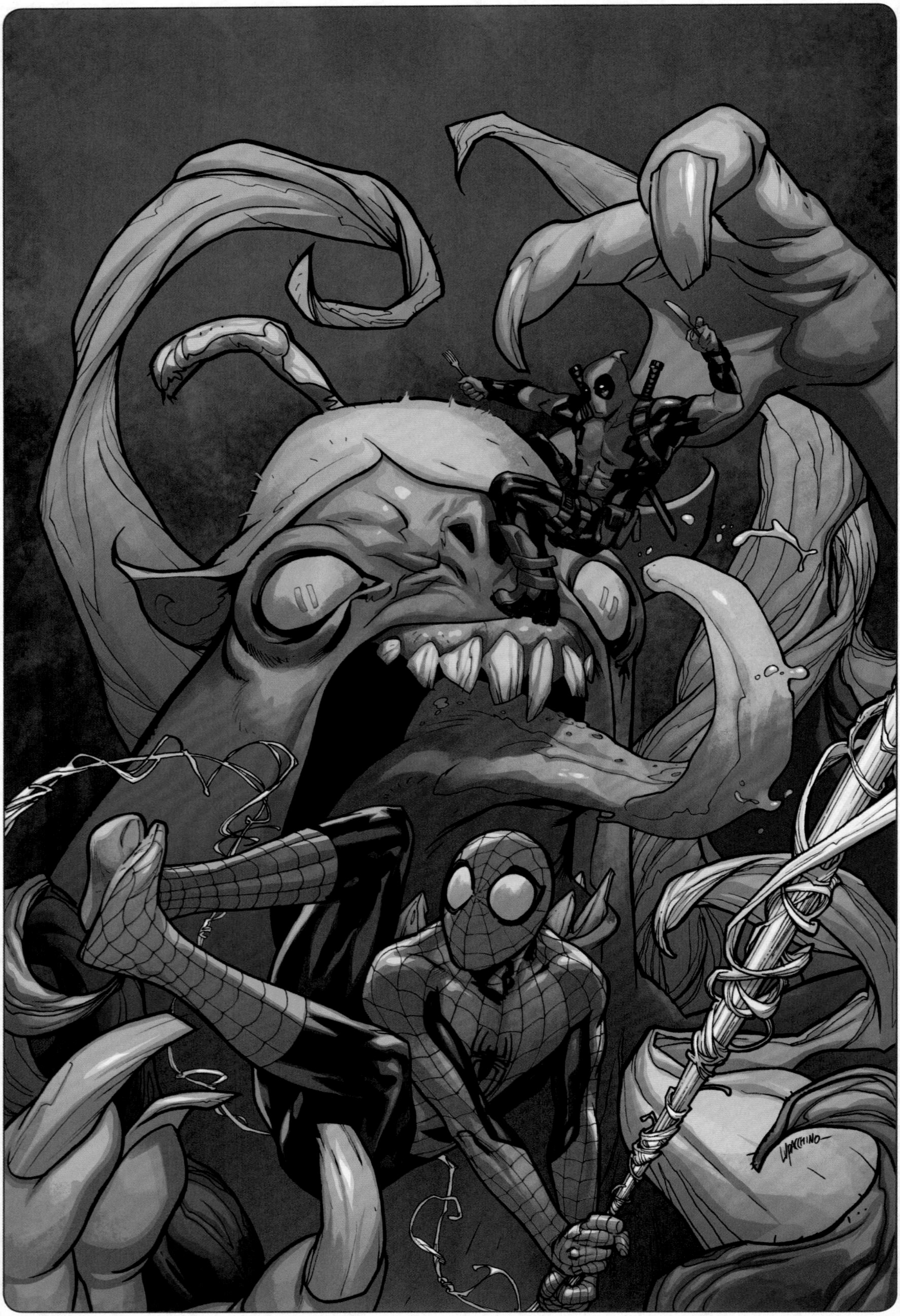
LUPACCHINO

1.MU VARIANT BY
EMANUELA LUPACCHINO

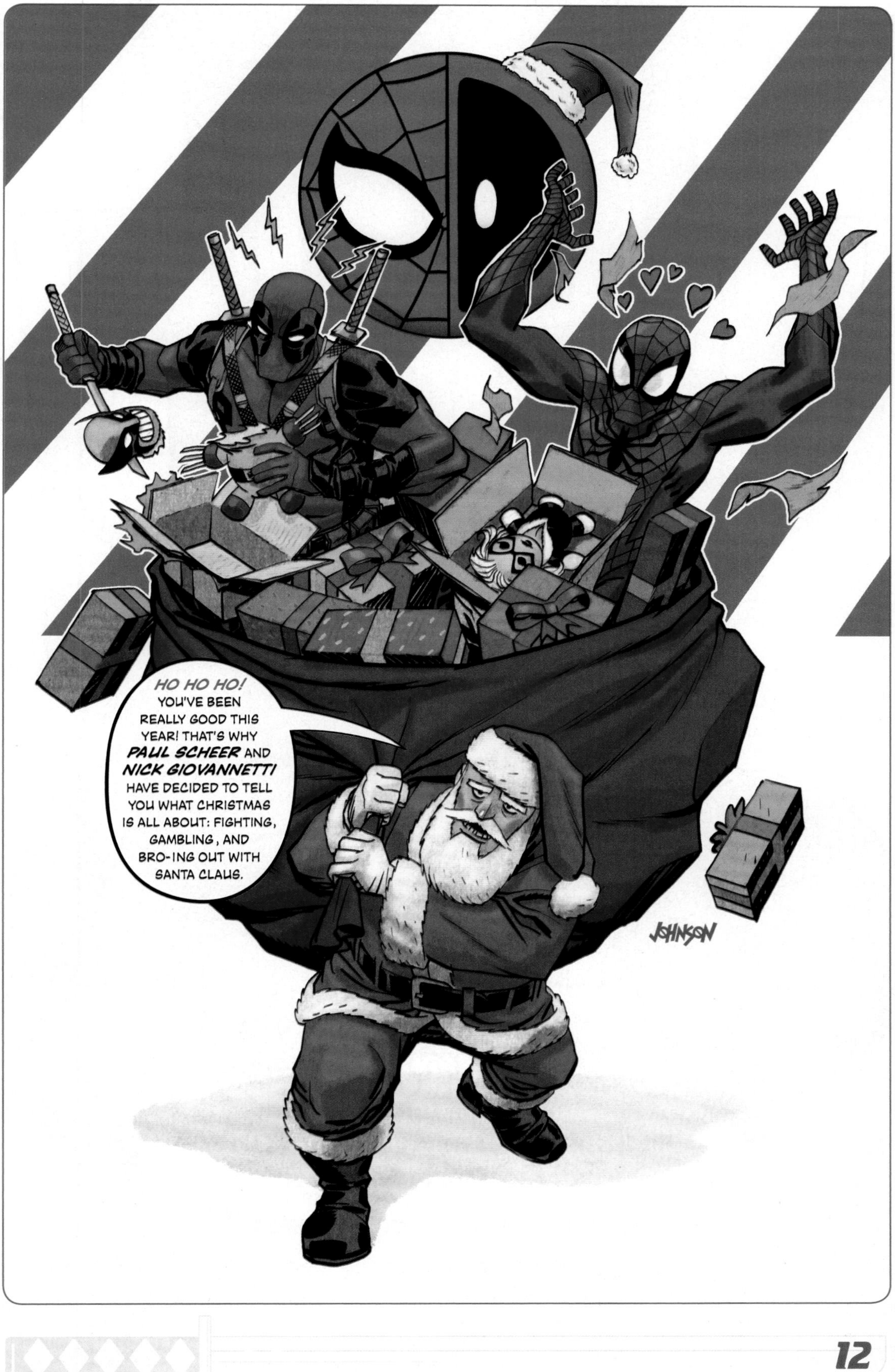
HO HO HO! YOU'VE BEEN REALLY GOOD THIS YEAR! THAT'S WHY PAUL SCHEER AND NICK GIOVANNETTI HAVE DECIDED TO TELL YOU WHAT CHRISTMAS IS ALL ABOUT: FIGHTING, GAMBLING, AND BRO-ING OUT WITH SANTA CLAUS.
JOHNSON

Dear Santa,

It's me, your friendly neighborhood Spider-Man. I've been very good this year, saving the world and all that, and there's a few things I would like for the holidays. I would love a lunch date with Neil deGrasse Tyson and Stephen Hawking, the ultimate science bros. Also, a subscription to *Crochet World Magazine*, for Aunt May. But what I really want is homes for the homeless, food for the hungry, and peace on earth. Also, I'd really love some *Hamilton* tickets.

Best regards,

The AMAZING SPIDER-MAN

Dear Krampus,

It's Christmas, which means it's time to cough up some gifts for your good pal Deadpool, number one on your naughty list. I want a *Family Matters* action figure set. I want a subscription to *Cat Fancy Magazine*, including the swimsuit issue. I want bullets, like one for every person who has ever done the Mannequin Challenge (I'd like them stop moving permanen... a walrus costume. I want a lock of Bea Arthur's silver hair... how about some *Hamilton* tick...

XOXO,

DEADPOOL

MARVEL

MERRILY PRESENTS

THE SPIDER-MAN/DEADPOOL HO-HO-HOLIDAY SPECIAL!

NICK GIOVANNETTI & PAUL SCHEER
WRITERS

TODD NAUCK
ARTIST

RACHELLE ROSENBERG
COLOR ARTIST

VC'S JOE SABINO
LETTERER

DAVE JOHNSON
COVER

ANTHONY GAMBINO
RECAP PAGE ART

ALLISON STOCK
ASSISTANT EDITOR

DEVIN LEWIS
ASSOCIATE EDITOR

JORDAN D. WHITE & NICK LOWE
EDITORS

AXEL ALONSO EDITOR IN CHIEF   **JOE QUESADA** CHIEF CREATIVE OFFICER   **DAN BUCKLEY** PUBLISHER   **ALAN FINE** EXECUTIVE PRODUCER

SPIDER-MAN CREATED BY **STAN LEE** AND **STEVE DITKO**   **DEADPOOL** CREATED BY **ROB LIEFELD** AND **FABIAN NICIEZA**

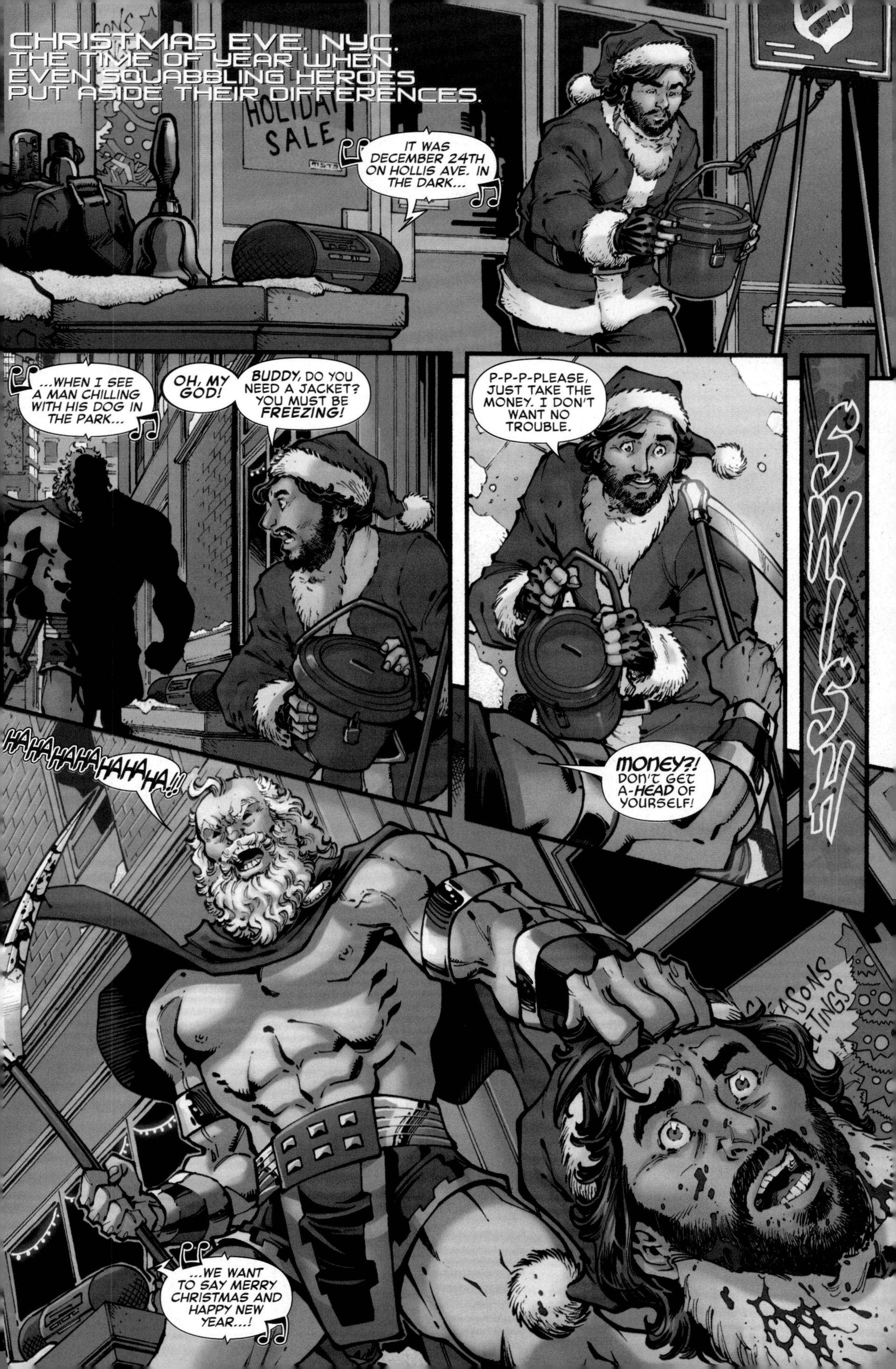
CHRISTMAS EVE, NYC.
THE TIME OF YEAR WHEN EVEN SQUABBLING HEROES PUT ASIDE THEIR DIFFERENCES.
HOLIDAY SALE
IT WAS DECEMBER 24TH ON HOLLIS AVE. IN THE DARK...
...WHEN I SEE A MAN CHILLING WITH HIS DOG IN THE PARK...
OH, MY GOD!
BUDDY, DO YOU NEED A JACKET? YOU MUST BE FREEZING!
P-P-P-PLEASE, JUST TAKE THE MONEY. I DON'T WANT NO TROUBLE.
SWISH!
MONEY?! DON'T GET A-HEAD OF YOURSELF!
HAHAHAHAHAHAHA!!
...WE WANT TO SAY MERRY CHRISTMAS AND HAPPY NEW YEAR...!

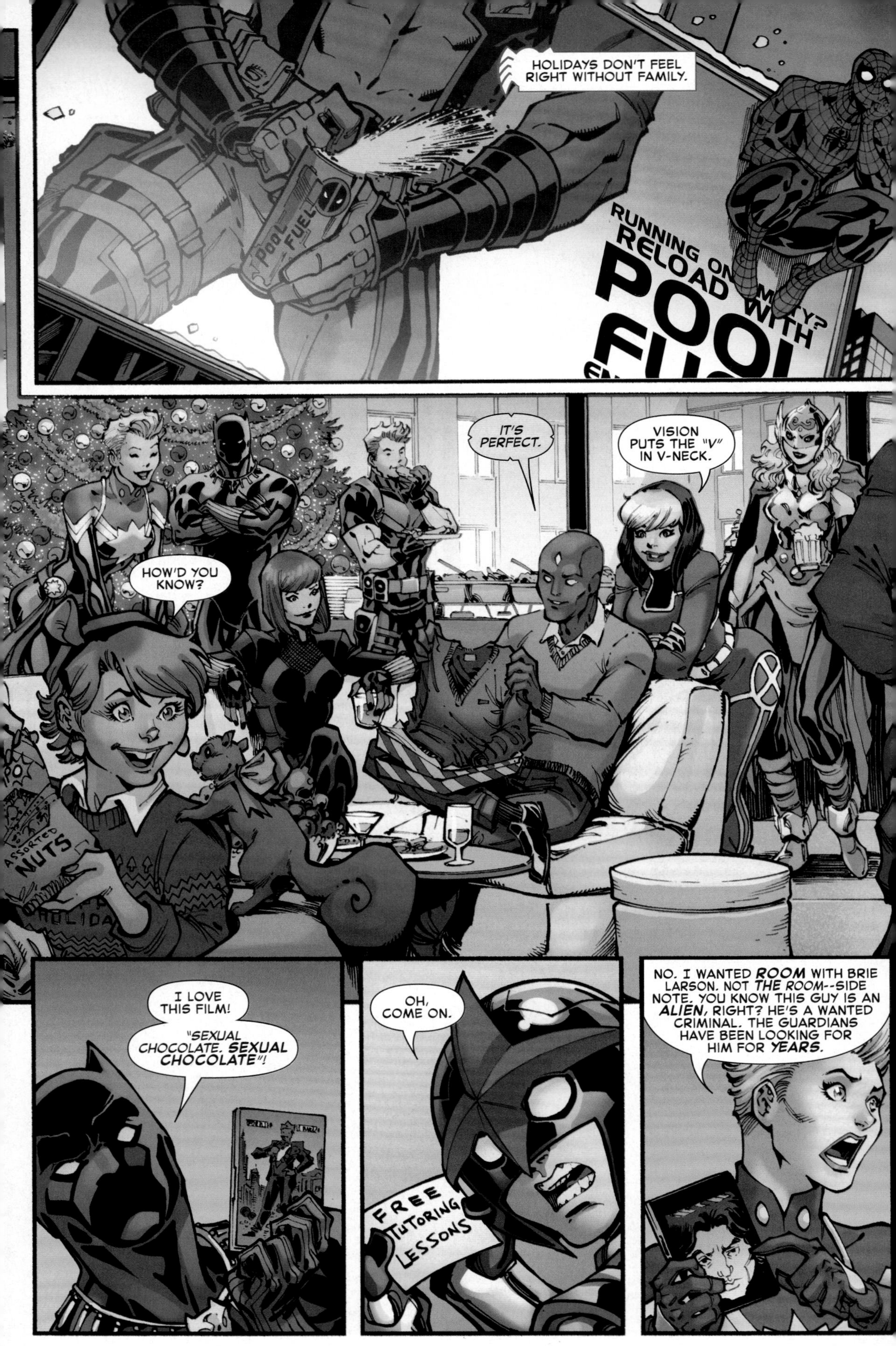
HOLIDAYS DON'T FEEL RIGHT WITHOUT FAMILY.
POOL FUEL
RUNNING ON E...? RELOAD WITH POOL FU...
IT'S PERFECT.
VISION PUTS THE "V" IN V-NECK.
HOW'D YOU KNOW?
ASSORTED NUTS
I LOVE THIS FILM!
"SEXUAL CHOCOLATE. SEXUAL CHOCOLATE"!
OH, COME ON.
FREE TUTORING LESSONS
NO. I WANTED ROOM WITH BRIE LARSON. NOT THE ROOM--SIDE NOTE. YOU KNOW THIS GUY IS AN ALIEN, RIGHT? HE'S A WANTED CRIMINAL. THE GUARDIANS HAVE BEEN LOOKING FOR HIM FOR YEARS.

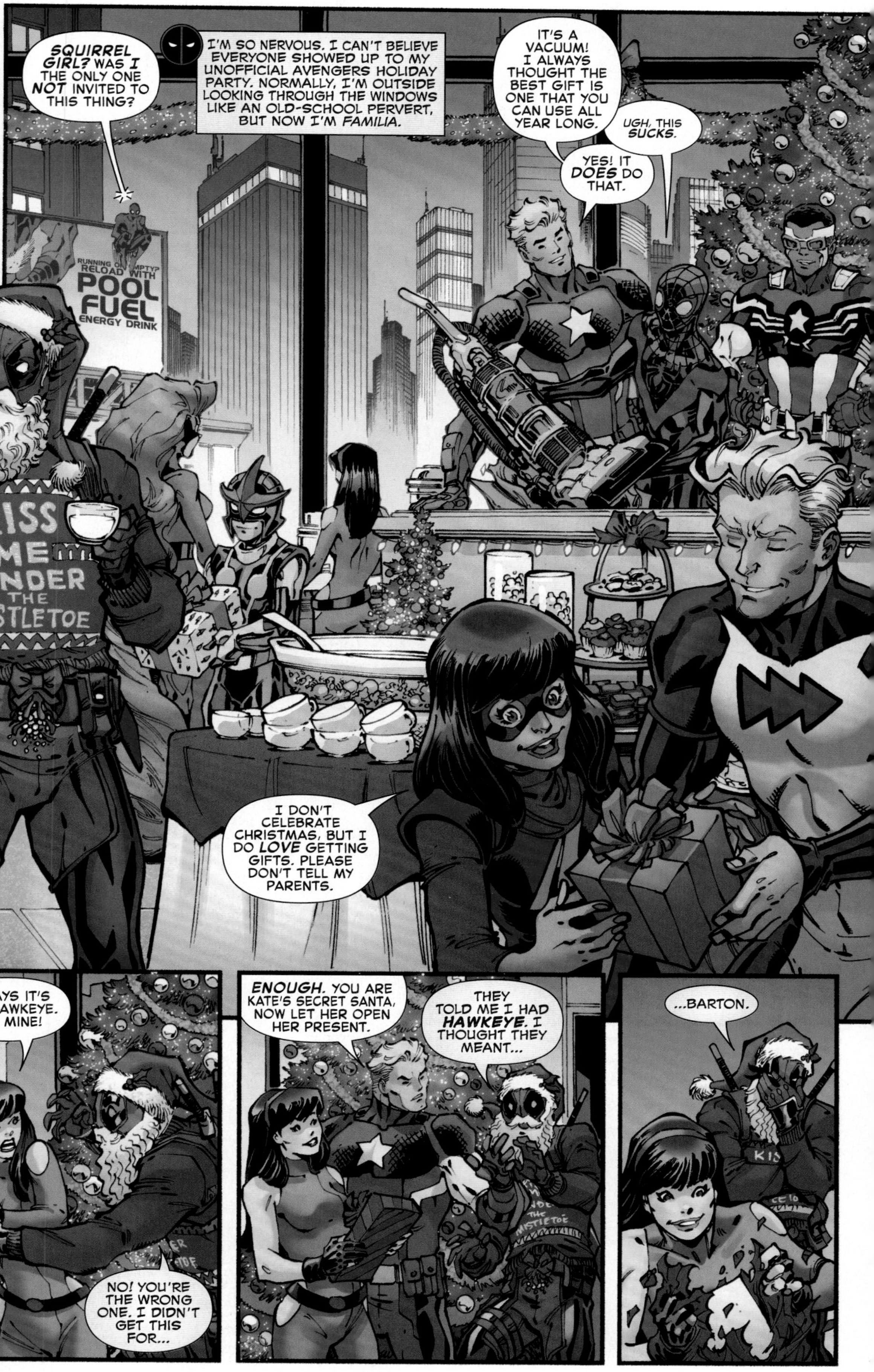
SQUIRREL GIRL? WAS I THE ONLY ONE NOT INVITED TO THIS THING?
I'M SO NERVOUS. I CAN'T BELIEVE EVERYONE SHOWED UP TO MY UNOFFICIAL AVENGERS HOLIDAY PARTY. NORMALLY, I'M OUTSIDE LOOKING THROUGH THE WINDOWS LIKE AN OLD-SCHOOL PERVERT, BUT NOW I'M FAMILIA.
IT'S A VACUUM! I ALWAYS THOUGHT THE BEST GIFT IS ONE THAT YOU CAN USE ALL YEAR LONG.
UGH, THIS SUCKS.
YES! IT DOES DO THAT.
RELOAD WITH
POOL FUEL
ENERGY DRINK
KISS ME UNDER THE MISTLETOE
I DON'T CELEBRATE CHRISTMAS, BUT I DO LOVE GETTING GIFTS. PLEASE DON'T TELL MY PARENTS.
IT SAYS IT'S FOR HAWKEYE. IT'S MINE!
NO! YOU'RE THE WRONG ONE. I DIDN'T GET THIS FOR...
ENOUGH. YOU ARE KATE'S SECRET SANTA, NOW LET HER OPEN HER PRESENT.
THEY TOLD ME I HAD HAWKEYE. I THOUGHT THEY MEANT...
...BARTON.

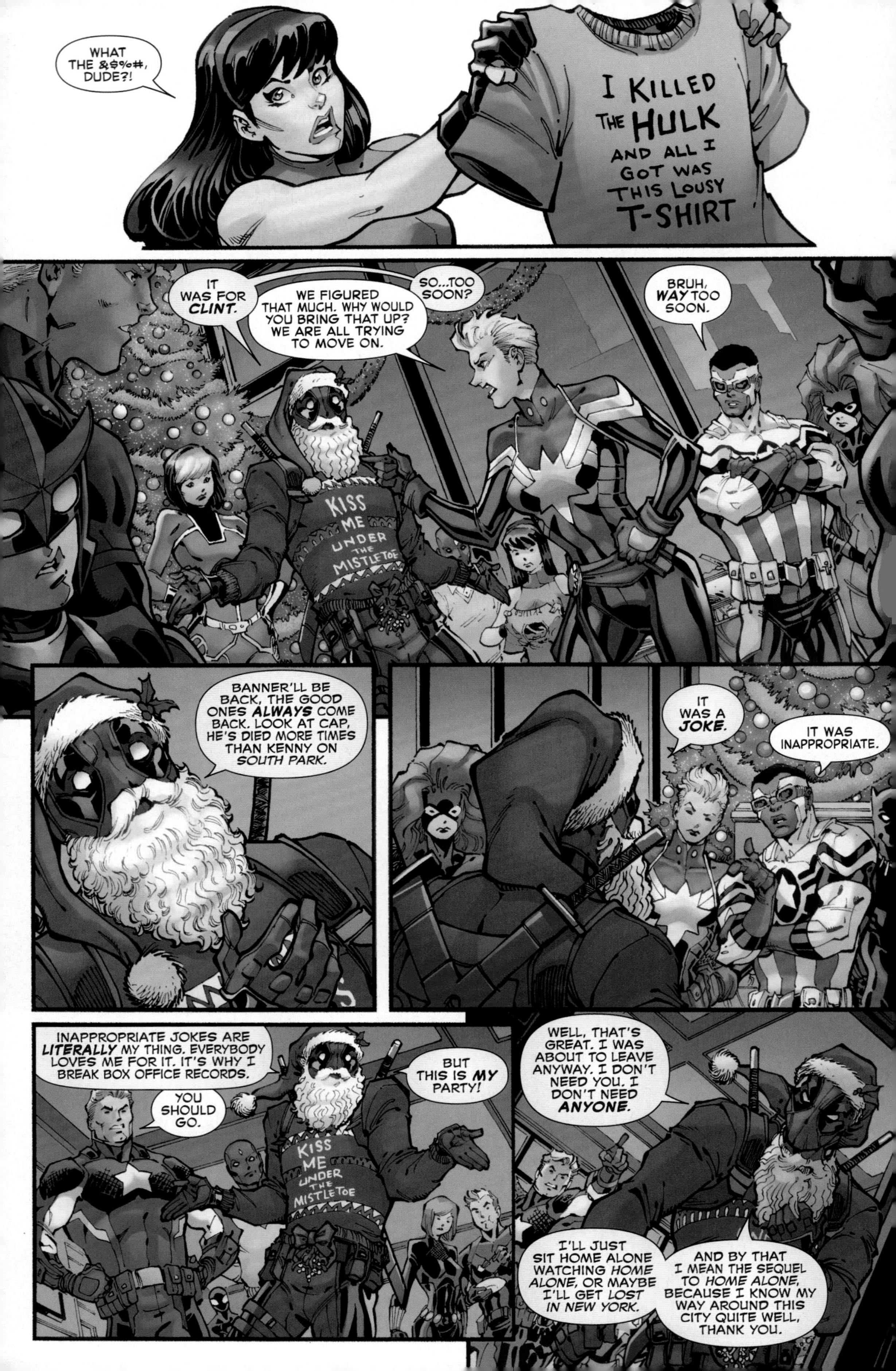
WHAT THE &$%#, DUDE?!
I KILLED THE HULK AND ALL I GOT WAS THIS LOUSY T-SHIRT
IT WAS FOR CLINT.
WE FIGURED THAT MUCH. WHY WOULD YOU BRING THAT UP? WE ARE ALL TRYING TO MOVE ON.
SO...TOO SOON?
BRUH, WAY TOO SOON.
KISS ME UNDER THE MISTLETOE
BANNER'LL BE BACK, THE GOOD ONES ALWAYS COME BACK. LOOK AT CAP, HE'S DIED MORE TIMES THAN KENNY ON SOUTH PARK.
IT WAS A JOKE.
IT WAS INAPPROPRIATE.
INAPPROPRIATE JOKES ARE LITERALLY MY THING. EVERYBODY LOVES ME FOR IT. IT'S WHY I BREAK BOX OFFICE RECORDS.
YOU SHOULD GO.
BUT THIS IS MY PARTY!
KISS ME UNDER THE MISTLETOE
WELL, THAT'S GREAT. I WAS ABOUT TO LEAVE ANYWAY. I DON'T NEED YOU. I DON'T NEED ANYONE.
I'LL JUST SIT HOME ALONE WATCHING HOME ALONE, OR MAYBE I'LL GET LOST IN NEW YORK.
AND BY THAT I MEAN THE SEQUEL TO HOME ALONE, BECAUSE I KNOW MY WAY AROUND THIS CITY QUITE WELL, THANK YOU.

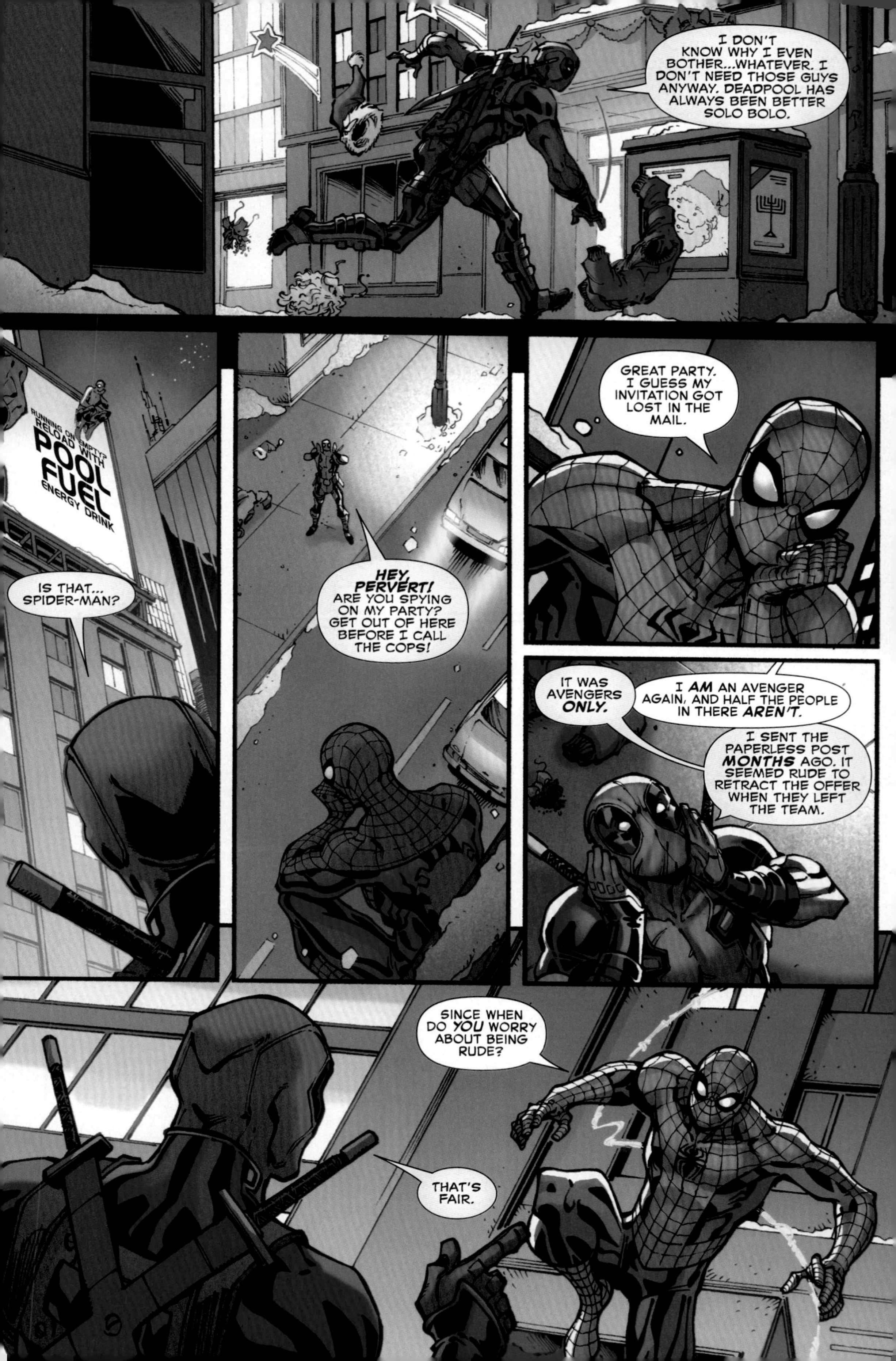
I DON'T KNOW WHY I EVEN BOTHER...WHATEVER. I DON'T NEED THOSE GUYS ANYWAY. DEADPOOL HAS ALWAYS BEEN BETTER SOLO BOLO.
RUNNING ON EMPTY? RELOAD WITH POOL FUEL ENERGY DRINK
IS THAT... SPIDER-MAN?
HEY, PERVERT! ARE YOU SPYING ON MY PARTY? GET OUT OF HERE BEFORE I CALL THE COPS!
GREAT PARTY. I GUESS MY INVITATION GOT LOST IN THE MAIL.
IT WAS AVENGERS ONLY.
I AM AN AVENGER AGAIN, AND HALF THE PEOPLE IN THERE AREN'T.
I SENT THE PAPERLESS POST MONTHS AGO. IT SEEMED RUDE TO RETRACT THE OFFER WHEN THEY LEFT THE TEAM.
SINCE WHEN DO YOU WORRY ABOUT BEING RUDE?
THAT'S FAIR.

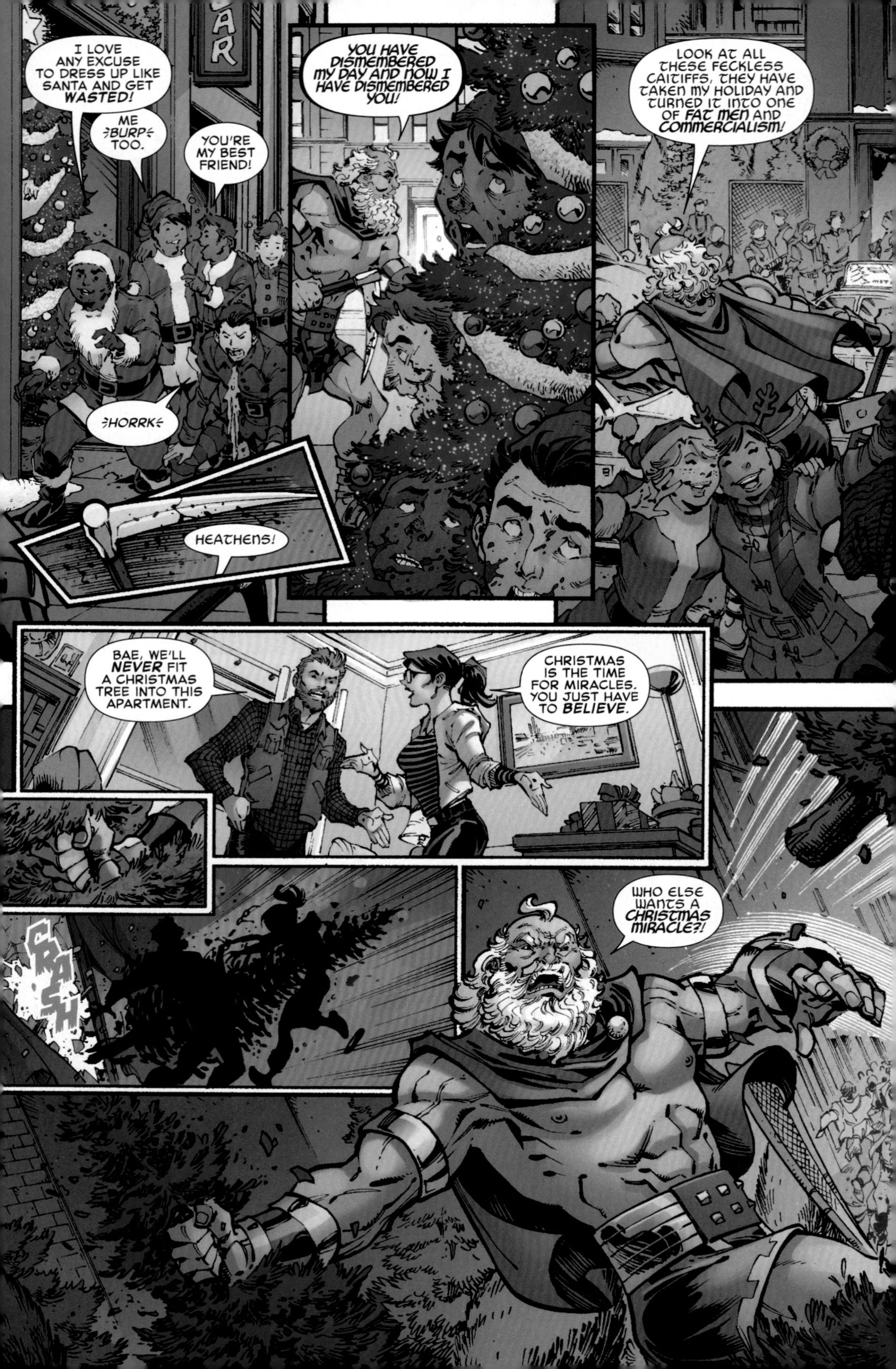

I LOVE ANY EXCUSE TO DRESS UP LIKE SANTA AND GET WASTED!
ME *BURP* TOO.
YOU'RE MY BEST FRIEND!
HORRK
HEATHENS!
YOU HAVE DISMEMBERED MY DAY AND NOW I HAVE DISMEMBERED YOU!
LOOK AT ALL THESE FECKLESS CAITIFFS, THEY HAVE TAKEN MY HOLIDAY AND TURNED IT INTO ONE OF FAT MEN AND COMMERCIALISM!
BAE, WE'LL NEVER FIT A CHRISTMAS TREE INTO THIS APARTMENT.
CHRISTMAS IS THE TIME FOR MIRACLES. YOU JUST HAVE TO BELIEVE.
CRASH
WHO ELSE WANTS A CHRISTMAS MIRACLE?!

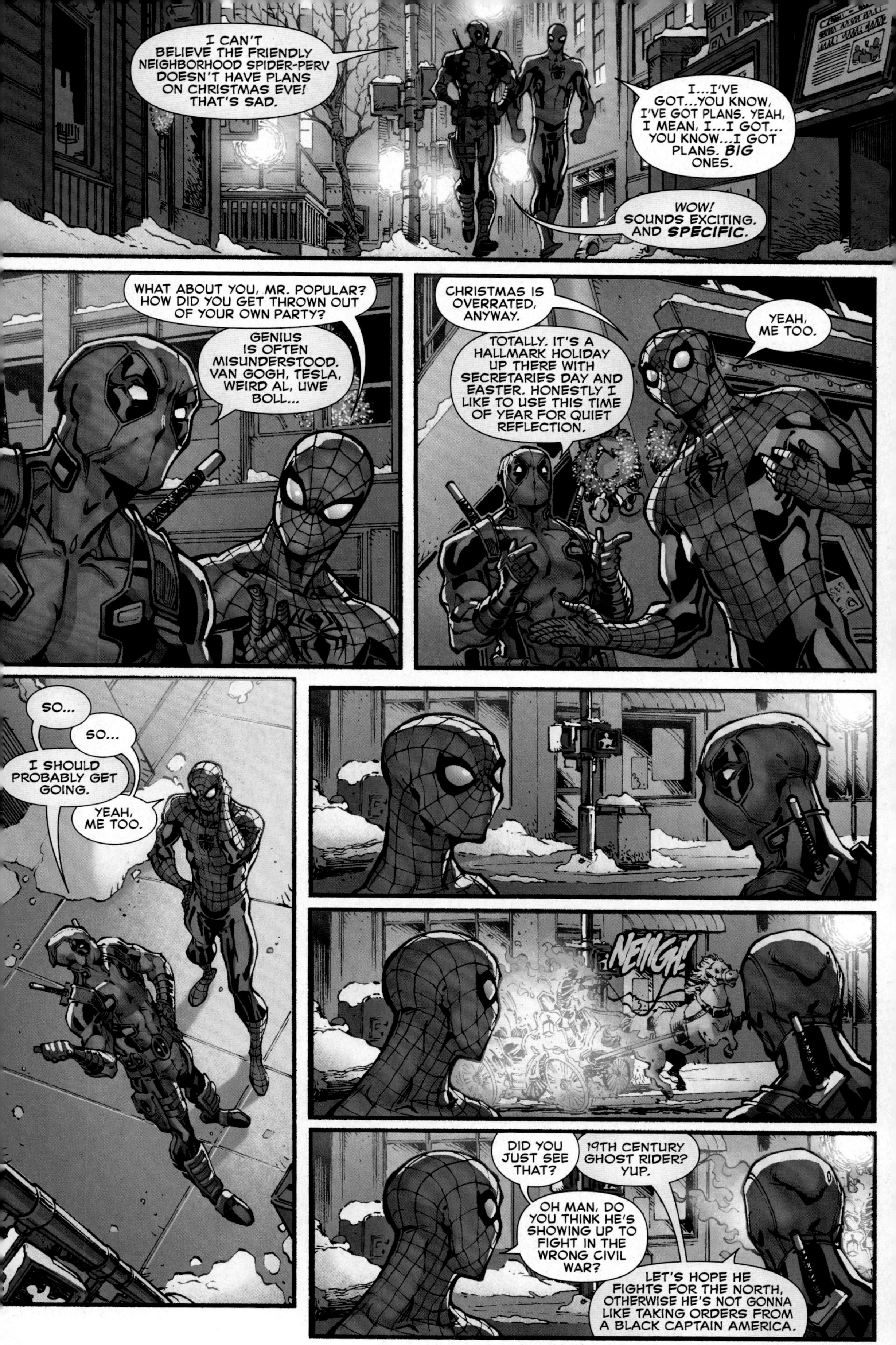
I CAN'T BELIEVE THE FRIENDLY NEIGHBORHOOD SPIDER-PERV DOESN'T HAVE PLANS ON CHRISTMAS EVE! THAT'S SAD.
I...I'VE GOT...YOU KNOW, I'VE GOT PLANS. YEAH, I MEAN, I...I GOT... YOU KNOW...I GOT PLANS. BIG ONES.
WOW! SOUNDS EXCITING. AND SPECIFIC.
WHAT ABOUT YOU, MR. POPULAR? HOW DID YOU GET THROWN OUT OF YOUR OWN PARTY?
GENIUS IS OFTEN MISUNDERSTOOD. VAN GOGH, TESLA, WEIRD AL, UWE BOLL...
CHRISTMAS IS OVERRATED, ANYWAY.
YEAH, ME TOO.
TOTALLY. IT'S A HALLMARK HOLIDAY UP THERE WITH SECRETARIES DAY AND EASTER. HONESTLY I LIKE TO USE THIS TIME OF YEAR FOR QUIET REFLECTION.
SO...
SO...
I SHOULD PROBABLY GET GOING.
YEAH, ME TOO.
NEIGH!
DID YOU JUST SEE THAT?
19TH CENTURY GHOST RIDER? YUP.
OH MAN, DO YOU THINK HE'S SHOWING UP TO FIGHT IN THE WRONG CIVIL WAR?
LET'S HOPE HE FIGHTS FOR THE NORTH, OTHERWISE HE'S NOT GONNA LIKE TAKING ORDERS FROM A BLACK CAPTAIN AMERICA.

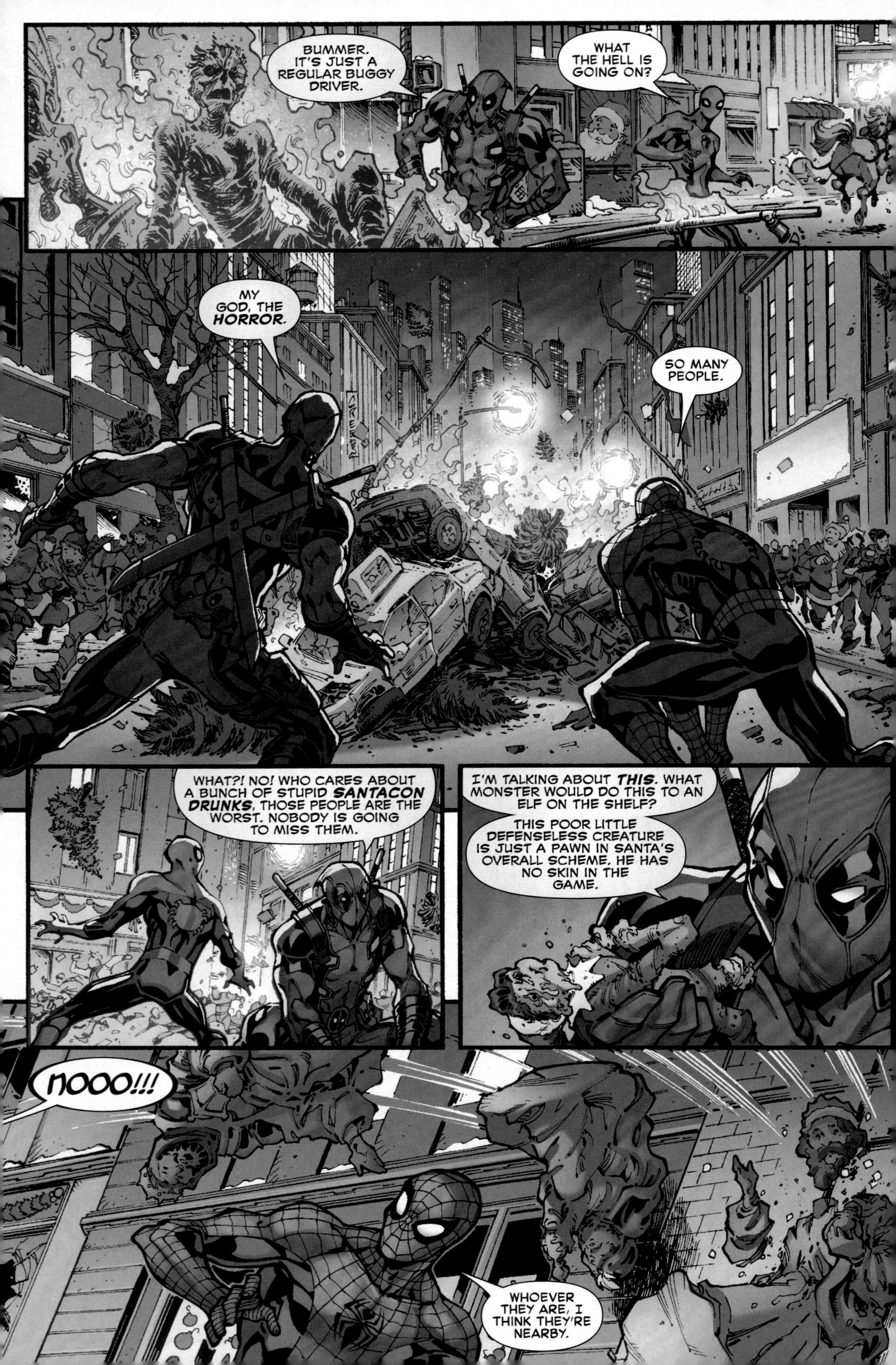
BUMMER. IT'S JUST A REGULAR BUGGY DRIVER.
WHAT THE HELL IS GOING ON?
MY GOD, THE HORROR.
SO MANY PEOPLE.
WHAT?! NO! WHO CARES ABOUT A BUNCH OF STUPID SANTACON DRUNKS, THOSE PEOPLE ARE THE WORST. NOBODY IS GOING TO MISS THEM.
I'M TALKING ABOUT THIS. WHAT MONSTER WOULD DO THIS TO AN ELF ON THE SHELF?
THIS POOR LITTLE DEFENSELESS CREATURE IS JUST A PAWN IN SANTA'S OVERALL SCHEME. HE HAS NO SKIN IN THE GAME.
NOOO!!!
WHOEVER THEY ARE, I THINK THEY'RE NEARBY.

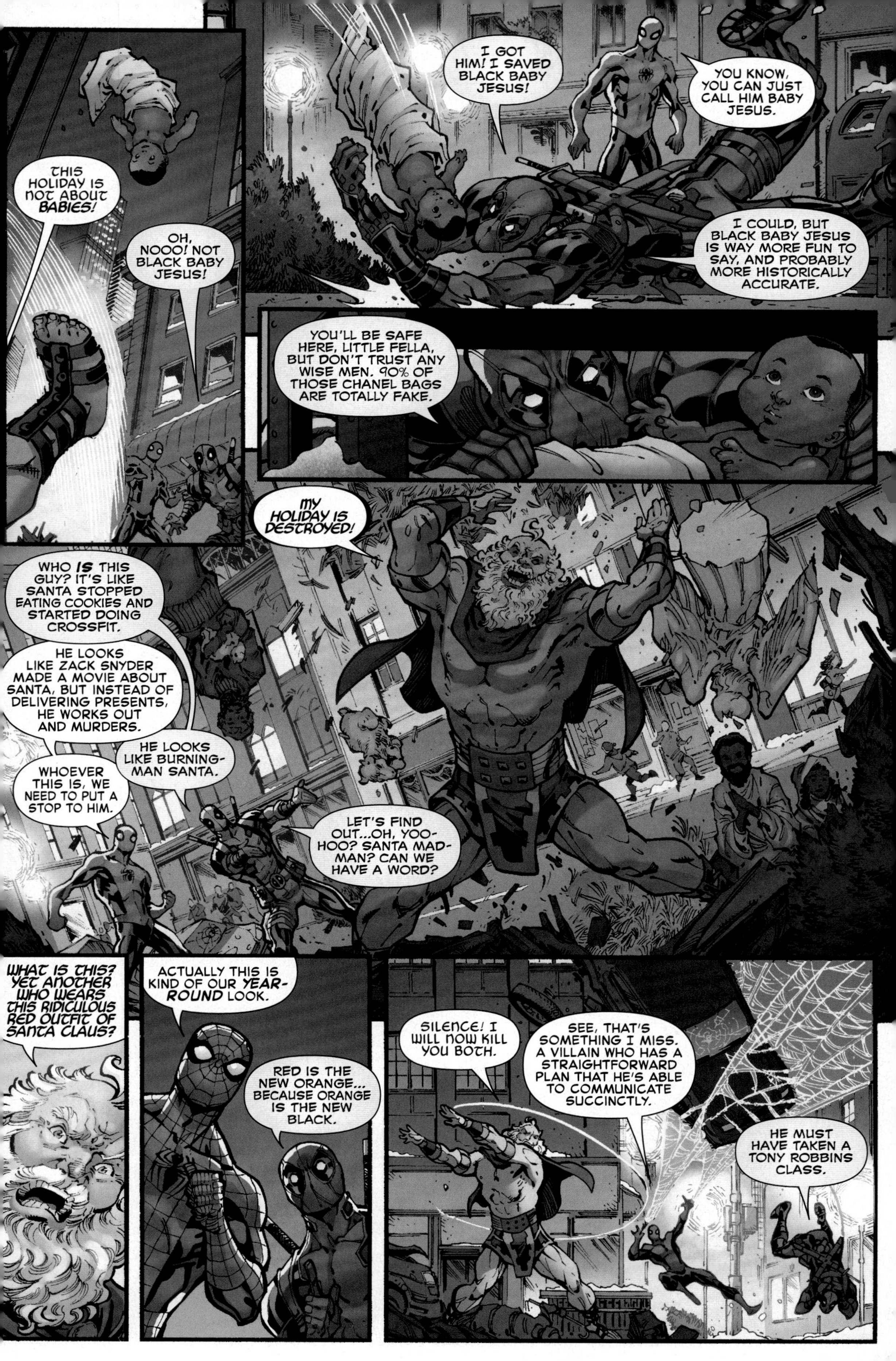
THIS HOLIDAY IS NOT ABOUT BABIES!
OH, NOOO! NOT BLACK BABY JESUS!
I GOT HIM! I SAVED BLACK BABY JESUS!
YOU KNOW, YOU CAN JUST CALL HIM BABY JESUS.
I COULD, BUT BLACK BABY JESUS IS WAY MORE FUN TO SAY, AND PROBABLY MORE HISTORICALLY ACCURATE.
YOU'LL BE SAFE HERE, LITTLE FELLA, BUT DON'T TRUST ANY WISE MEN. 90% OF THOSE CHANEL BAGS ARE TOTALLY FAKE.
MY HOLIDAY IS DESTROYED!
WHO IS THIS GUY? IT'S LIKE SANTA STOPPED EATING COOKIES AND STARTED DOING CROSSFIT.
HE LOOKS LIKE ZACK SNYDER MADE A MOVIE ABOUT SANTA, BUT INSTEAD OF DELIVERING PRESENTS, HE WORKS OUT AND MURDERS.
HE LOOKS LIKE BURNING-MAN SANTA.
WHOEVER THIS IS, WE NEED TO PUT A STOP TO HIM.
LET'S FIND OUT...OH, YOO-HOO? SANTA MAD-MAN? CAN WE HAVE A WORD?
WHAT IS THIS? YET ANOTHER WHO WEARS THIS RIDICULOUS RED OUTFIT OF SANTA CLAUS?
ACTUALLY THIS IS KIND OF OUR YEAR-ROUND LOOK.
RED IS THE NEW ORANGE... BECAUSE ORANGE IS THE NEW BLACK.
SILENCE! I WILL NOW KILL YOU BOTH.
SEE, THAT'S SOMETHING I MISS. A VILLAIN WHO HAS A STRAIGHTFORWARD PLAN THAT HE'S ABLE TO COMMUNICATE SUCCINCTLY.
HE MUST HAVE TAKEN A TONY ROBBINS CLASS.

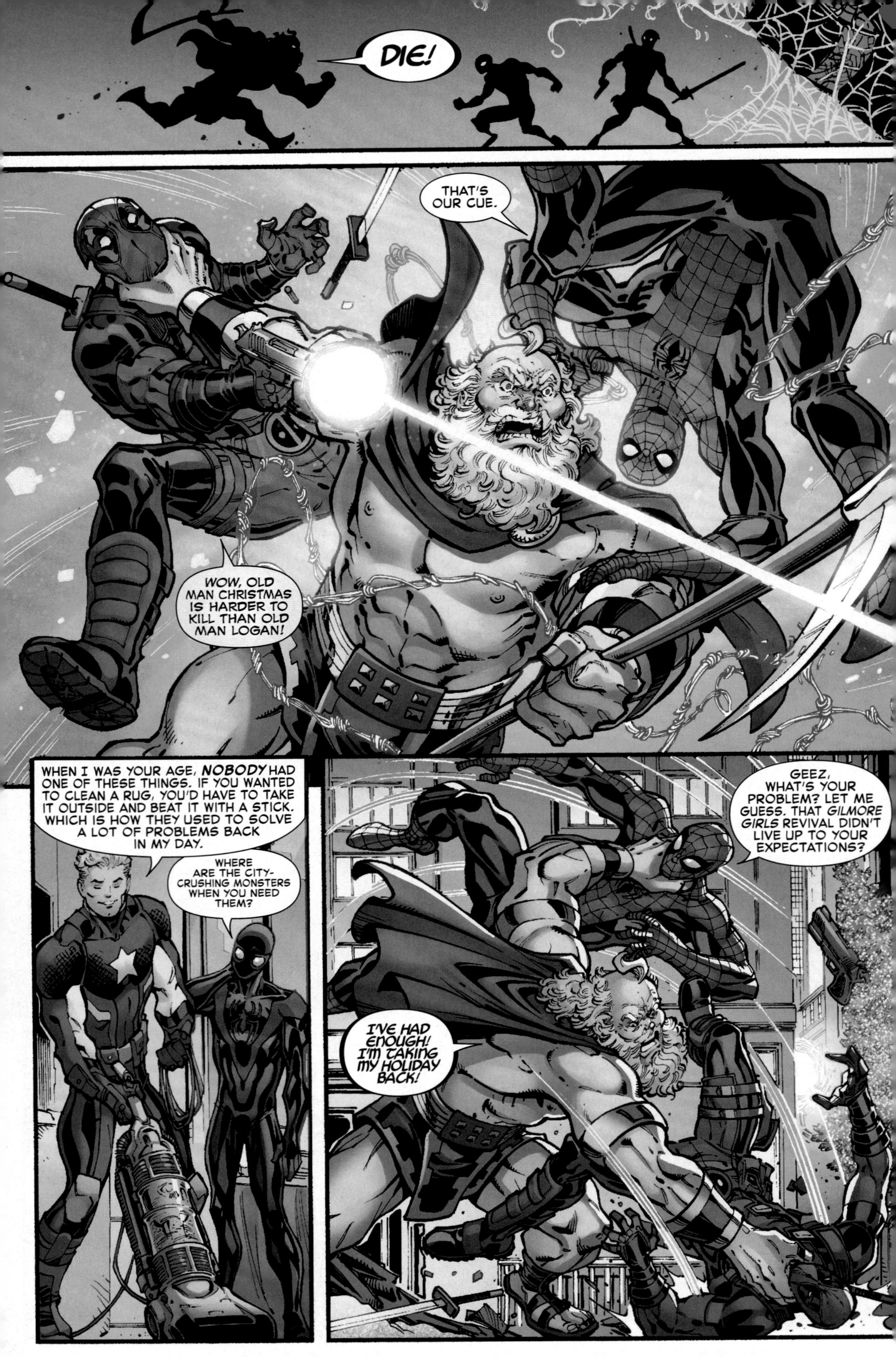
DIE!
THAT'S OUR CUE.
WOW, OLD MAN CHRISTMAS IS HARDER TO KILL THAN OLD MAN LOGAN!
WHEN I WAS YOUR AGE, NOBODY HAD ONE OF THESE THINGS. IF YOU WANTED TO CLEAN A RUG, YOU'D HAVE TO TAKE IT OUTSIDE AND BEAT IT WITH A STICK. WHICH IS HOW THEY USED TO SOLVE A LOT OF PROBLEMS BACK IN MY DAY.
WHERE ARE THE CITY-CRUSHING MONSTERS WHEN YOU NEED THEM?
GEEZ, WHAT'S YOUR PROBLEM? LET ME GUESS. THAT GILMORE GIRLS REVIVAL DIDN'T LIVE UP TO YOUR EXPECTATIONS?
I'VE HAD ENOUGH! I'M TAKING MY HOLIDAY BACK!

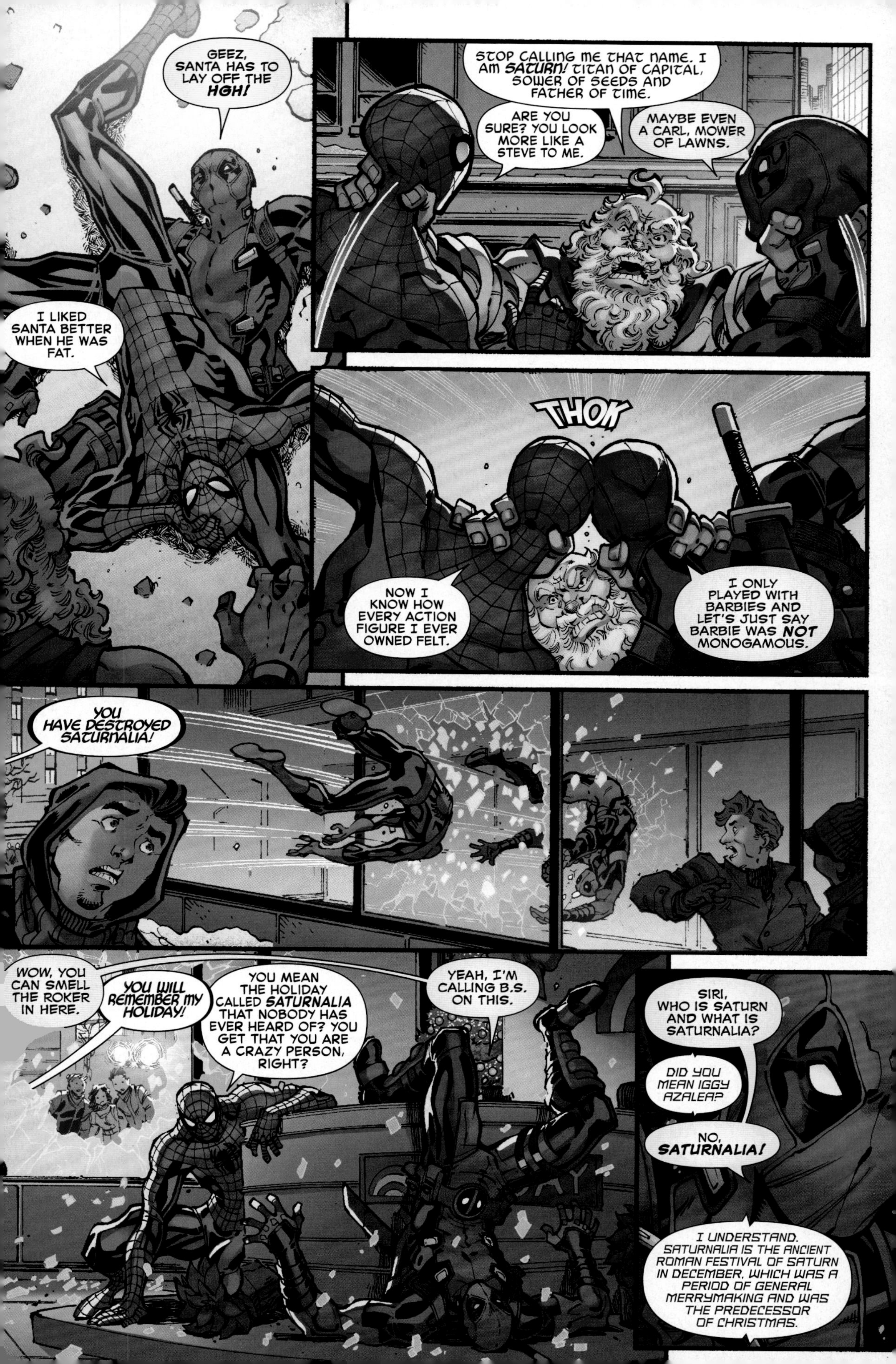

GEEZ, SANTA HAS TO LAY OFF THE HGH!
I LIKED SANTA BETTER WHEN HE WAS FAT.
STOP CALLING ME THAT NAME. I AM SATURN! TITAN OF CAPITAL, SOWER OF SEEDS AND FATHER OF TIME.
ARE YOU SURE? YOU LOOK MORE LIKE A STEVE TO ME.
MAYBE EVEN A CARL, MOWER OF LAWNS.
THOK
NOW I KNOW HOW EVERY ACTION FIGURE I EVER OWNED FELT.
I ONLY PLAYED WITH BARBIES AND LET'S JUST SAY BARBIE WAS NOT MONOGAMOUS.
YOU HAVE DESTROYED SATURNALIA!
WOW, YOU CAN SMELL THE ROKER IN HERE.
YOU WILL REMEMBER MY HOLIDAY!
YOU MEAN THE HOLIDAY CALLED SATURNALIA THAT NOBODY HAS EVER HEARD OF? YOU GET THAT YOU ARE A CRAZY PERSON, RIGHT?
YEAH, I'M CALLING B.S. ON THIS.
SIRI, WHO IS SATURN AND WHAT IS SATURNALIA?
DID YOU MEAN IGGY AZALEA?
NO, SATURNALIA!
I UNDERSTAND. SATURNALIA IS THE ANCIENT ROMAN FESTIVAL OF SATURN IN DECEMBER, WHICH WAS A PERIOD OF GENERAL MERRYMAKING AND WAS THE PREDECESSOR OF CHRISTMAS.

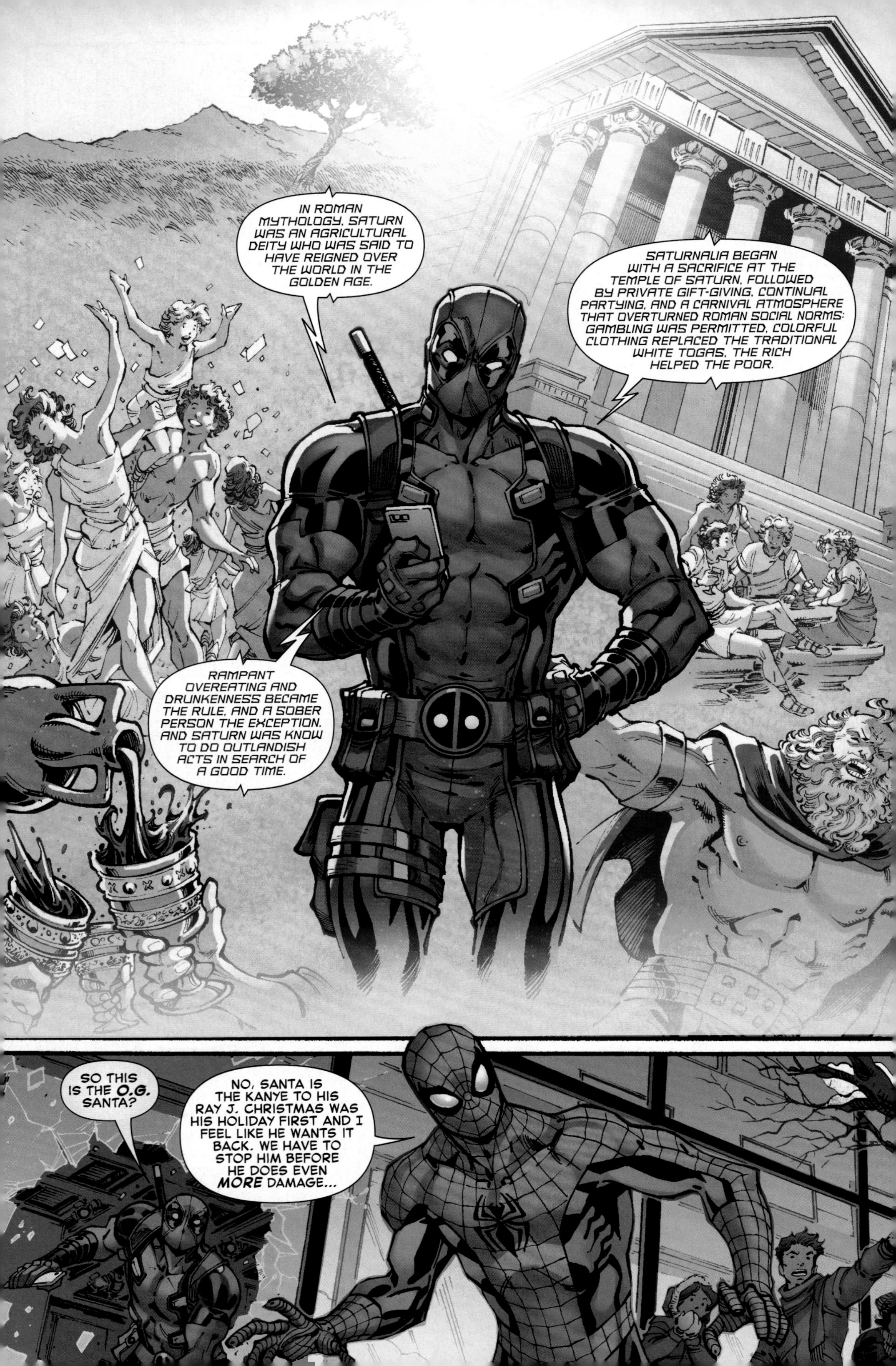
IN ROMAN MYTHOLOGY, SATURN WAS AN AGRICULTURAL DEITY WHO WAS SAID TO HAVE REIGNED OVER THE WORLD IN THE GOLDEN AGE.
SATURNALIA BEGAN WITH A SACRIFICE AT THE TEMPLE OF SATURN, FOLLOWED BY PRIVATE GIFT-GIVING, CONTINUAL PARTYING, AND A CARNIVAL ATMOSPHERE THAT OVERTURNED ROMAN SOCIAL NORMS: GAMBLING WAS PERMITTED, COLORFUL CLOTHING REPLACED THE TRADITIONAL WHITE TOGAS, THE RICH HELPED THE POOR.
RAMPANT OVEREATING AND DRUNKENNESS BECAME THE RULE, AND A SOBER PERSON THE EXCEPTION. AND SATURN WAS KNOW TO DO OUTLANDISH ACTS IN SEARCH OF A GOOD TIME.
SO THIS IS THE O.G. SANTA?
NO, SANTA IS THE KANYE TO HIS RAY J. CHRISTMAS WAS HIS HOLIDAY FIRST AND I FEEL LIKE HE WANTS IT BACK. WE HAVE TO STOP HIM BEFORE HE DOES EVEN MORE DAMAGE...

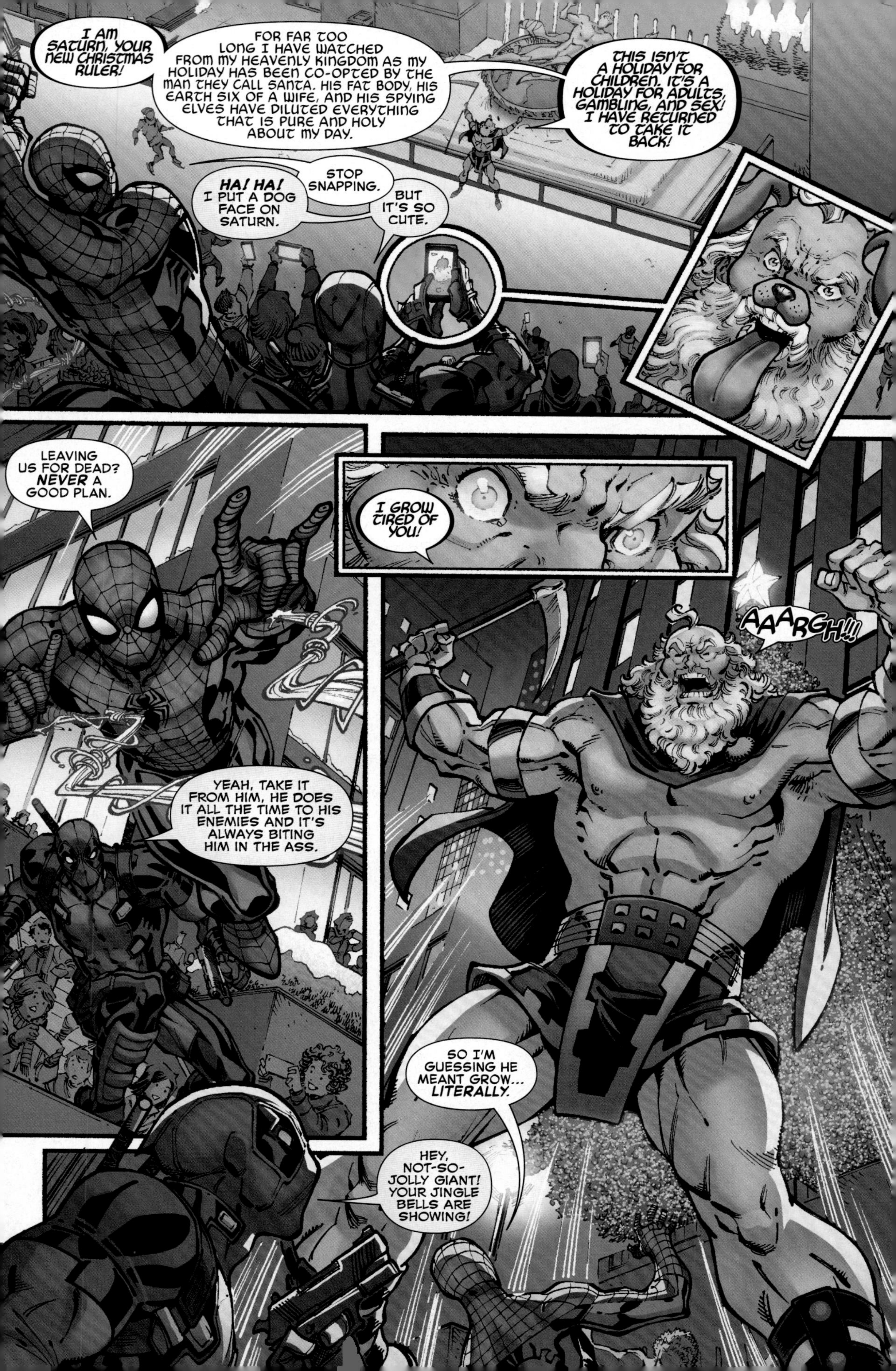
I AM SATURN, YOUR NEW CHRISTMAS RULER!
FOR FAR TOO LONG I HAVE WATCHED FROM MY HEAVENLY KINGDOM AS MY HOLIDAY HAS BEEN CO-OPTED BY THE MAN THEY CALL SANTA. HIS FAT BODY, HIS EARTH SIX OF A WIFE, AND HIS SPYING ELVES HAVE DILUTED EVERYTHING THAT IS PURE AND HOLY ABOUT MY DAY.
THIS ISN'T A HOLIDAY FOR CHILDREN. IT'S A HOLIDAY FOR ADULTS, GAMBLING, AND SEX! I HAVE RETURNED TO TAKE IT BACK!
HA! HA! I PUT A DOG FACE ON SATURN.
STOP SNAPPING.
BUT IT'S SO CUTE.
LEAVING US FOR DEAD? NEVER A GOOD PLAN.
YEAH, TAKE IT FROM HIM, HE DOES IT ALL THE TIME TO HIS ENEMIES AND IT'S ALWAYS BITING HIM IN THE ASS.
I GROW TIRED OF YOU!
AAARGH!!!
SO I'M GUESSING HE MEANT GROW... LITERALLY.
HEY, NOT-SO-JOLLY GIANT! YOUR JINGLE BELLS ARE SHOWING!

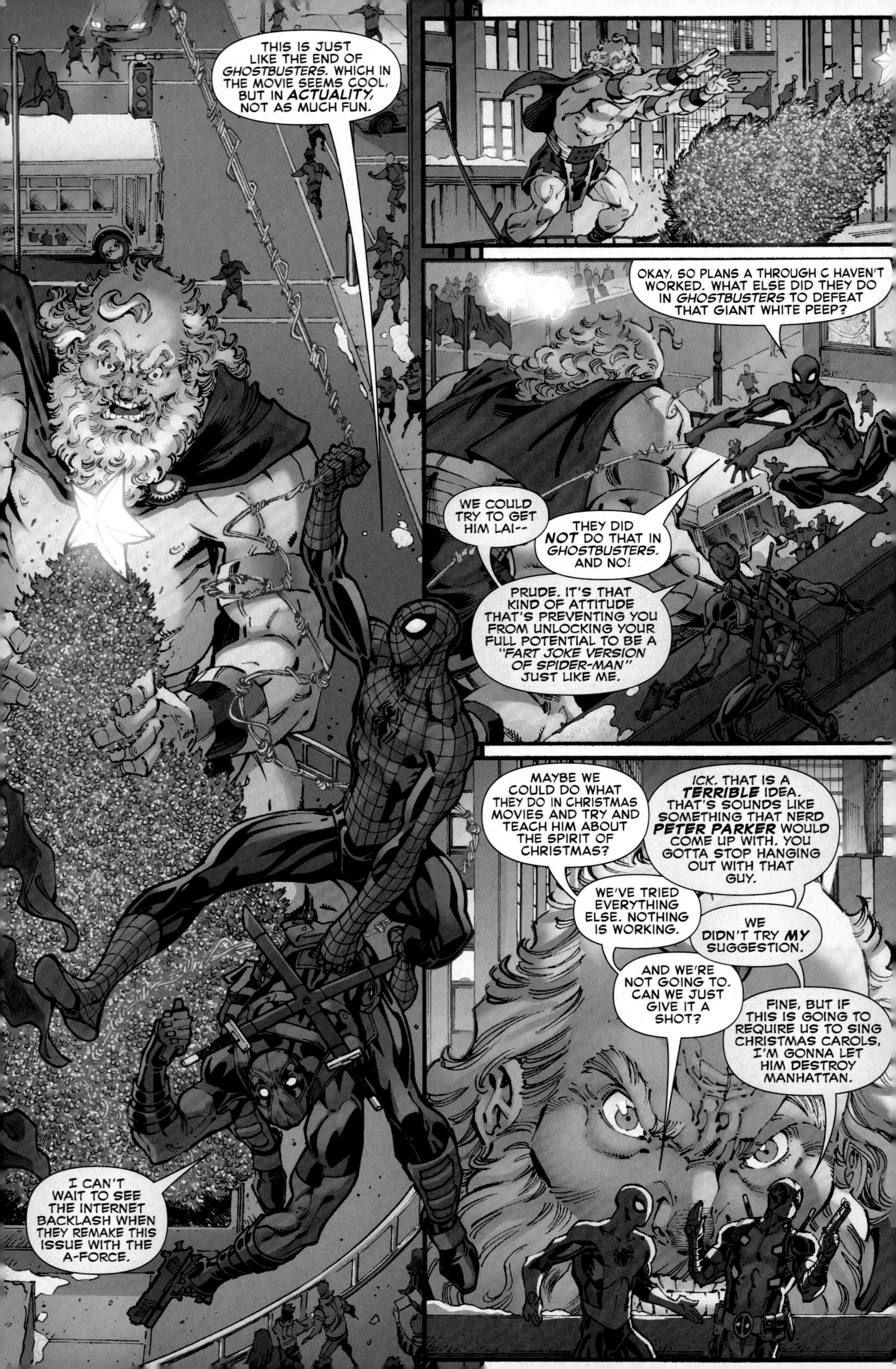
THIS IS JUST LIKE THE END OF GHOSTBUSTERS. WHICH IN THE MOVIE SEEMS COOL, BUT IN ACTUALITY, NOT AS MUCH FUN.
I CAN'T WAIT TO SEE THE INTERNET BACKLASH WHEN THEY REMAKE THIS ISSUE WITH THE A-FORCE.
OKAY, SO PLANS A THROUGH C HAVEN'T WORKED. WHAT ELSE DID THEY DO IN GHOSTBUSTERS TO DEFEAT THAT GIANT WHITE PEEP?
WE COULD TRY TO GET HIM LAI--
THEY DID NOT DO THAT IN GHOSTBUSTERS. AND NO!
PRUDE. IT'S THAT KIND OF ATTITUDE THAT'S PREVENTING YOU FROM UNLOCKING YOUR FULL POTENTIAL TO BE A "FART JOKE VERSION OF SPIDER-MAN" JUST LIKE ME.
MAYBE WE COULD DO WHAT THEY DO IN CHRISTMAS MOVIES AND TRY AND TEACH HIM ABOUT THE SPIRIT OF CHRISTMAS?
ICK. THAT IS A TERRIBLE IDEA. THAT'S SOUNDS LIKE SOMETHING THAT NERD PETER PARKER WOULD COME UP WITH. YOU GOTTA STOP HANGING OUT WITH THAT GUY.
WE'VE TRIED EVERYTHING ELSE. NOTHING IS WORKING.
WE DIDN'T TRY MY SUGGESTION.
AND WE'RE NOT GOING TO. CAN WE JUST GIVE IT A SHOT?
FINE, BUT IF THIS IS GOING TO REQUIRE US TO SING CHRISTMAS CAROLS, I'M GONNA LET HIM DESTROY MANHATTAN.

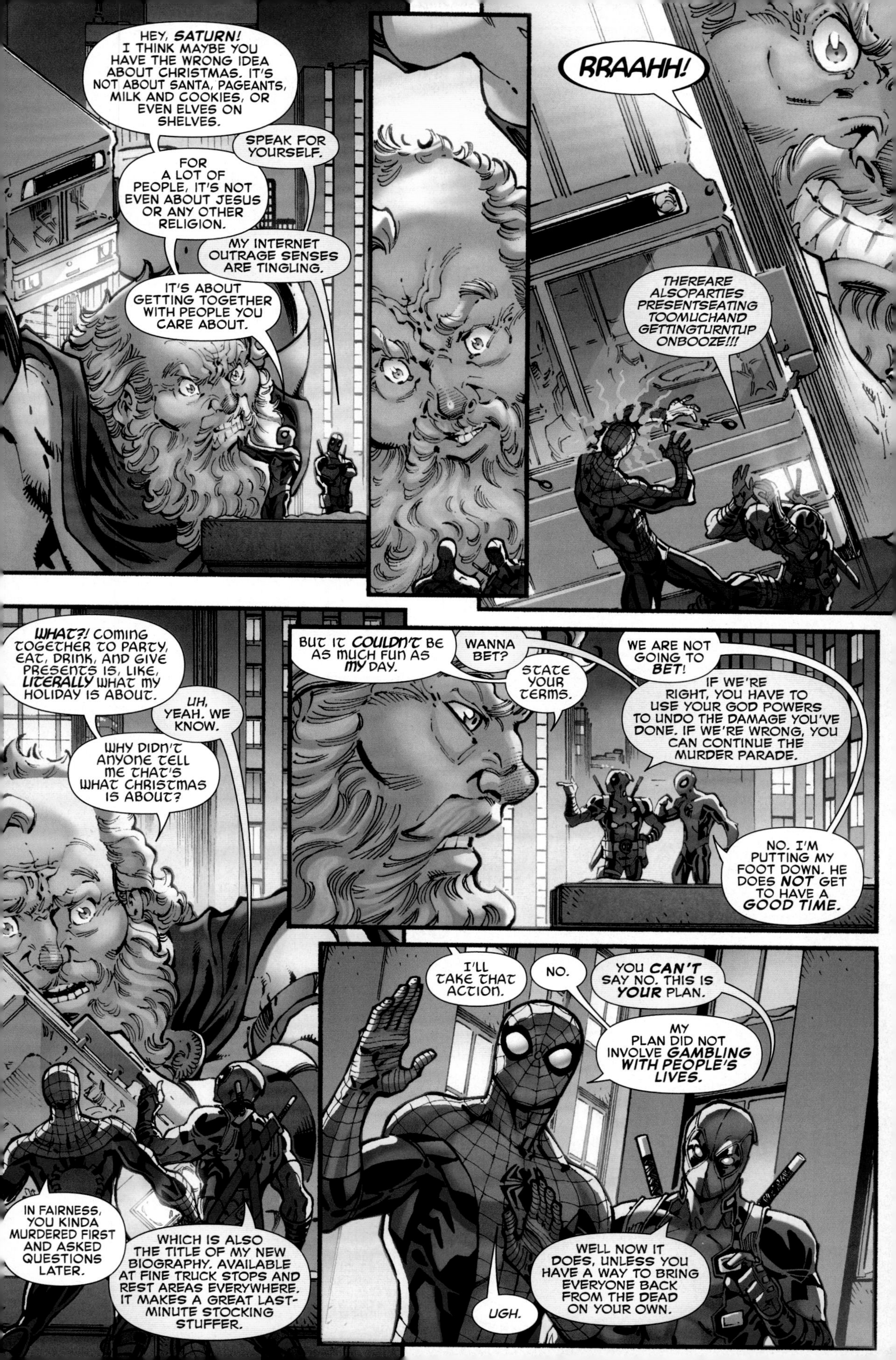

HEY, SATURN! I THINK MAYBE YOU HAVE THE WRONG IDEA ABOUT CHRISTMAS. IT'S NOT ABOUT SANTA, PAGEANTS, MILK AND COOKIES, OR EVEN ELVES ON SHELVES.
SPEAK FOR YOURSELF.
FOR A LOT OF PEOPLE, IT'S NOT EVEN ABOUT JESUS OR ANY OTHER RELIGION.
MY INTERNET OUTRAGE SENSES ARE TINGLING.
IT'S ABOUT GETTING TOGETHER WITH PEOPLE YOU CARE ABOUT.
BRAAHH!
THEREARE ALSOPARTIES PRESENTSEATING TOOMUCHAND GETTINGTURNTUP ONBOOZE!!!
WHAT?! COMING TOGETHER TO PARTY, EAT, DRINK, AND GIVE PRESENTS IS, LIKE, LITERALLY WHAT MY HOLIDAY IS ABOUT.
UH, YEAH. WE KNOW.
WHY DIDN'T ANYONE TELL ME THAT'S WHAT CHRISTMAS IS ABOUT?
IN FAIRNESS, YOU KINDA MURDERED FIRST AND ASKED QUESTIONS LATER.
WHICH IS ALSO THE TITLE OF MY NEW BIOGRAPHY. AVAILABLE AT FINE TRUCK STOPS AND REST AREAS EVERYWHERE. IT MAKES A GREAT LAST-MINUTE STOCKING STUFFER.
BUT IT COULDN'T BE AS MUCH FUN AS MY DAY.
WANNA BET?
STATE YOUR TERMS.
WE ARE NOT GOING TO BET!
IF WE'RE RIGHT, YOU HAVE TO USE YOUR GOD POWERS TO UNDO THE DAMAGE YOU'VE DONE. IF WE'RE WRONG, YOU CAN CONTINUE THE MURDER PARADE.
NO. I'M PUTTING MY FOOT DOWN. HE DOES NOT GET TO HAVE A GOOD TIME.
I'LL TAKE THAT ACTION.
NO.
YOU CAN'T SAY NO. THIS IS YOUR PLAN.
MY PLAN DID NOT INVOLVE GAMBLING WITH PEOPLE'S LIVES.
WELL NOW IT DOES, UNLESS YOU HAVE A WAY TO BRING EVERYONE BACK FROM THE DEAD ON YOUR OWN.
UGH.

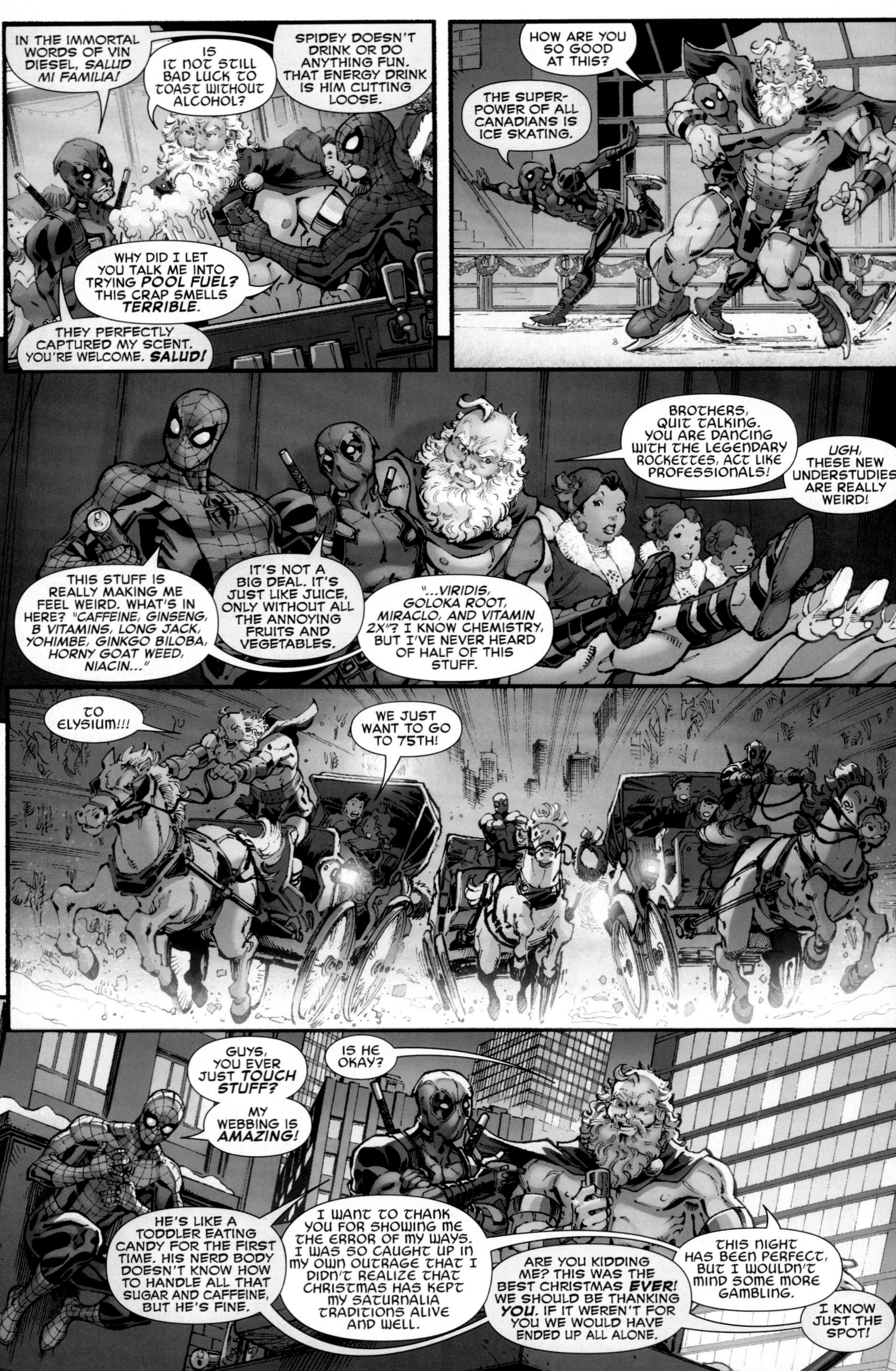
IN THE IMMORTAL WORDS OF VIN DIESEL, *SALUD MI FAMILIA!*
IS IT NOT STILL BAD LUCK TO TOAST WITHOUT ALCOHOL?
SPIDEY DOESN'T DRINK OR DO ANYTHING FUN. THAT ENERGY DRINK IS HIM CUTTING LOOSE.
WHY DID I LET YOU TALK ME INTO TRYING ***POOL FUEL?*** THIS CRAP SMELLS ***TERRIBLE***.
THEY PERFECTLY CAPTURED MY SCENT. YOU'RE WELCOME. ***SALUD!***
HOW ARE YOU SO GOOD AT THIS?
THE SUPER-POWER OF ALL CANADIANS IS ICE SKATING.
BROTHERS, QUIT TALKING. YOU ARE DANCING WITH THE LEGENDARY ROCKETTES, ACT LIKE PROFESSIONALS!
UGH, THESE NEW UNDERSTUDIES ARE REALLY WEIRD!
THIS STUFF IS REALLY MAKING ME FEEL WEIRD. WHAT'S IN HERE? *"CAFFEINE, GINSENG, B VITAMINS, LONG JACK, YOHIMBE, GINKGO BILOBA, HORNY GOAT WEED, NIACIN..."*
IT'S NOT A BIG DEAL. IT'S JUST LIKE JUICE, ONLY WITHOUT ALL THE ANNOYING FRUITS AND VEGETABLES.
"...VIRIDIS, GOLOKA ROOT, MIRACLO, AND VITAMIN 2X"? I KNOW CHEMISTRY, BUT I'VE NEVER HEARD OF HALF OF THIS STUFF.
TO ELYSIUM!!!
WE JUST WANT TO GO TO 75TH!
GUYS, YOU EVER JUST ***TOUCH STUFF?***
MY WEBBING IS ***AMAZING!***
IS HE OKAY?
HE'S LIKE A TODDLER EATING CANDY FOR THE FIRST TIME. HIS NERD BODY DOESN'T KNOW HOW TO HANDLE ALL THAT SUGAR AND CAFFEINE, BUT HE'S FINE.
I WANT TO THANK YOU FOR SHOWING ME THE ERROR OF MY WAYS. I WAS SO CAUGHT UP IN MY OWN OUTRAGE THAT I DIDN'T REALIZE THAT CHRISTMAS HAS KEPT MY SATURNALIA TRADITIONS ALIVE AND WELL.
ARE YOU KIDDING ME? THIS WAS THE BEST CHRISTMAS ***EVER!*** WE SHOULD BE THANKING ***YOU***. IF IT WEREN'T FOR YOU WE WOULD HAVE ENDED UP ALL ALONE.
THIS NIGHT HAS BEEN PERFECT, BUT I WOULDN'T MIND SOME MORE GAMBLING.
I KNOW JUST THE SPOT!

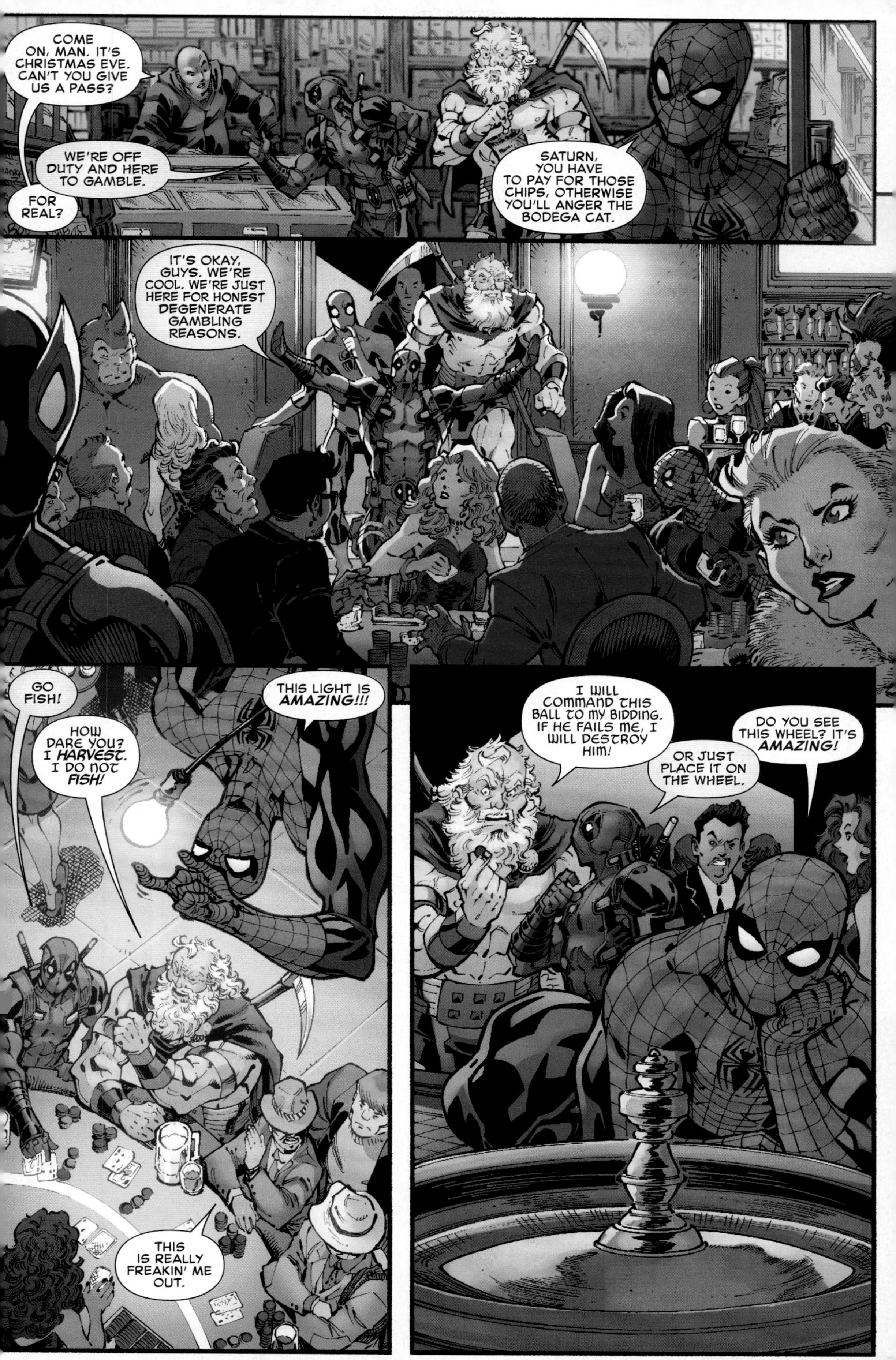
COME ON, MAN. IT'S CHRISTMAS EVE. CAN'T YOU GIVE US A PASS?
WE'RE OFF DUTY AND HERE TO GAMBLE.
FOR REAL?
SATURN, YOU HAVE TO PAY FOR THOSE CHIPS, OTHERWISE YOU'LL ANGER THE BODEGA CAT.
IT'S OKAY, GUYS. WE'RE COOL. WE'RE JUST HERE FOR HONEST DEGENERATE GAMBLING REASONS.
GO FISH!
HOW DARE YOU? I *HARVEST*. I DO NOT *FISH*!
THIS LIGHT IS *AMAZING!!!*
THIS IS REALLY FREAKIN' ME OUT.
I WILL COMMAND THIS BALL TO MY BIDDING. IF HE FAILS ME, I WILL DESTROY HIM!
OR JUST PLACE IT ON THE WHEEL.
DO YOU SEE THIS WHEEL? IT'S *AMAZING!*

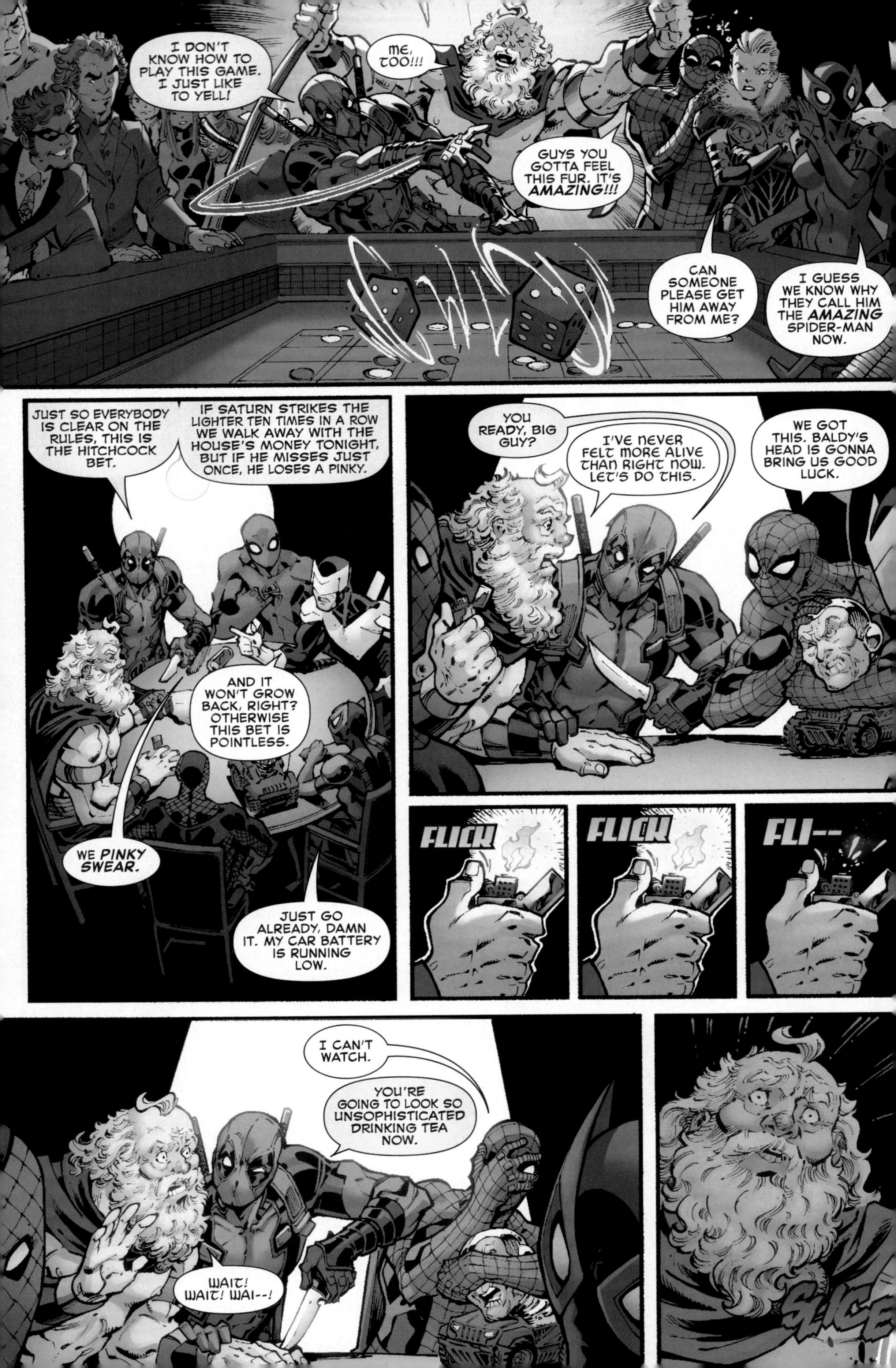
I DON'T KNOW HOW TO PLAY THIS GAME. I JUST LIKE TO YELL!
ME, TOO!!!
GUYS YOU GOTTA FEEL THIS FUR. IT'S AMAZING!!!
CAN SOMEONE PLEASE GET HIM AWAY FROM ME?
I GUESS WE KNOW WHY THEY CALL HIM THE AMAZING SPIDER-MAN NOW.
JUST SO EVERYBODY IS CLEAR ON THE RULES, THIS IS THE HITCHCOCK BET.
IF SATURN STRIKES THE LIGHTER TEN TIMES IN A ROW WE WALK AWAY WITH THE HOUSE'S MONEY TONIGHT, BUT IF HE MISSES JUST ONCE, HE LOSES A PINKY.
AND IT WON'T GROW BACK, RIGHT? OTHERWISE THIS BET IS POINTLESS.
WE PINKY SWEAR.
JUST GO ALREADY, DAMN IT. MY CAR BATTERY IS RUNNING LOW.
YOU READY, BIG GUY?
I'VE NEVER FELT MORE ALIVE THAN RIGHT NOW. LET'S DO THIS.
WE GOT THIS. BALDY'S HEAD IS GONNA BRING US GOOD LUCK.
FLICK
FLICK
FLI--
I CAN'T WATCH.
YOU'RE GOING TO LOOK SO UNSOPHISTICATED DRINKING TEA NOW.
WAIT! WAIT! WAI--!
SLICE

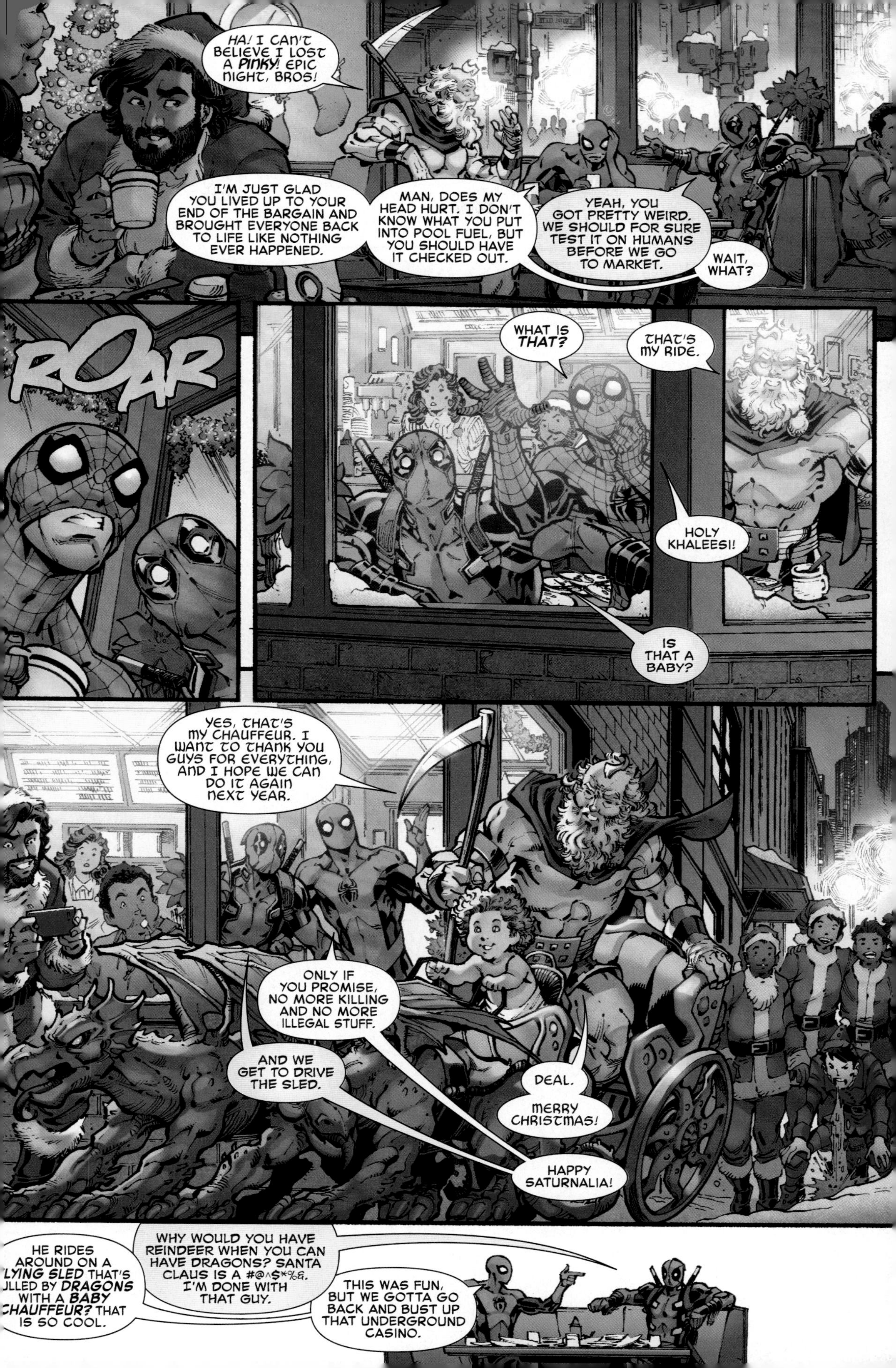
HA! I CAN'T BELIEVE I LOST A PINKY! EPIC NIGHT, BROS!
I'M JUST GLAD YOU LIVED UP TO YOUR END OF THE BARGAIN AND BROUGHT EVERYONE BACK TO LIFE LIKE NOTHING EVER HAPPENED.
MAN, DOES MY HEAD HURT. I DON'T KNOW WHAT YOU PUT INTO POOL FUEL, BUT YOU SHOULD HAVE IT CHECKED OUT.
YEAH, YOU GOT PRETTY WEIRD. WE SHOULD FOR SURE TEST IT ON HUMANS BEFORE WE GO TO MARKET.
WAIT, WHAT?
ROAR
WHAT IS THAT?
THAT'S MY RIDE.
HOLY KHALEESI!
IS THAT A BABY?
YES, THAT'S MY CHAUFFEUR. I WANT TO THANK YOU GUYS FOR EVERYTHING, AND I HOPE WE CAN DO IT AGAIN NEXT YEAR.
ONLY IF YOU PROMISE, NO MORE KILLING AND NO MORE ILLEGAL STUFF.
AND WE GET TO DRIVE THE SLED.
DEAL.
MERRY CHRISTMAS!
HAPPY SATURNALIA!
HE RIDES AROUND ON A LYING SLED THAT'S ULLED BY DRAGONS WITH A BABY CHAUFFEUR? THAT IS SO COOL.
WHY WOULD YOU HAVE REINDEER WHEN YOU CAN HAVE DRAGONS? SANTA CLAUS IS A #@^$*%&. I'M DONE WITH THAT GUY.
THIS WAS FUN, BUT WE GOTTA GO BACK AND BUST UP THAT UNDERGROUND CASINO.

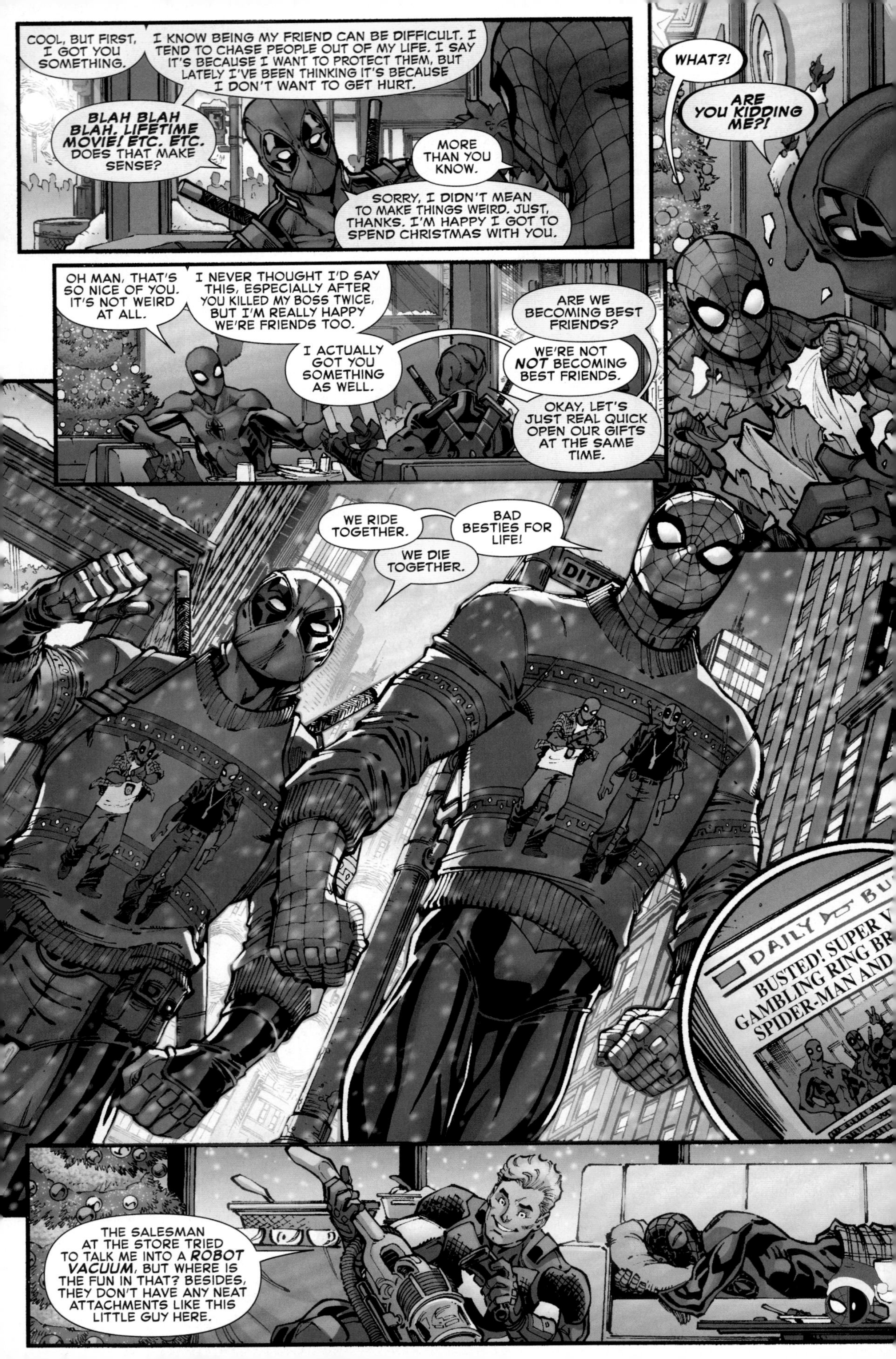

COOL, BUT FIRST, I GOT YOU SOMETHING.
I KNOW BEING MY FRIEND CAN BE DIFFICULT. I TEND TO CHASE PEOPLE OUT OF MY LIFE. I SAY IT'S BECAUSE I WANT TO PROTECT THEM, BUT LATELY I'VE BEEN THINKING IT'S BECAUSE I DON'T WANT TO GET HURT.
BLAH BLAH BLAH. LIFETIME MOVIE! ETC. ETC. DOES THAT MAKE SENSE?
MORE THAN YOU KNOW.
SORRY, I DIDN'T MEAN TO MAKE THINGS WEIRD. JUST, THANKS. I'M HAPPY I GOT TO SPEND CHRISTMAS WITH YOU.
OH MAN, THAT'S SO NICE OF YOU. IT'S NOT WEIRD AT ALL.
I NEVER THOUGHT I'D SAY THIS, ESPECIALLY AFTER YOU KILLED MY BOSS TWICE, BUT I'M REALLY HAPPY WE'RE FRIENDS TOO.
I ACTUALLY GOT YOU SOMETHING AS WELL.
ARE WE BECOMING BEST FRIENDS?
WE'RE NOT NOT BECOMING BEST FRIENDS.
OKAY, LET'S JUST REAL QUICK OPEN OUR GIFTS AT THE SAME TIME.
WHAT?!
ARE YOU KIDDING ME?!
WE RIDE TOGETHER.
WE DIE TOGETHER.
BAD BESTIES FOR LIFE!
DAILY
BUSTED! SUPER
GAMBLING RING
SPIDER-MAN AND
THE SALESMAN AT THE STORE TRIED TO TALK ME INTO A ROBOT VACUUM, BUT WHERE IS THE FUN IN THAT? BESIDES, THEY DON'T HAVE ANY NEAT ATTACHMENTS LIKE THIS LITTLE GUY HERE.

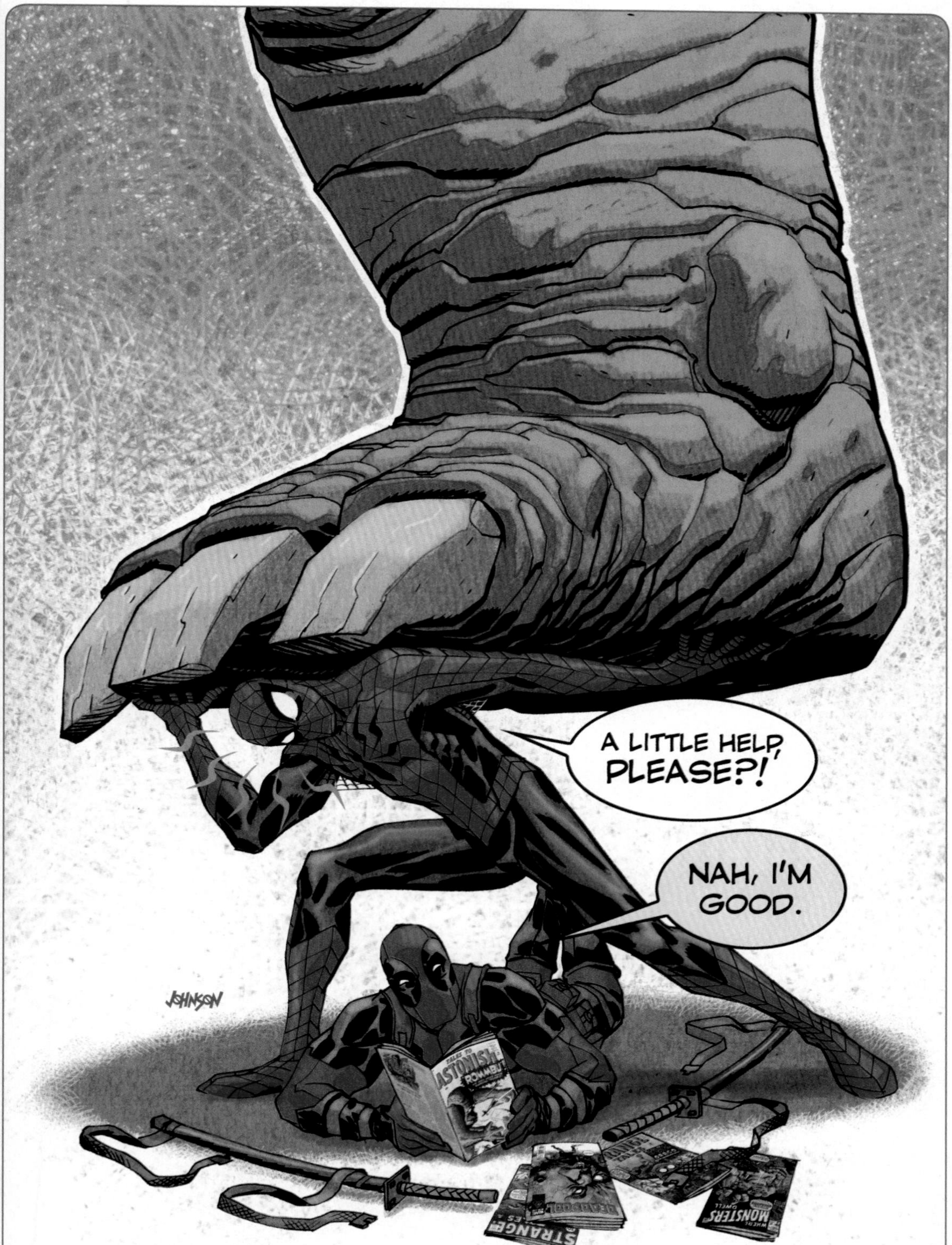
A LITTLE HELP, PLEASE?!
NAH, I'M GOOD.
JOHNSON

SPIDER-MAN/ DEADPOOL

MONSTERS UNLEASHED!

WHEN GIANT MONSTERS KNOWN AS LEVIATHONS START RAINING FROM THE SKY AND WREAKING HAVOC ALL OVER THE WORLD, IT IS UP TO THE HEROES OF EARTH TO STOP THEM. BUT EVEN WORKING TOGETHER, THE AVENGERS, CHAMPIONS, X-MEN, GUARDIANS OF THE GALAXY, AND INHUMANS MIGHT BE UP AGAINST A THREAT TOO LARGE FOR THEM TO TACKLE. WAVE AFTER WAVE OF LEVIATHONS ATTACK, INTENT ON RAZING THE WORLD, AND IT SEEMS LIKE ONLY A MIRACLE CAN SAVE THE EARTH NOW... A MIRACLE NAMED SPIDER-MAN!

...AND ANOTHER MIRACLE NAMED DEADPOOL!

JOSHUA CORIN -- *WRITER*
TIGH WALKER -- *ARTIST*
RACHELLE ROSENBERG -- *COLOR ARTIST*
VC's JOE SABINO -- *LETTERER*

DAVE JOHNSON -- *COVER ART*

GUSTAVO DUARTE -- *GWENSTER VARIANT COVER ART*

ALLISON STOCK -- *ASSISTANT EDITOR*
DEVIN LEWIS -- *ASSOCIATE EDITOR*
JORDAN D. WHITE & NICK LOWE -- *EDITORS*

AXEL ALONSO
EDITOR IN CHIEF

JOE QUESADA
CHIEF CREATIVE OFFICER

DAN BUCKLEY
PUBLISHER

ALAN FINE
EXECUTIVE PRODUCER

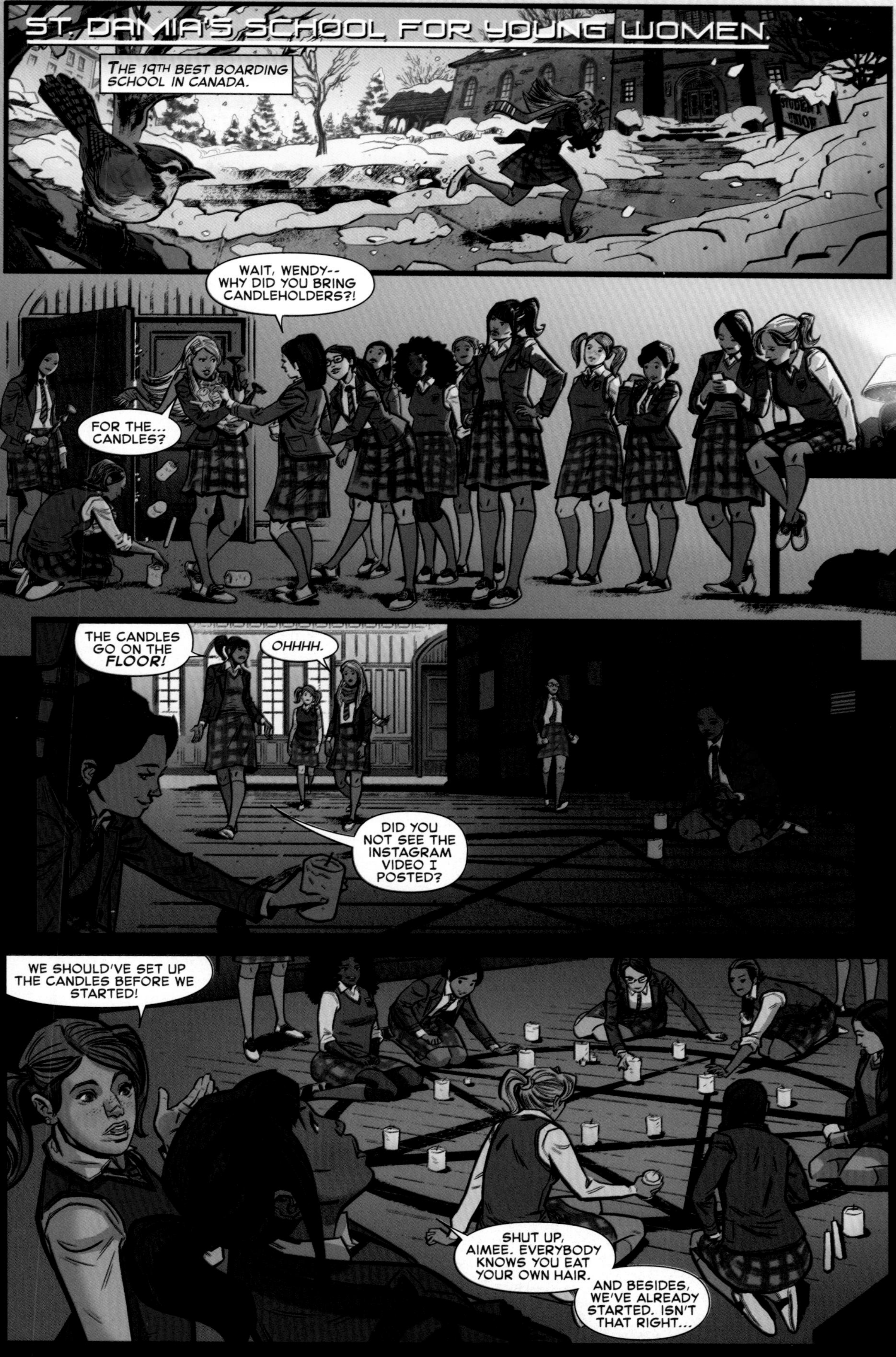
ST. DAMIA'S SCHOOL FOR YOUNG WOMEN.
THE 19TH BEST BOARDING SCHOOL IN CANADA.
WAIT, WENDY-- WHY DID YOU BRING CANDLEHOLDERS?!
FOR THE... CANDLES?
THE CANDLES GO ON THE FLOOR!
OHHHH.
DID YOU NOT SEE THE INSTAGRAM VIDEO I POSTED?
WE SHOULD'VE SET UP THE CANDLES BEFORE WE STARTED!
SHUT UP, AIMEE. EVERYBODY KNOWS YOU EAT YOUR OWN HAIR.
AND BESIDES, WE'VE ALREADY STARTED. ISN'T THAT RIGHT...

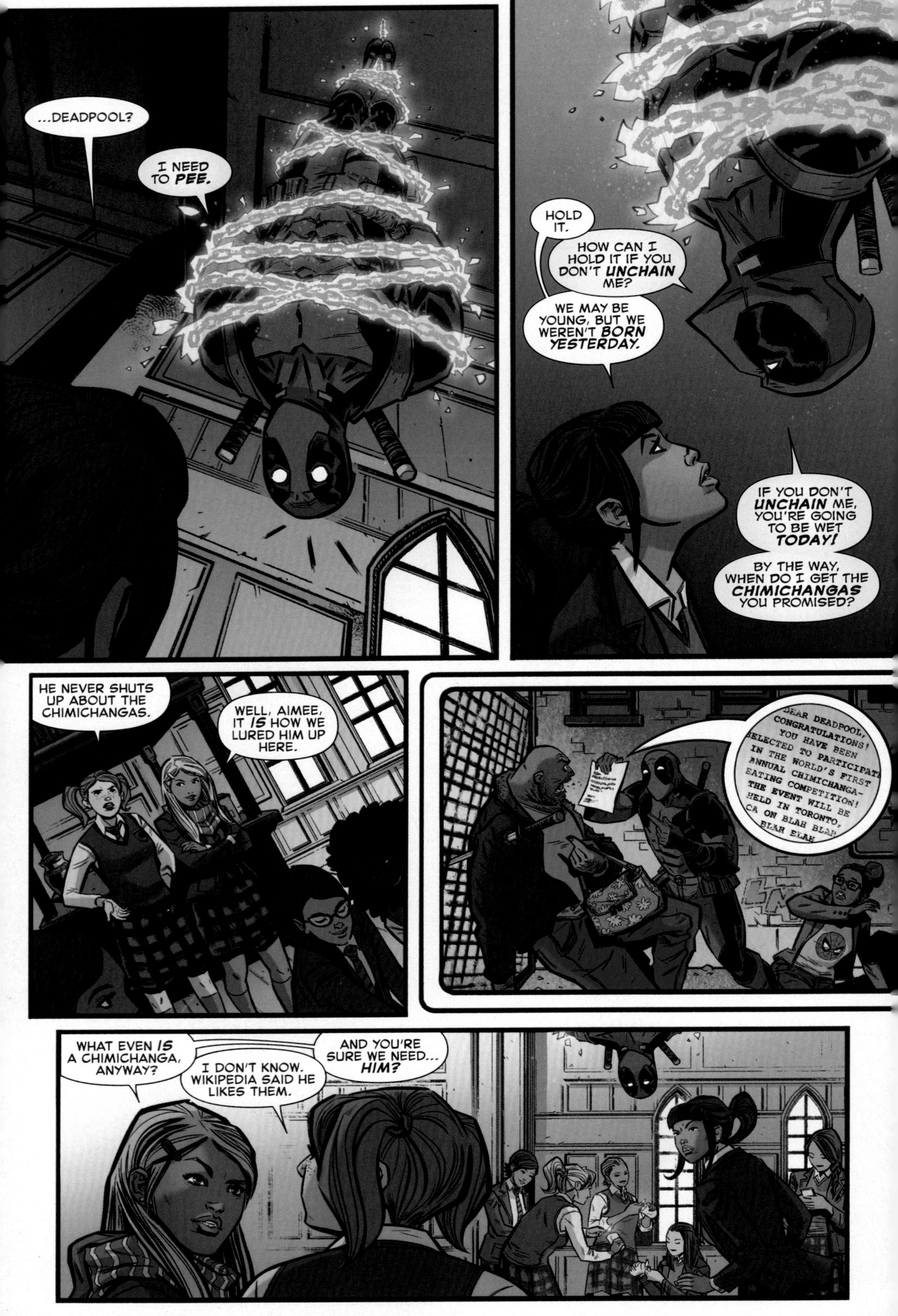
...DEADPOOL?
I NEED TO *PEE.*
HOLD IT.
HOW CAN I HOLD IT IF YOU DON'T *UNCHAIN* ME?
WE MAY BE YOUNG, BUT WE WEREN'T *BORN YESTERDAY.*
IF YOU DON'T *UNCHAIN* ME, YOU'RE GOING TO BE WET *TODAY!*
BY THE WAY, WHEN DO I GET THE *CHIMICHANGAS* YOU PROMISED?
HE NEVER SHUTS UP ABOUT THE CHIMICHANGAS.
WELL, AIMEE, IT *IS* HOW WE LURED HIM UP HERE.
DEAR DEADPOOL, CONGRATULATIONS! YOU HAVE BEEN SELECTED TO PARTICIPAT IN THE WORLD'S FIRST ANNUAL CHIMICHANGA-EATING COMPETITION! THE EVENT WILL BE HELD IN TORONTO, CA ON BLAH BLAH BLAH BLAH
WHAT EVEN *IS* A CHIMICHANGA, ANYWAY?
I DON'T KNOW. WIKIPEDIA SAID HE LIKES THEM.
AND YOU'RE SURE WE NEED... *HIM?*

YES, WENDY! IF WE TRY TO SUMMON THE *SUCCUBUS QUEEN SHIKLAH* WITHOUT THE PRESENCE OF HER HEARTMATE, SHE'LL PROBABLY TEAR US ALL APART! STARTING WITH *YOU!*

WAIT, WHAT DO YOU WANT WITH MY SEXY-SEXY DEMON-SPOUSE, SHIKLAH?

OUR BELOVED LEADER, *HEADMISTRESS SOO,* DIED LAST WEEK AFTER TRAGICALLY *CHOKING* ON A *HOCKEY PUCK.*

SHE WAS A *POWERFUL WITCH,* AND SO REQUIRES A *POWERFUL VESSEL* WHEN WE BRING HER SPIRIT BACK.

YOU'RE MAKING THIS VERY DIFFICULT FOR ME...I DON'T REALLY WANT TO HAVE TO KILL A BUNCH OF GIRLS...

WE'RE NOT A *BUNCH OF GIRLS*-- WE'RE A *COVEN OF WITCHES!*

OH.

IN THAT CASE...

ONE SEC.

POP!

EXCUSE ME, BUT CAN I BORROW YOUR KNIFE? I PROMISE TO RETURN IT.

MAYBE I SHOULD HAVE BEEN MORE SPECIFIC.

HIS BLOOD IS DRAWN! QUICK! CAST THE SPELL!

O, MOTHER EARTH AND SISTER SKY...

...HEAR YOUR DAUGHTERS' PLAINTIVE CRY...

...WE GIFT YOU WITH THIS HUMAN WINE...

...NOW SEND ITS HEARTMATE TO OUR SIGN!

SSSSSSSSSSSSS!

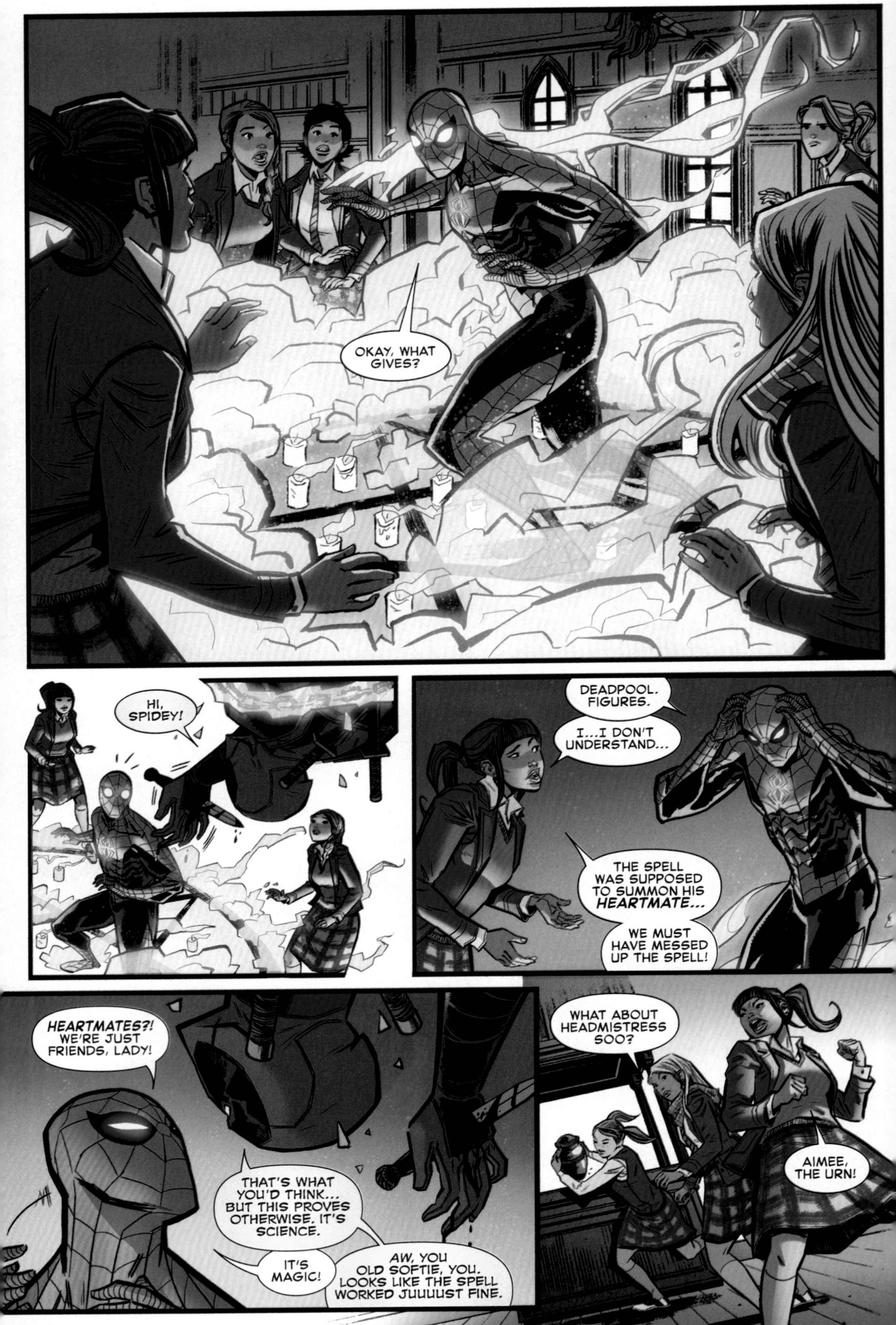
OKAY, WHAT GIVES?
HI, SPIDEY!
DEADPOOL. FIGURES.
I...I DON'T UNDERSTAND...
THE SPELL WAS SUPPOSED TO SUMMON HIS *HEARTMATE...*
WE MUST HAVE MESSED UP THE SPELL!
HEARTMATES?! WE'RE JUST FRIENDS, LADY!
THAT'S WHAT YOU'D THINK... BUT THIS PROVES OTHERWISE. IT'S SCIENCE.
IT'S MAGIC!
AW, YOU OLD SOFTIE, YOU. LOOKS LIKE THE SPELL WORKED JUUUUST FINE.
WHAT ABOUT HEADMISTRESS SOO?
AIMEE, THE URN!

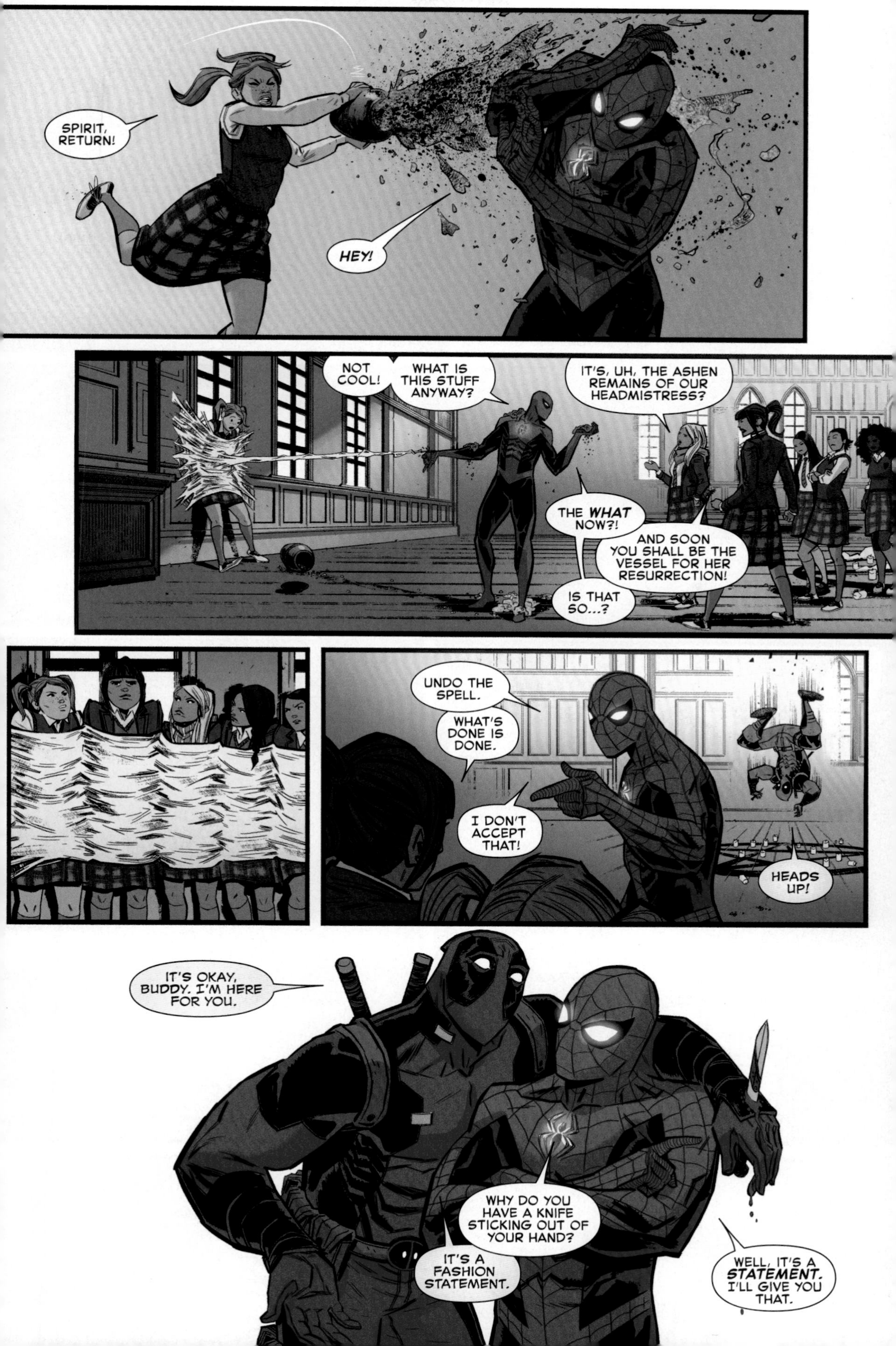
SPIRIT, RETURN!
HEY!
NOT COOL!
WHAT IS THIS STUFF ANYWAY?
IT'S, UH, THE ASHEN REMAINS OF OUR HEADMISTRESS?
THE WHAT NOW?!
AND SOON YOU SHALL BE THE VESSEL FOR HER RESURRECTION!
IS THAT SO...?
UNDO THE SPELL.
WHAT'S DONE IS DONE.
I DON'T ACCEPT THAT!
HEADS UP!
IT'S OKAY, BUDDY. I'M HERE FOR YOU.
WHY DO YOU HAVE A KNIFE STICKING OUT OF YOUR HAND?
IT'S A FASHION STATEMENT.
WELL, IT'S A STATEMENT. I'LL GIVE YOU THAT.

WHAT ARE YOU **DOING**?!

MAKING SURE YOU'RE STILL YOU.

I'M STILL ME! JEEZ!

OKAY, JUST TURN YOUR HEAD AND COUGH. THIS MIGHT FEEL A LITTLE UNCOMFORTABLE...

CHECK-UP COMPLETE. THAT'S TOTALLY STILL SPIDEY.

ONLY FOR THE NEXT FEW MINUTES. YOU MAY WANT TO SAY YOUR GOODBYES.

EXCUSE ME! MR. SPIDER-MAN! I NEED TO PEE...

AHA! HOW DO **YOU** LIKE IT?

JEEZ--WHERE THE HECK ARE WE, ANYWAY? ALASKA?

TORONTO.

TORONTO?! OH, NO!

I NEED TO GET BACK TO PHILADELPHIA! THERE ARE **MONSTERS** FALLING FROM THE SKY!

MONSTERS FALLING FROM THE SKY?!

YEAH, PHILADELPHIA IS CRAZY.

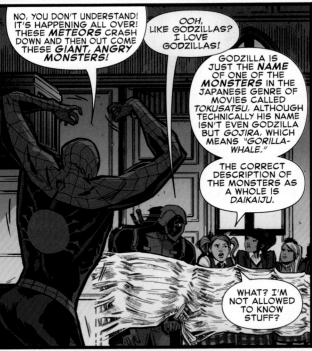

NO, YOU DON'T UNDERSTAND! IT'S HAPPENING ALL OVER! THESE **METEORS** CRASH DOWN AND THEN OUT COME THESE **GIANT, ANGRY MONSTERS**!

OOH, LIKE GODZILLAS? I LOVE GODZILLAS!

GODZILLA IS JUST THE **NAME** OF ONE OF THE **MONSTERS** IN THE JAPANESE GENRE OF MOVIES CALLED *TOKUSATSU*, ALTHOUGH TECHNICALLY HIS NAME ISN'T EVEN GODZILLA BUT *GOJIRA*, WHICH MEANS "GORILLA-WHALE."

THE CORRECT DESCRIPTION OF THE MONSTERS AS A WHOLE IS *DAIKAIJU*.

WHAT? I'M NOT ALLOWED TO KNOW STUFF?

THESE GIANT, ANGRY MONSTERS CRASH DOWN AS METEORS, YOU SAID?

YEAH... WHY?

...

NO REASON.

CRASH

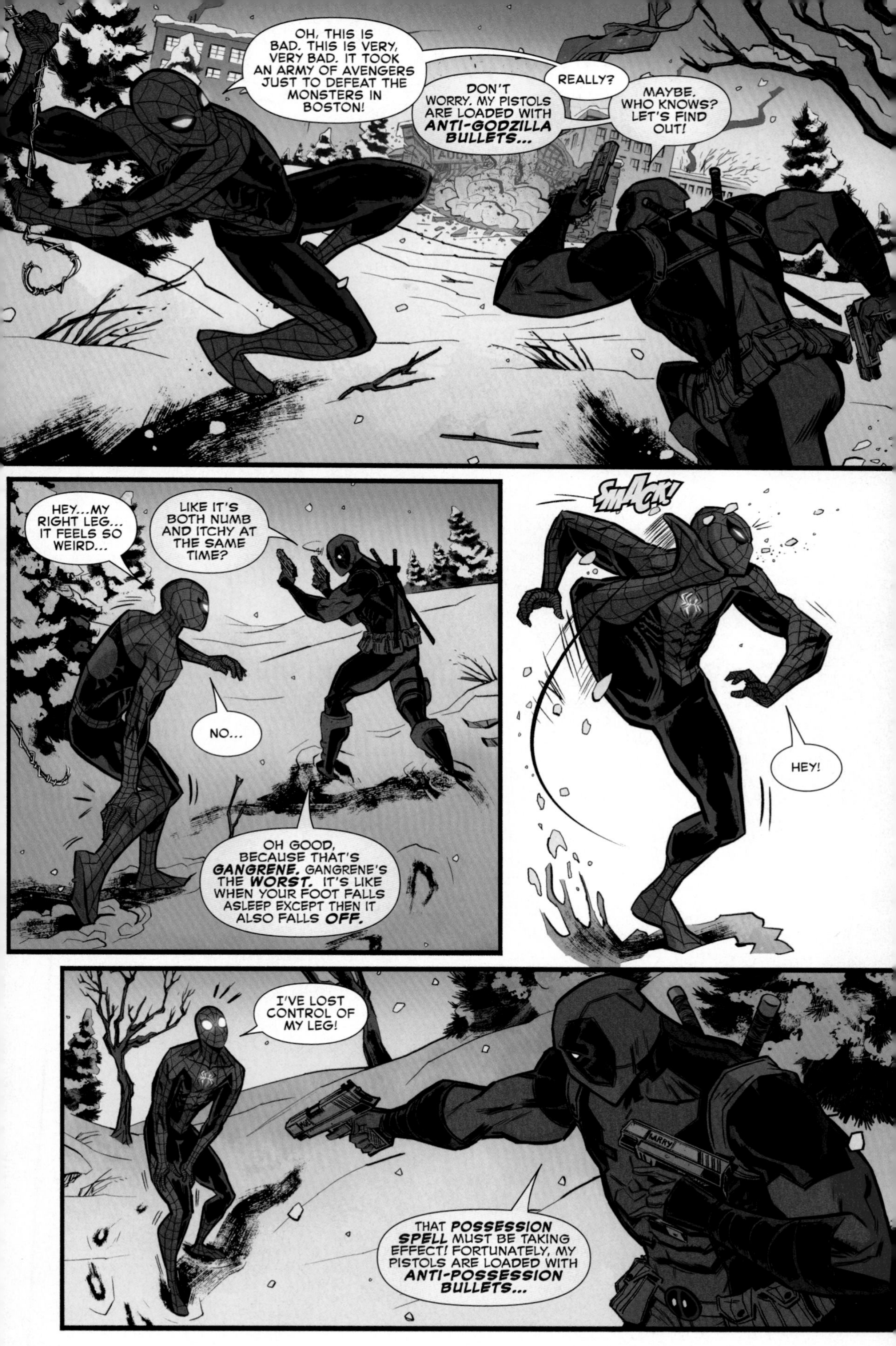
OH, THIS IS BAD. THIS IS VERY, VERY BAD. IT TOOK AN ARMY OF AVENGERS JUST TO DEFEAT THE MONSTERS IN BOSTON!
DON'T WORRY. MY PISTOLS ARE LOADED WITH ANTI-GODZILLA BULLETS...
REALLY?
MAYBE. WHO KNOWS? LET'S FIND OUT!
HEY...MY RIGHT LEG... IT FEELS SO WEIRD...
LIKE IT'S BOTH NUMB AND ITCHY AT THE SAME TIME?
NO...
OH GOOD, BECAUSE THAT'S GANGRENE. GANGRENE'S THE WORST. IT'S LIKE WHEN YOUR FOOT FALLS ASLEEP EXCEPT THEN IT ALSO FALLS OFF.
SMACK!
HEY!
I'VE LOST CONTROL OF MY LEG!
THAT POSSESSION SPELL MUST BE TAKING EFFECT! FORTUNATELY, MY PISTOLS ARE LOADED WITH ANTI-POSSESSION BULLETS...

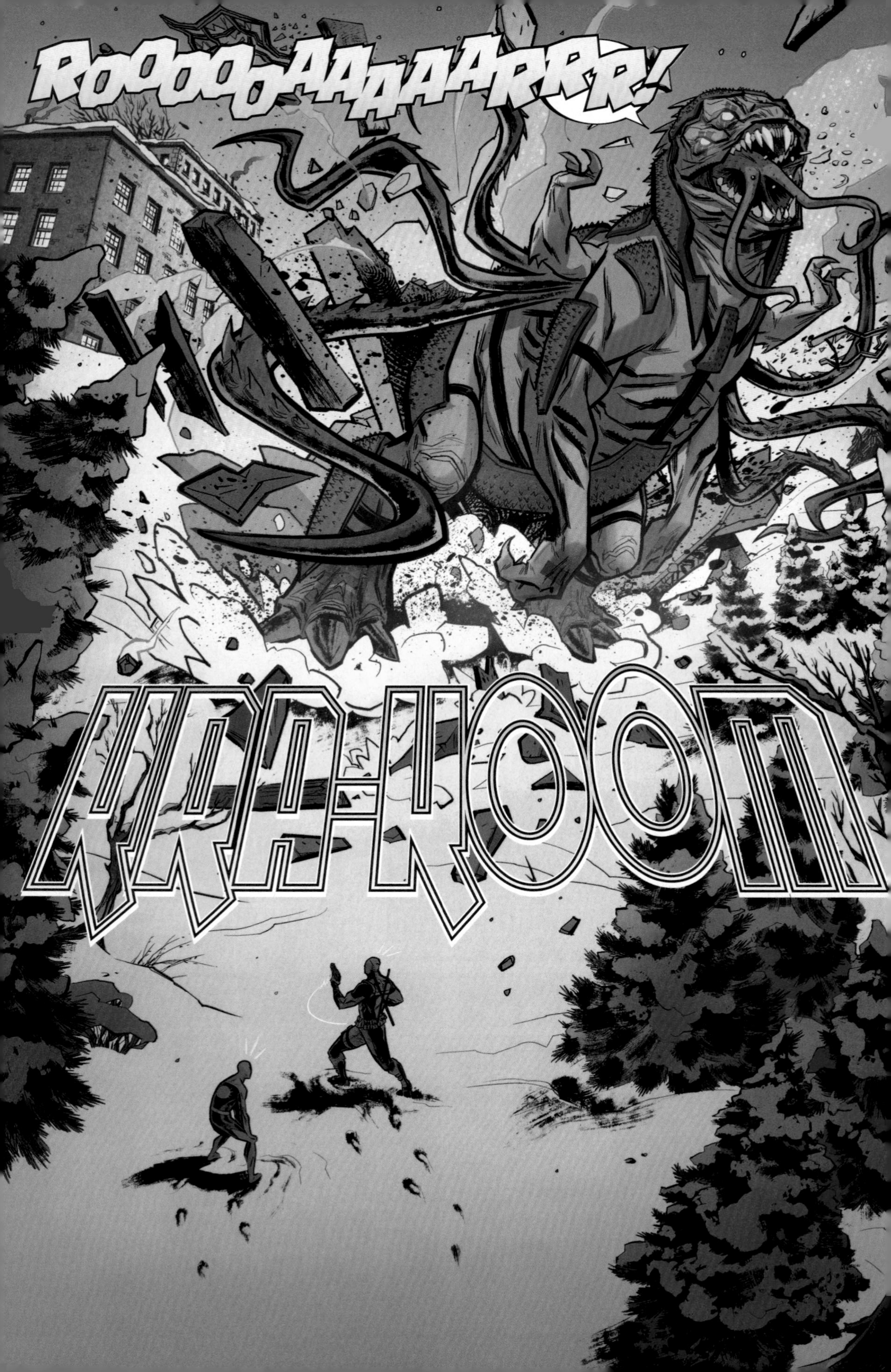
ROOOOOAAAAAARRR!
WHOOM

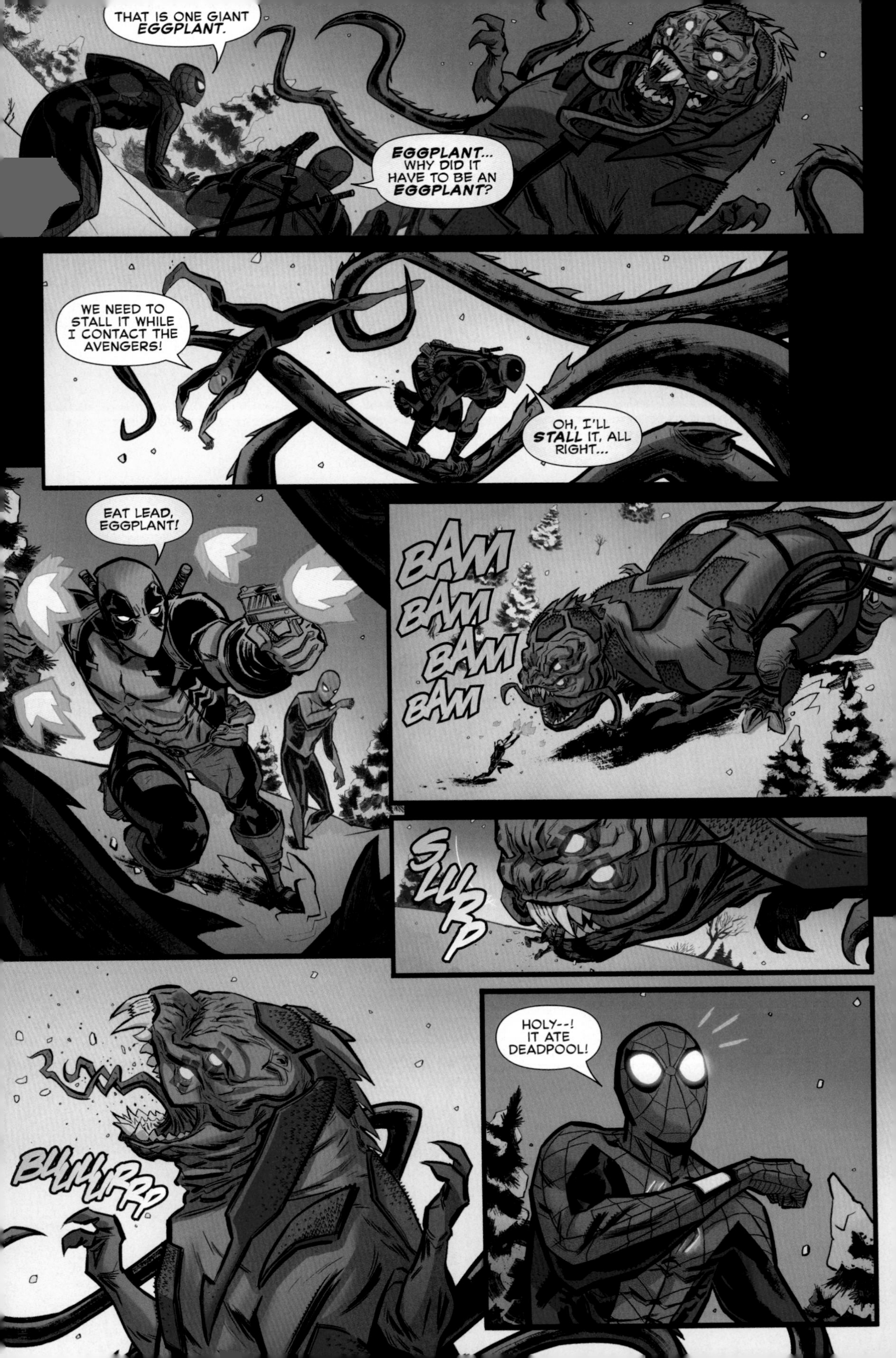

THAT IS ONE GIANT EGGPLANT.
EGGPLANT... WHY DID IT HAVE TO BE AN EGGPLANT?
WE NEED TO STALL IT WHILE I CONTACT THE AVENGERS!
OH, I'LL STALL IT, ALL RIGHT...
EAT LEAD, EGGPLANT!
BAM
BAM
BAM
BAM
SLURP
BLLLLURRP
HOLY--! IT ATE DEADPOOL!

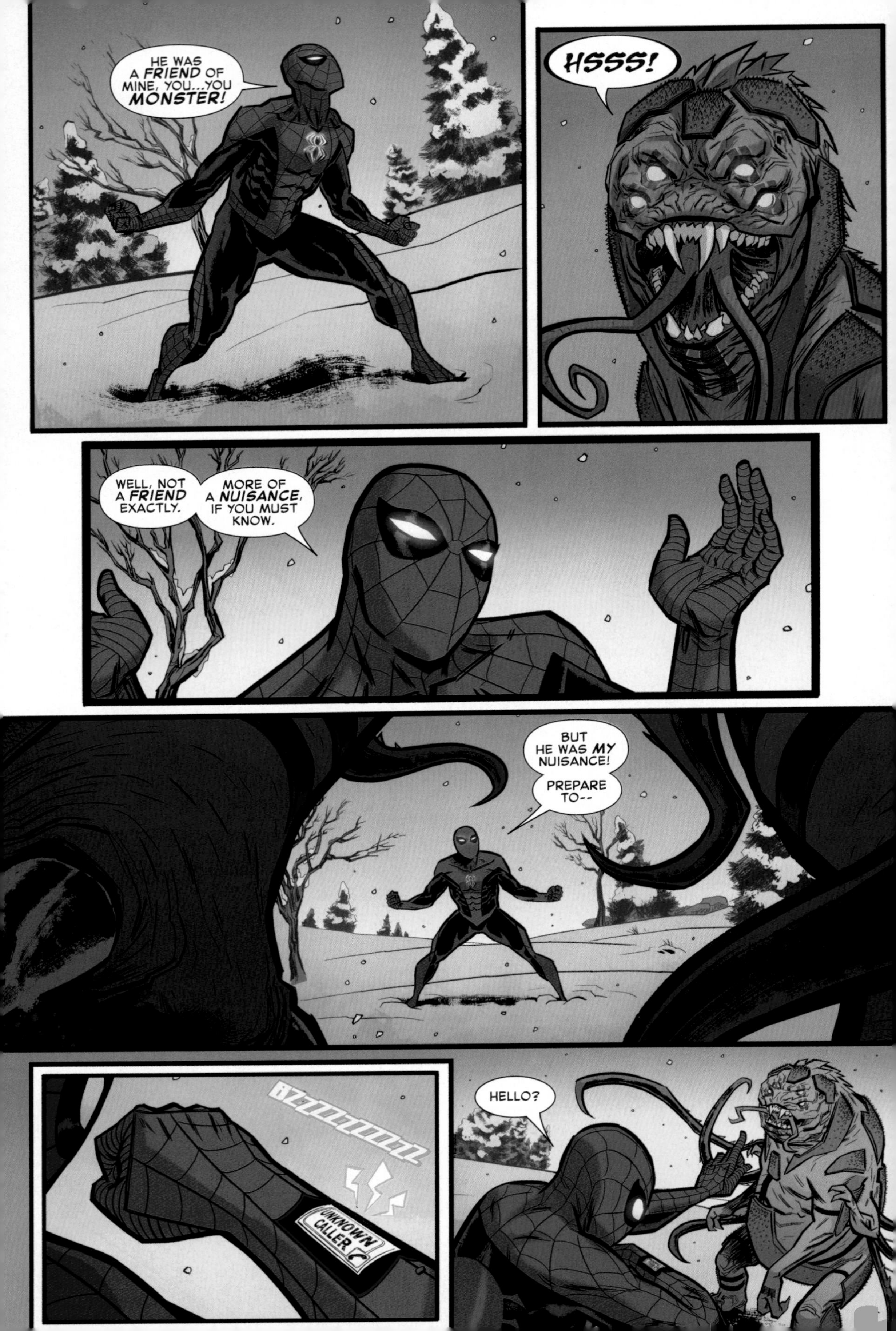
HE WAS A FRIEND OF MINE, YOU...YOU MONSTER!
HSSS!
WELL, NOT A FRIEND EXACTLY.
MORE OF A NUISANCE, IF YOU MUST KNOW.
BUT HE WAS MY NUISANCE!
PREPARE TO--
UNKNOWN CALLER
HELLO?

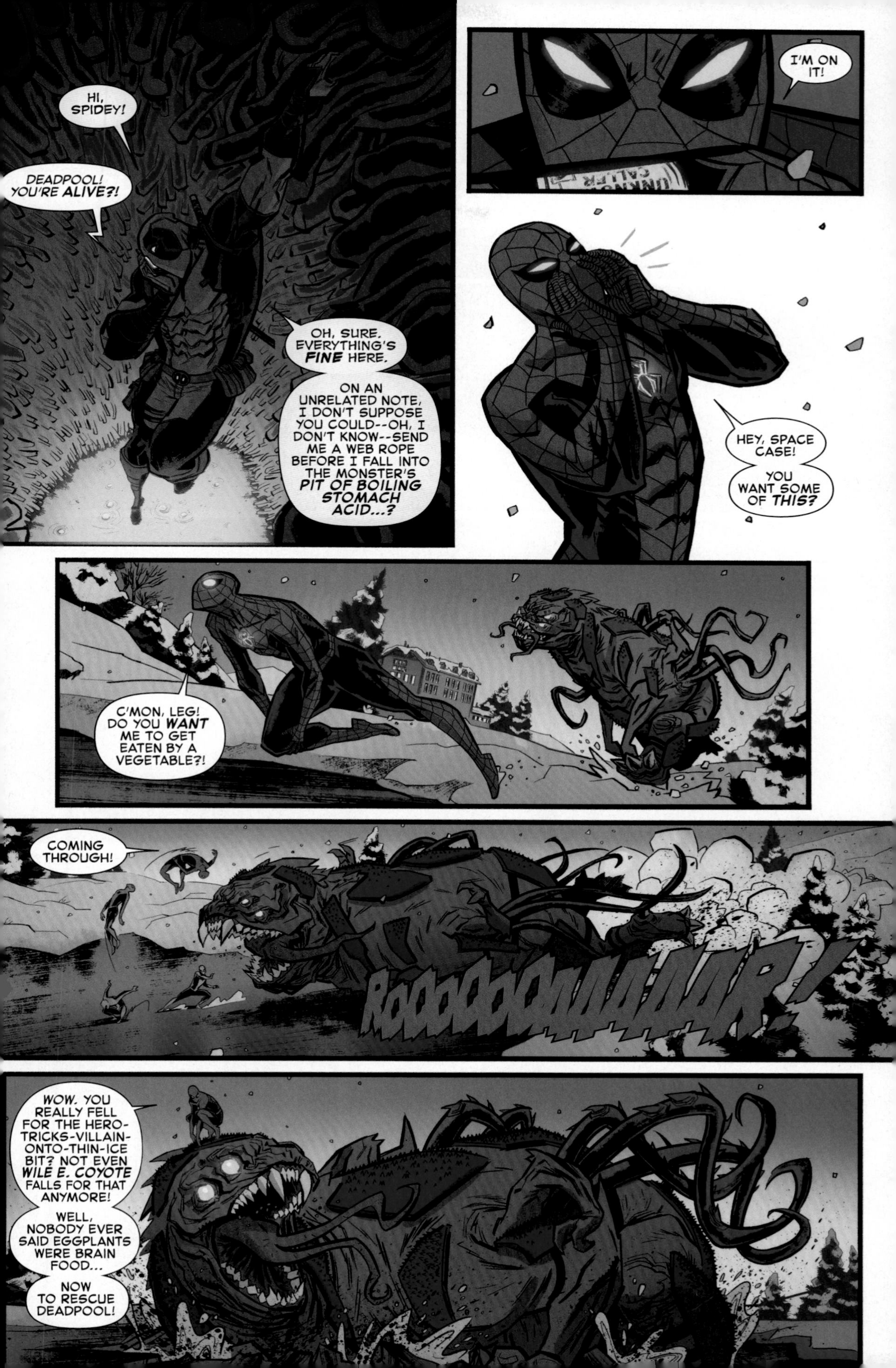
HI, SPIDEY!
DEADPOOL! YOU'RE ALIVE?!
OH, SURE. EVERYTHING'S FINE HERE.
ON AN UNRELATED NOTE, I DON'T SUPPOSE YOU COULD--SEND ME A WEB ROPE BEFORE I FALL INTO THE MONSTER'S PIT OF BOILING STOMACH ACID...?
I'M ON IT!
UNKNOWN CALLER
HEY, SPACE CASE!
YOU WANT SOME OF THIS?
C'MON, LEG! DO YOU WANT ME TO GET EATEN BY A VEGETABLE?!
COMING THROUGH!
ROOOOOAAAAAR!
WOW. YOU REALLY FELL FOR THE HERO-TRICKS-VILLAIN-ONTO-THIN-ICE BIT? NOT EVEN WILE E. COYOTE FALLS FOR THAT ANYMORE!
WELL, NOBODY EVER SAID EGGPLANTS WERE BRAIN FOOD...
NOW TO RESCUE DEADPOOL!

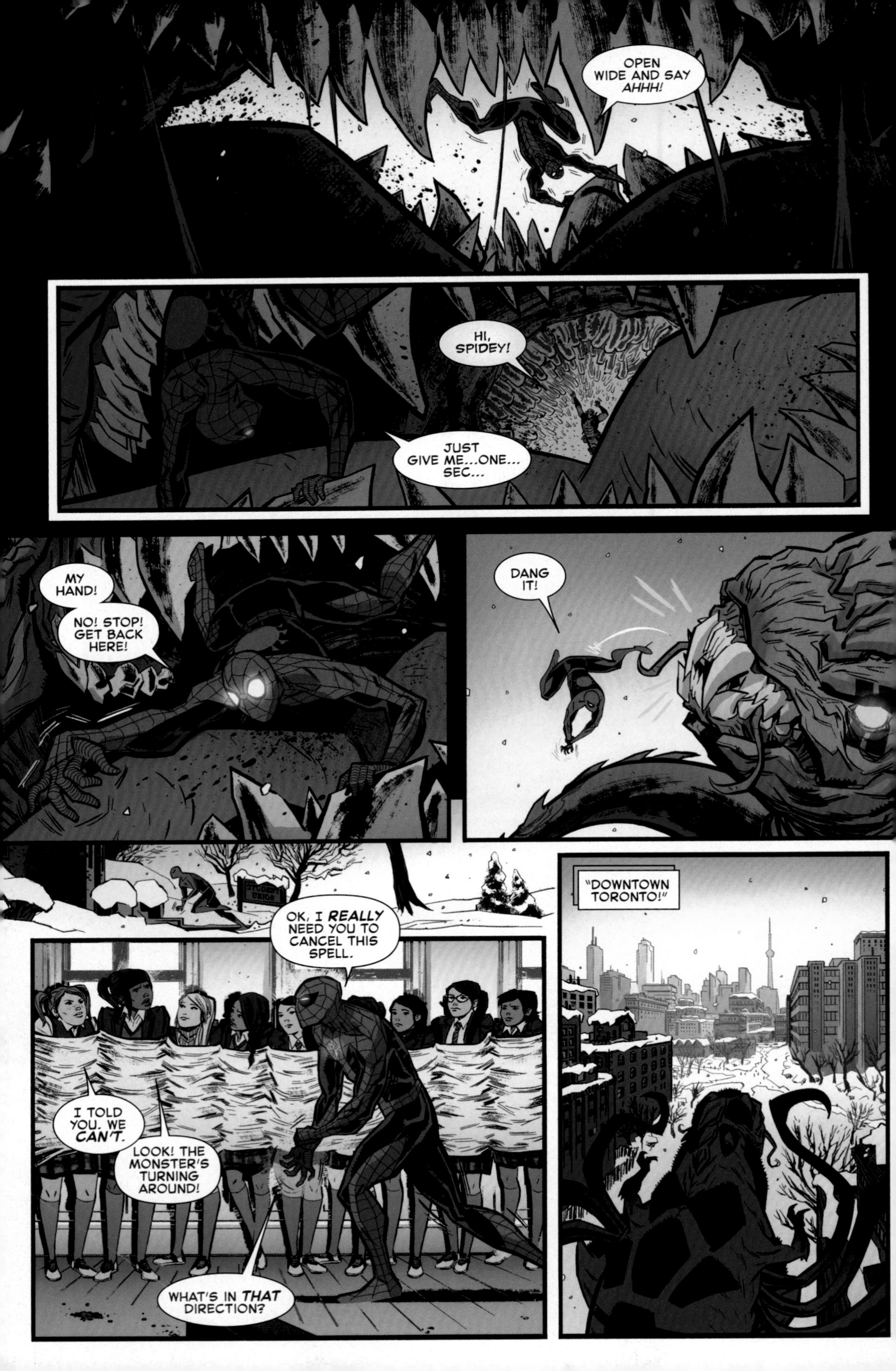
OPEN WIDE AND SAY AHHH!
HI, SPIDEY!
JUST GIVE ME...ONE... SEC...
MY HAND!
NO! STOP! GET BACK HERE!
DANG IT!
OK, I REALLY NEED YOU TO CANCEL THIS SPELL.
I TOLD YOU. WE CAN'T.
LOOK! THE MONSTER'S TURNING AROUND!
WHAT'S IN THAT DIRECTION?
"DOWNTOWN TORONTO!"

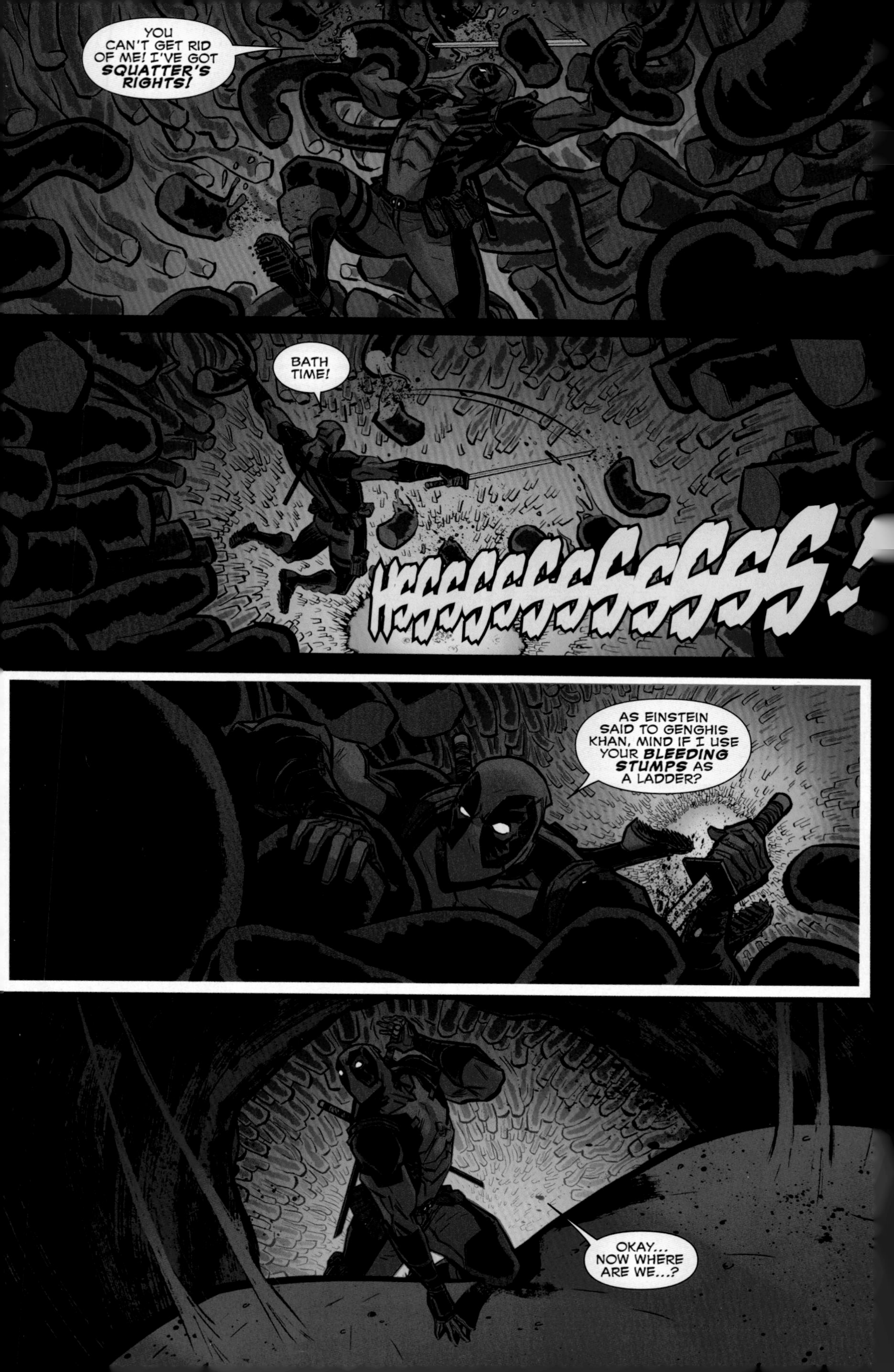
YOU CAN'T GET RID OF ME! I'VE GOT **SQUATTER'S RIGHTS!**
BATH TIME!
HSSSSSSSSSSS!
AS EINSTEIN SAID TO GENGHIS KHAN, MIND IF I USE YOUR **BLEEDING STUMPS** AS A LADDER?
OKAY... NOW WHERE ARE WE...?

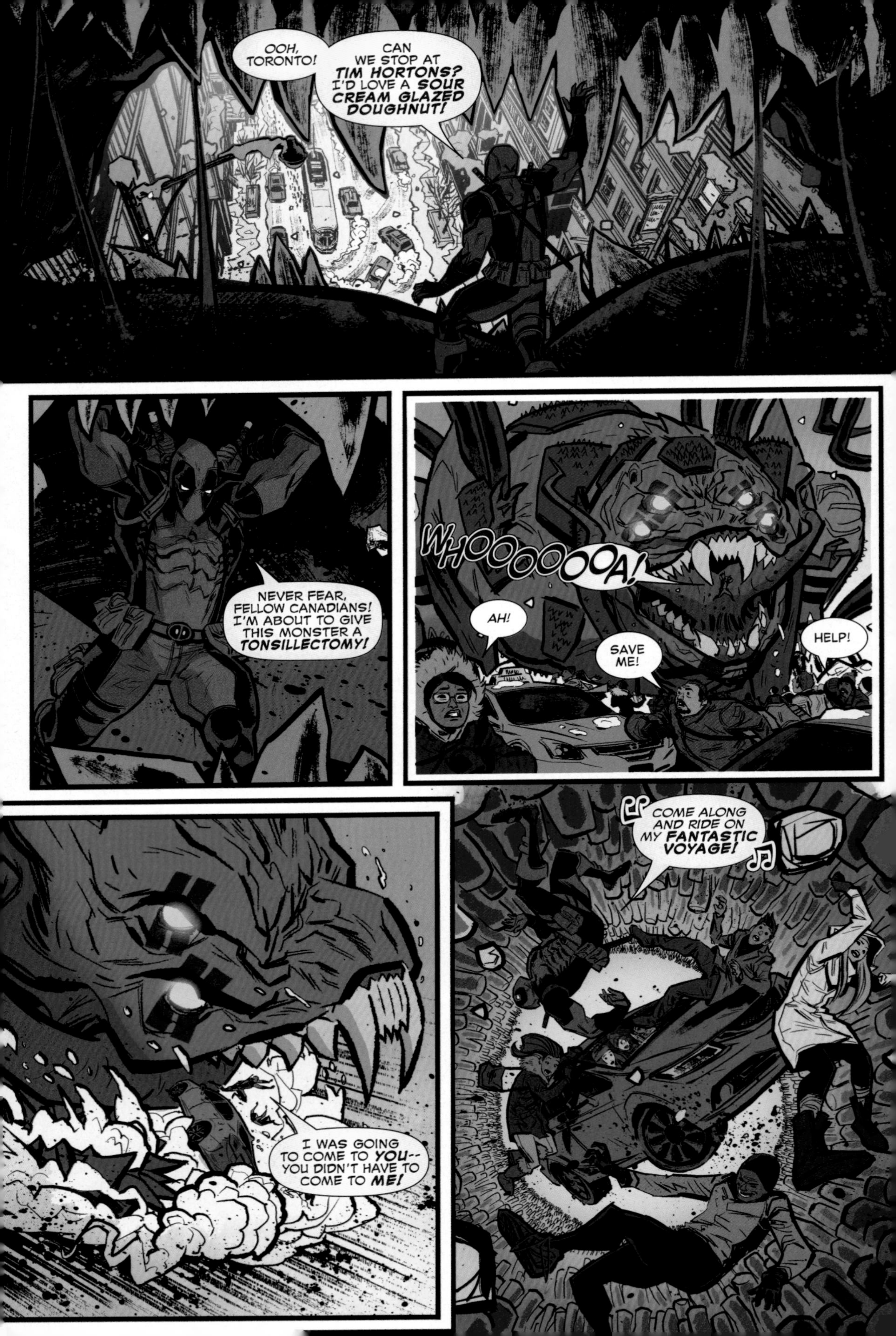
OOH, TORONTO!
CAN WE STOP AT TIM HORTONS? I'D LOVE A SOUR CREAM GLAZED DOUGHNUT!
NEVER FEAR, FELLOW CANADIANS! I'M ABOUT TO GIVE THIS MONSTER A TONSILLECTOMY!
WHOOOOOOOA!
AH!
SAVE ME!
HELP!
I WAS GOING TO COME TO YOU-- YOU DIDN'T HAVE TO COME TO ME!
COME ALONG AND RIDE ON MY FANTASTIC VOYAGE!

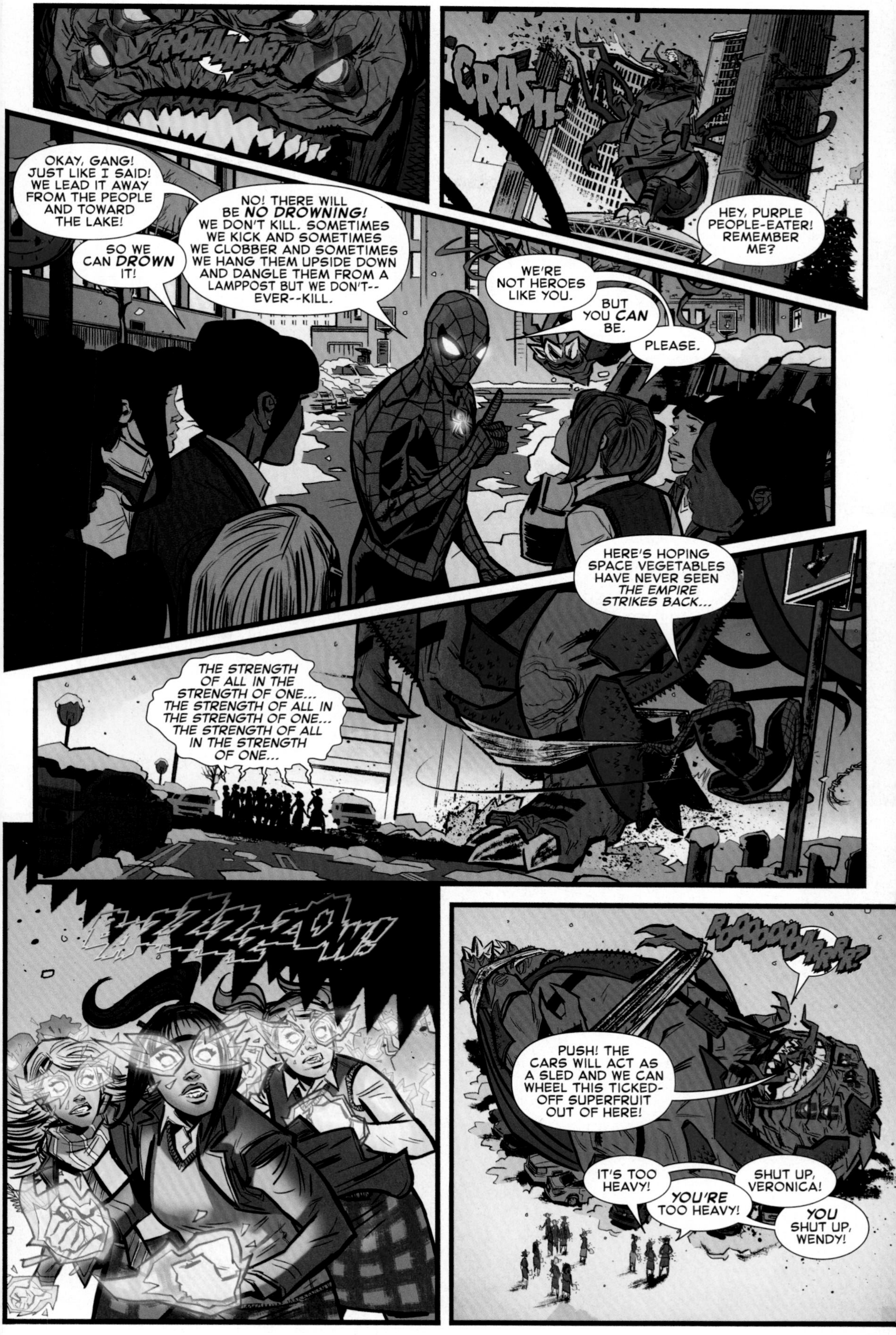
ROAAAAAR!
CRASH!
HEY, PURPLE PEOPLE-EATER! REMEMBER ME?
OKAY, GANG! JUST LIKE I SAID! WE LEAD IT AWAY FROM THE PEOPLE AND TOWARD THE LAKE!
SO WE CAN DROWN IT!
NO! THERE WILL BE NO DROWNING! WE DON'T KILL. SOMETIMES WE KICK AND SOMETIMES WE CLOBBER AND SOMETIMES WE HANG THEM UPSIDE DOWN AND DANGLE THEM FROM A LAMPPOST BUT WE DON'T-- EVER--KILL.
WE'RE NOT HEROES LIKE YOU.
BUT YOU CAN BE.
PLEASE.
HERE'S HOPING SPACE VEGETABLES HAVE NEVER SEEN THE EMPIRE STRIKES BACK...
THE STRENGTH OF ALL IN THE STRENGTH OF ONE... THE STRENGTH OF ALL IN THE STRENGTH OF ONE... THE STRENGTH OF ALL IN THE STRENGTH OF ONE...
RAAAAAARRR?
PUSH! THE CARS WILL ACT AS A SLED AND WE CAN WHEEL THIS TICKED-OFF SUPERFRUIT OUT OF HERE!
IT'S TOO HEAVY!
SHUT UP, VERONICA!
YOU'RE TOO HEAVY!
YOU SHUT UP, WENDY!

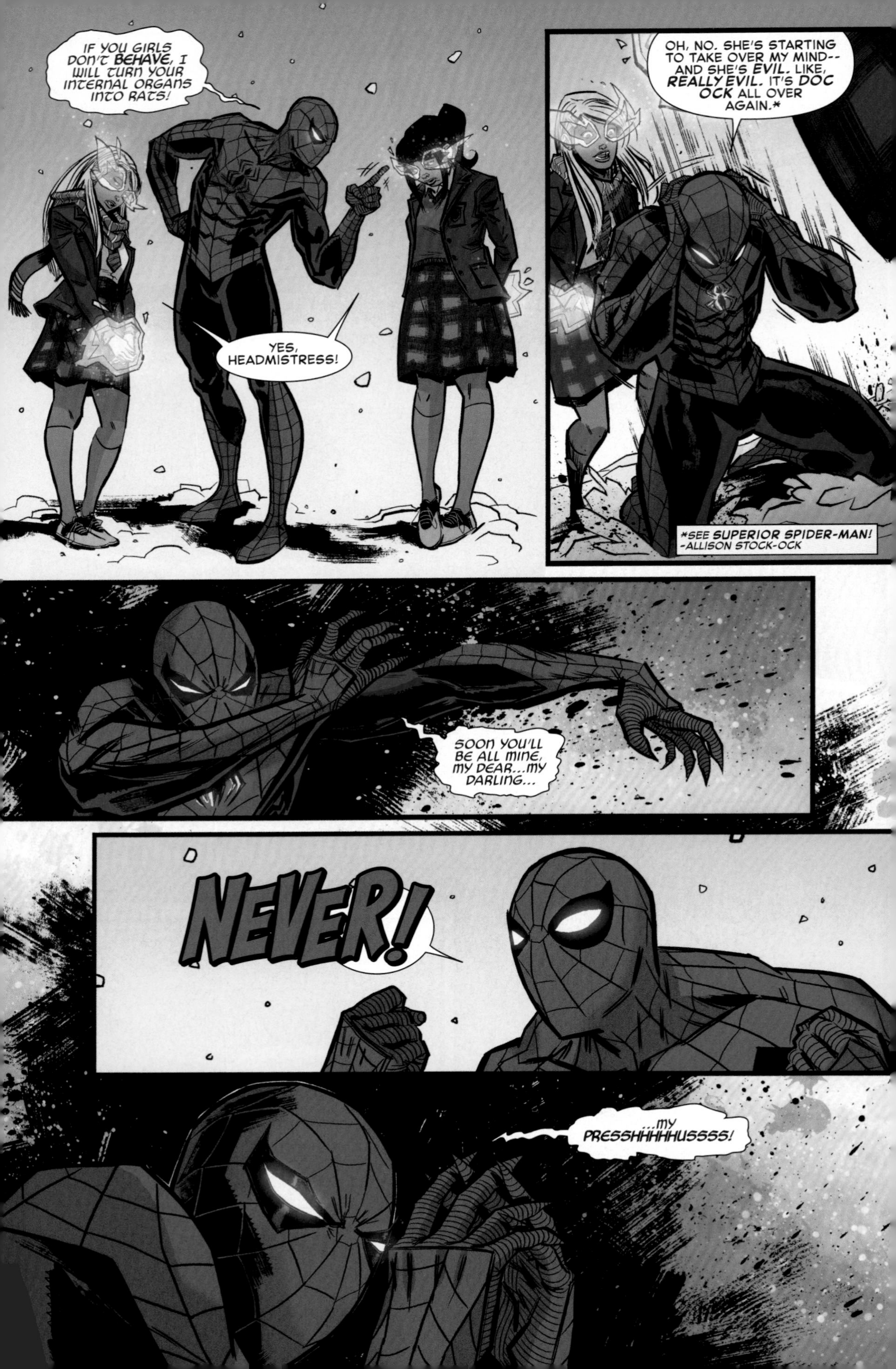
IF YOU GIRLS DON'T BEHAVE, I WILL TURN YOUR INTERNAL ORGANS INTO RATS!
YES, HEADMISTRESS!
OH, NO. SHE'S STARTING TO TAKE OVER MY MIND-- AND SHE'S EVIL. LIKE, REALLY EVIL. IT'S DOC OCK ALL OVER AGAIN.*
*SEE SUPERIOR SPIDER-MAN! -ALLISON STOCK-OCK
SOON YOU'LL BE ALL MINE, MY DEAR...MY DARLING...
NEVER!
...MY PRESSHHHHHUSSSS!

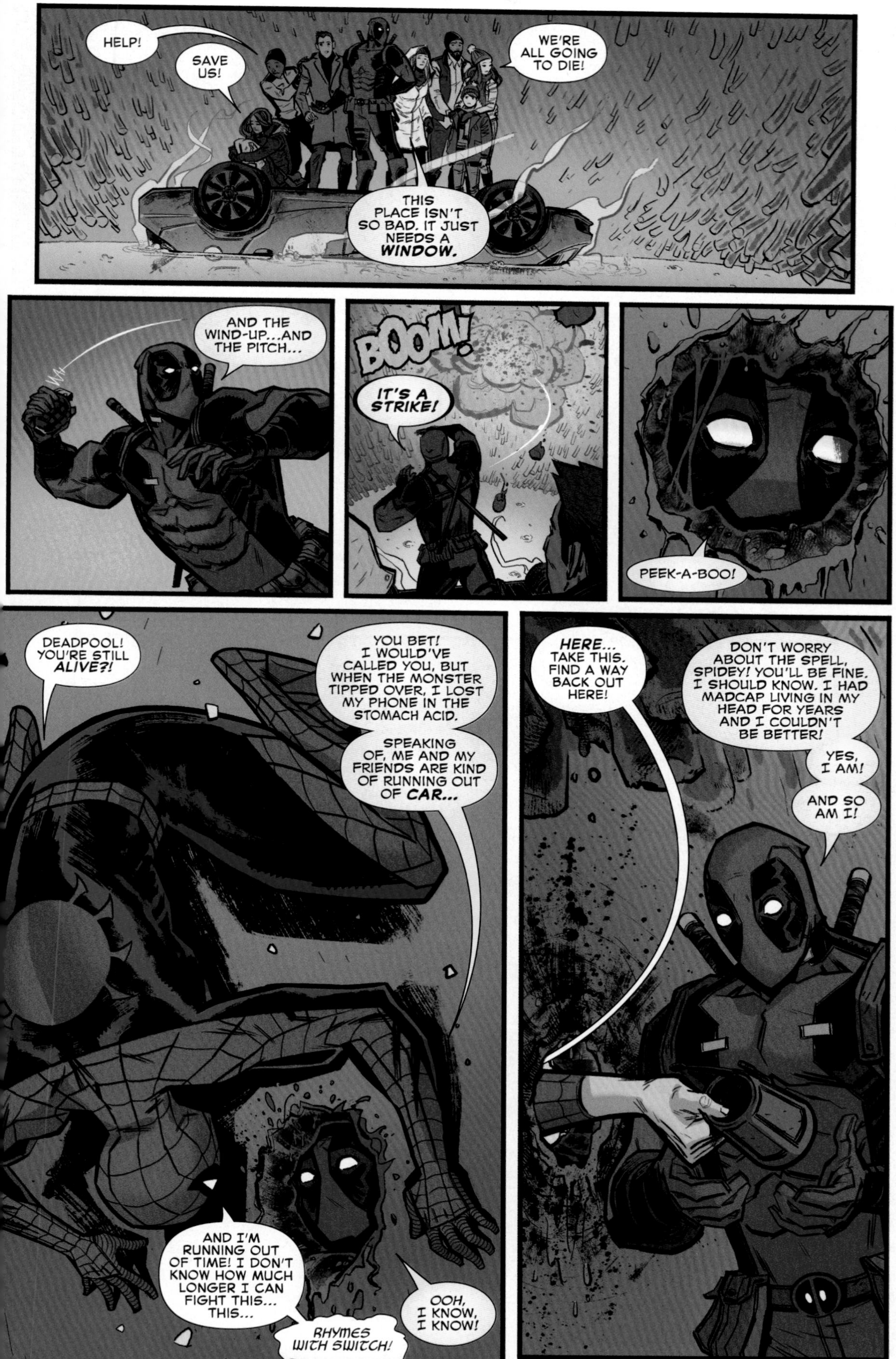

HELP!
SAVE US!
WE'RE ALL GOING TO DIE!
THIS PLACE ISN'T SO BAD. IT JUST NEEDS A **WINDOW.**
AND THE WIND-UP...AND THE PITCH...
BOOM!
IT'S A STRIKE!
PEEK-A-BOO!
DEADPOOL! YOU'RE STILL *ALIVE?!*
YOU BET! I WOULD'VE CALLED YOU, BUT WHEN THE MONSTER TIPPED OVER, I LOST MY PHONE IN THE STOMACH ACID.
SPEAKING OF, ME AND MY FRIENDS ARE KIND OF RUNNING OUT OF **CAR...**
AND I'M RUNNING OUT OF TIME! I DON'T KNOW HOW MUCH LONGER I CAN FIGHT THIS... THIS...
OOH, I KNOW, I KNOW!
RHYMES WITH SWITCH!
HERE... TAKE THIS. FIND A WAY BACK OUT HERE!
DON'T WORRY ABOUT THE SPELL, SPIDEY! YOU'LL BE FINE. I SHOULD KNOW. I HAD MADCAP LIVING IN MY HEAD FOR YEARS AND I COULDN'T BE BETTER!
YES, I AM!
AND SO AM I!

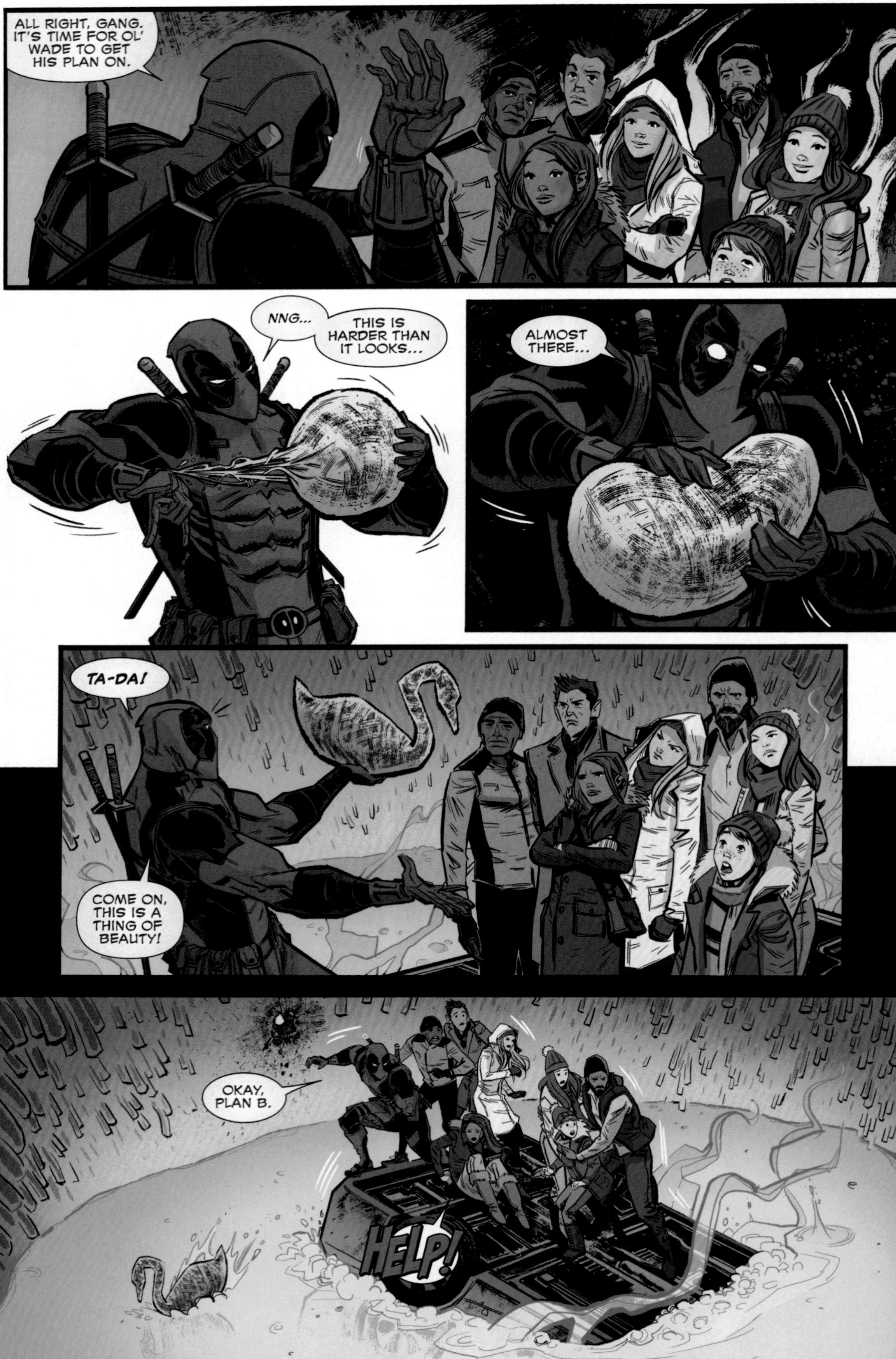
ALL RIGHT, GANG. IT'S TIME FOR OL' WADE TO GET HIS PLAN ON.
NNG...
THIS IS HARDER THAN IT LOOKS...
ALMOST THERE...
TA-DA!
COME ON, THIS IS A THING OF BEAUTY!
OKAY, PLAN B.
HELP!

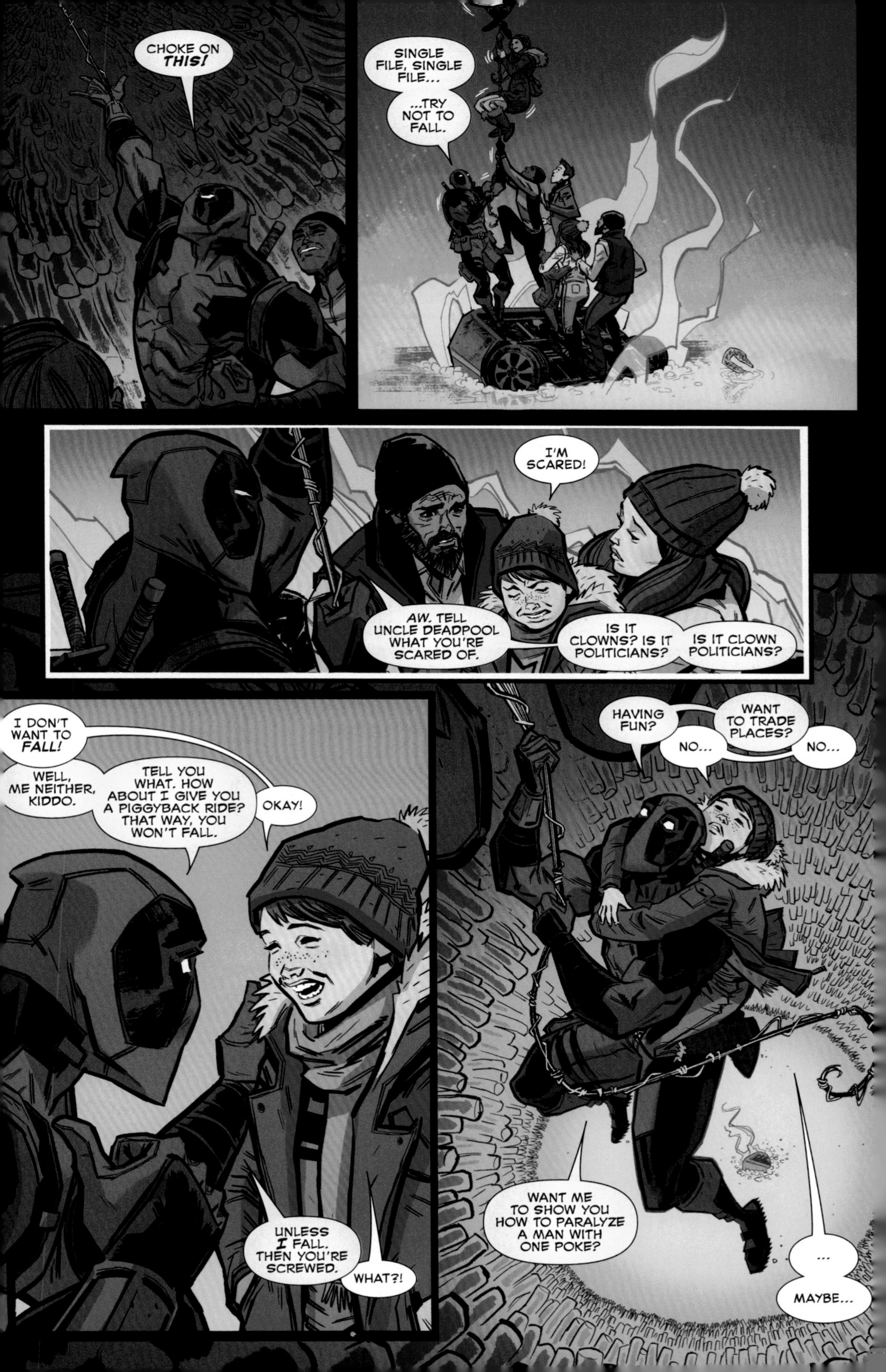
CHOKE ON *THIS!*
SINGLE FILE, SINGLE FILE...
...TRY NOT TO FALL.
I'M SCARED!
AW. TELL UNCLE DEADPOOL WHAT YOU'RE SCARED OF.
IS IT CLOWNS? IS IT POLITICIANS?
IS IT CLOWN POLITICIANS?
I DON'T WANT TO *FALL!*
WELL, ME NEITHER, KIDDO.
TELL YOU WHAT. HOW ABOUT I GIVE YOU A PIGGYBACK RIDE? THAT WAY, YOU WON'T FALL.
OKAY!
UNLESS *I* FALL. THEN YOU'RE SCREWED.
WHAT?!
HAVING FUN?
NO...
WANT TO TRADE PLACES?
NO...
WANT ME TO SHOW YOU HOW TO PARALYZE A MAN WITH ONE POKE?
...
MAYBE...

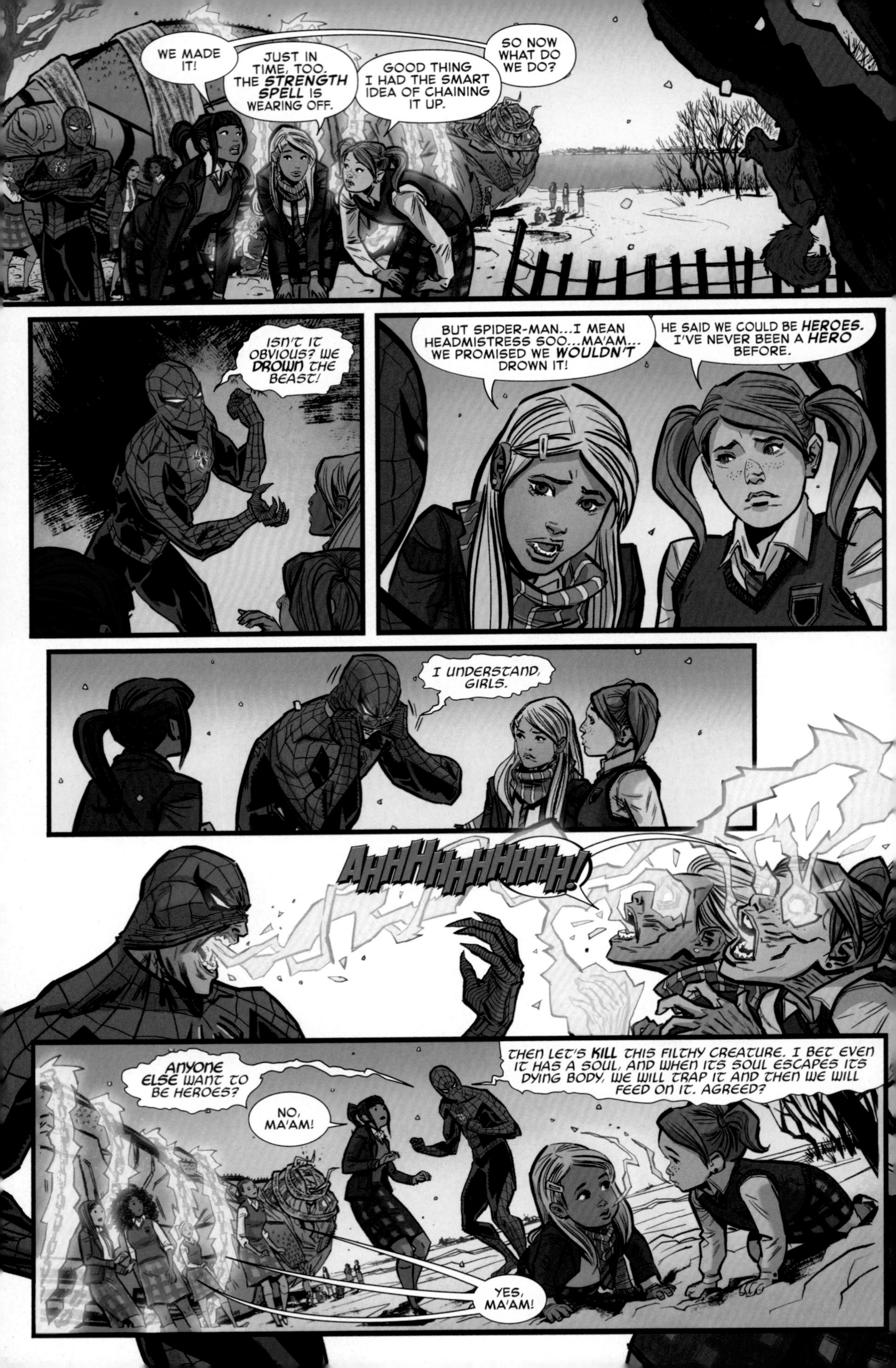
WE MADE IT!
JUST IN TIME, TOO. THE STRENGTH SPELL IS WEARING OFF.
GOOD THING I HAD THE SMART IDEA OF CHAINING IT UP.
SO NOW WHAT DO WE DO?
ISN'T IT OBVIOUS? WE DROWN THE BEAST!
BUT SPIDER-MAN...I MEAN HEADMISTRESS SOO...MA'AM... WE PROMISED WE WOULDN'T DROWN IT!
HE SAID WE COULD BE HEROES. I'VE NEVER BEEN A HERO BEFORE.
I UNDERSTAND, GIRLS.
AHHHHHHHHHH!
ANYONE ELSE WANT TO BE HEROES?
NO, MA'AM!
YES, MA'AM!
THEN LET'S KILL THIS FILTHY CREATURE. I BET EVEN IT HAS A SOUL, AND WHEN ITS SOUL ESCAPES ITS DYING BODY, WE WILL TRAP IT AND THEN WE WILL FEED ON IT. AGREED?

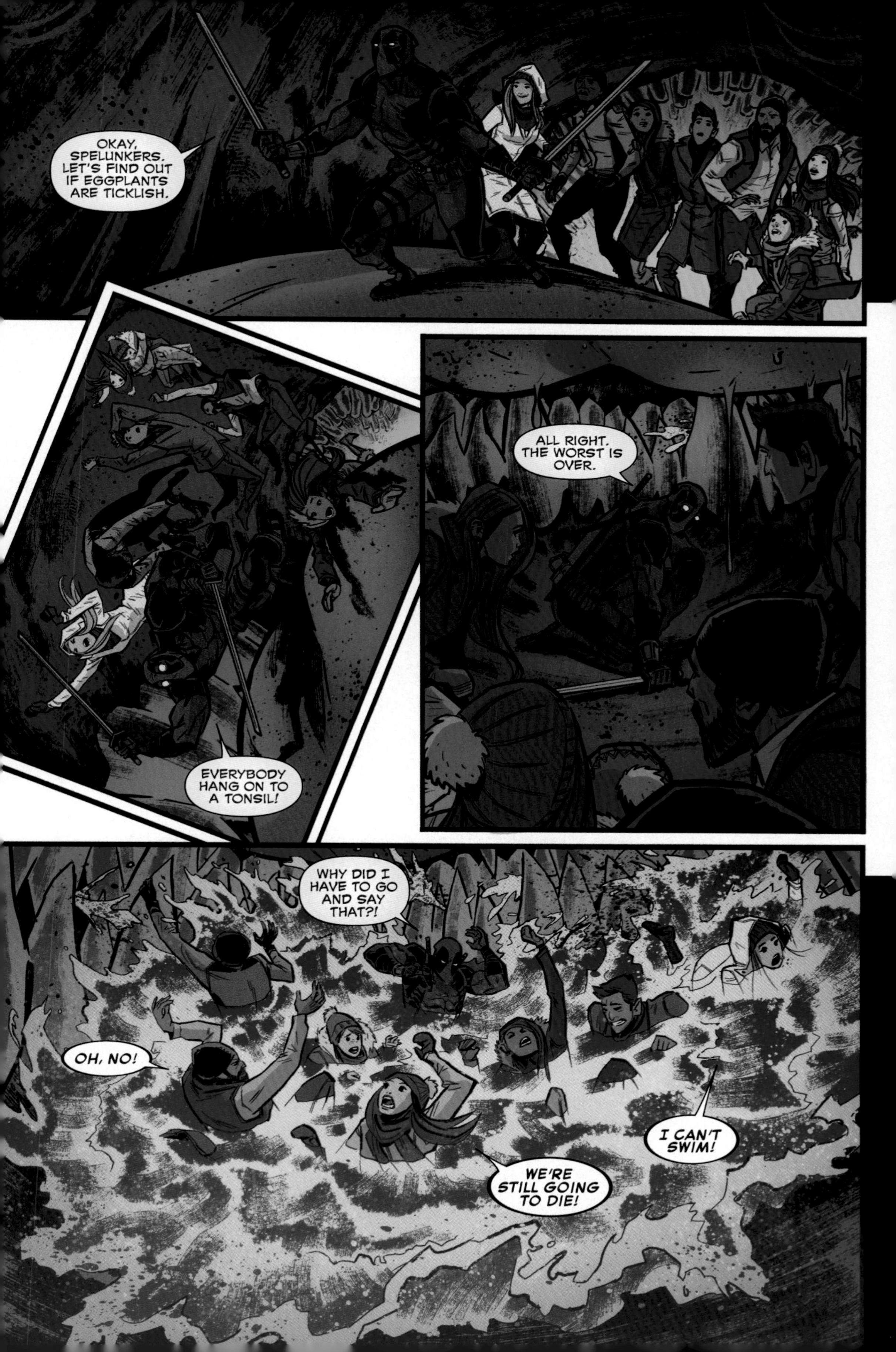
OKAY, SPELUNKERS. LET'S FIND OUT IF EGGPLANTS ARE TICKLISH.
EVERYBODY HANG ON TO A TONSIL!
ALL RIGHT. THE WORST IS OVER.
WHY DID I HAVE TO GO AND SAY THAT?!
OH, NO!
I CAN'T SWIM!
WE'RE STILL GOING TO DIE!

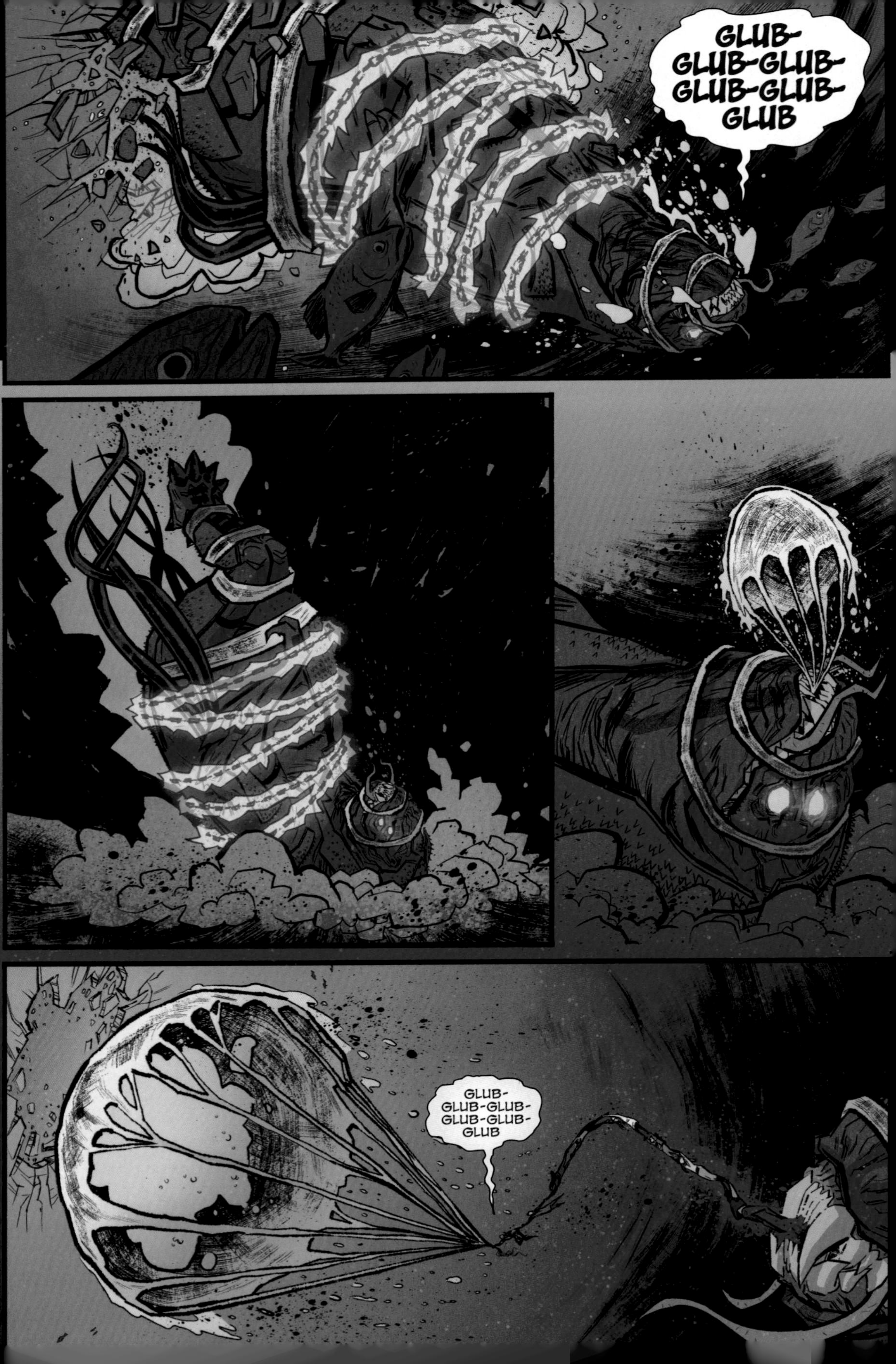
GLUB-
GLUB-GLUB-
GLUB-GLUB-
GLUB
GLUB-
GLUB-GLUB-
GLUB-GLUB-
GLUB

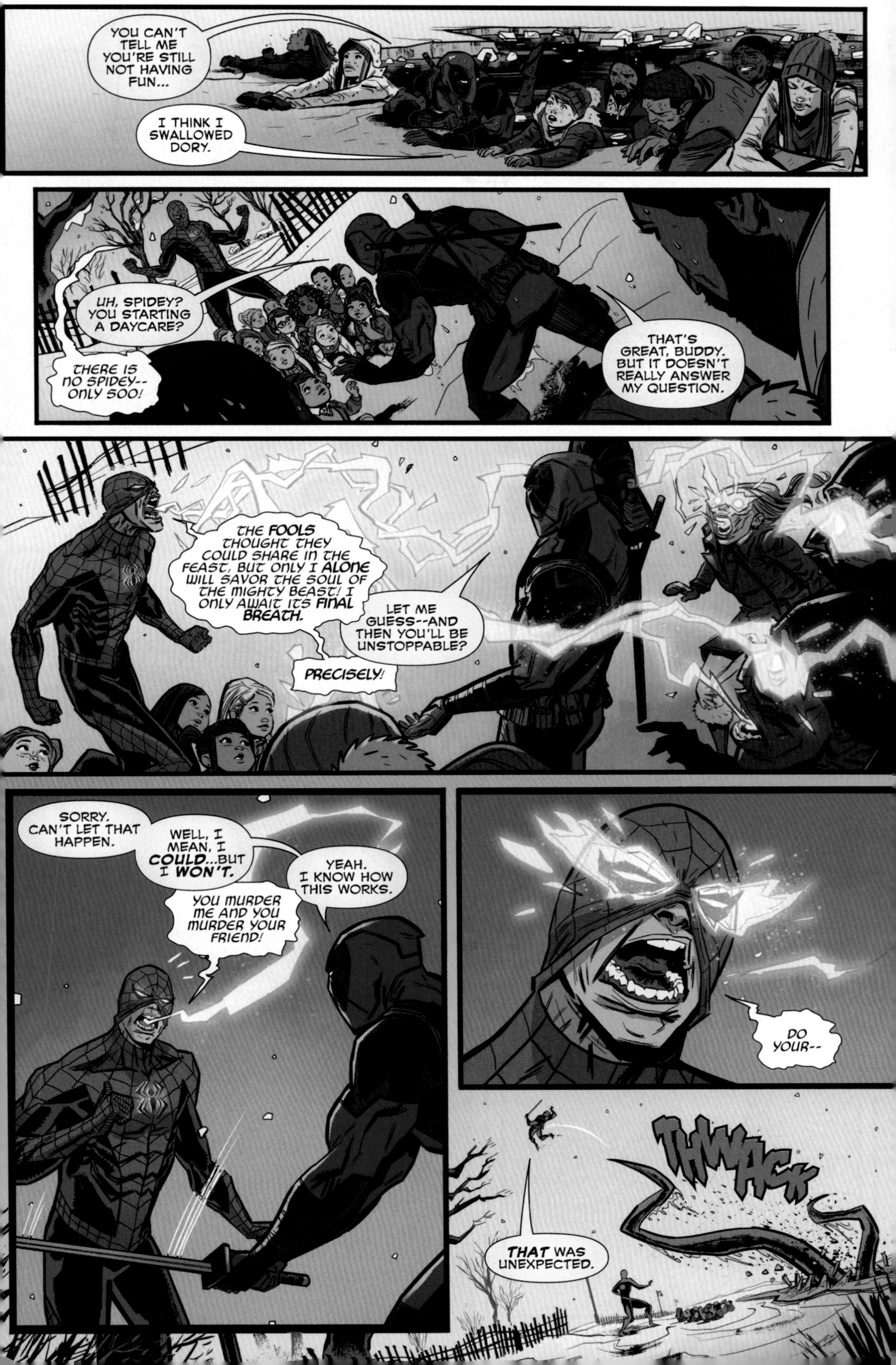
YOU CAN'T TELL ME YOU'RE STILL NOT HAVING FUN...
I THINK I SWALLOWED DORY.
UH, SPIDEY? YOU STARTING A DAYCARE?
THERE IS NO SPIDEY-- ONLY SOO!
THAT'S GREAT, BUDDY. BUT IT DOESN'T REALLY ANSWER MY QUESTION.
THE FOOLS THOUGHT THEY COULD SHARE IN THE FEAST, BUT ONLY I ALONE WILL SAVOR THE SOUL OF THE MIGHTY BEAST! I ONLY AWAIT ITS FINAL BREATH.
LET ME GUESS--AND THEN YOU'LL BE UNSTOPPABLE?
PRECISELY!
SORRY. CAN'T LET THAT HAPPEN.
WELL, I MEAN, I COULD...BUT I WON'T.
YOU MURDER ME AND YOU MURDER YOUR FRIEND!
YEAH. I KNOW HOW THIS WORKS.
DO YOUR--
THWACK
THAT WAS UNEXPECTED.

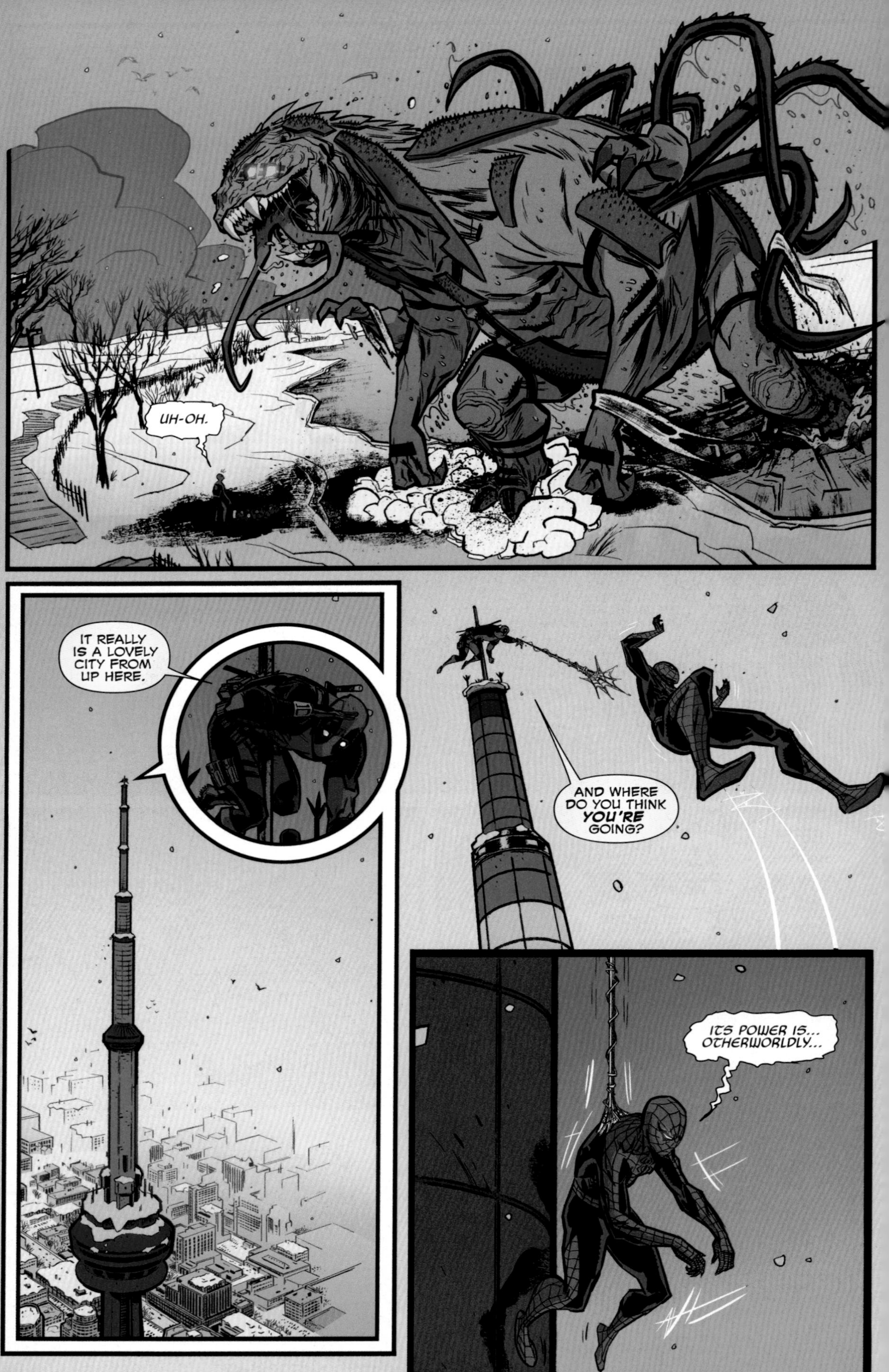
UH-OH.
IT REALLY IS A LOVELY CITY FROM UP HERE.
AND WHERE DO YOU THINK YOU'RE GOING?
ITS POWER IS... OTHERWORLDLY...

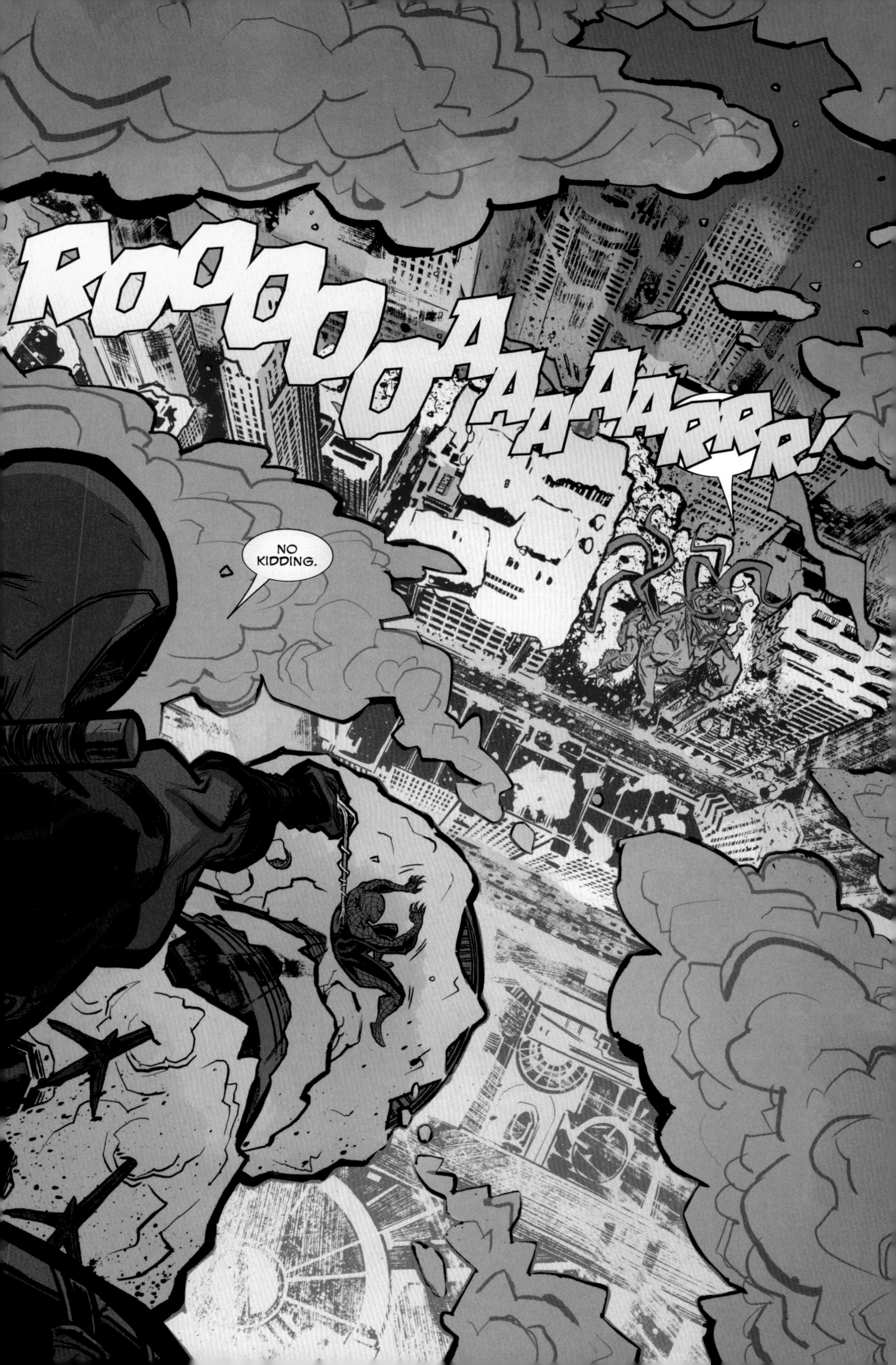
ROOOOOAAAAARRRR!
NO KIDDING.

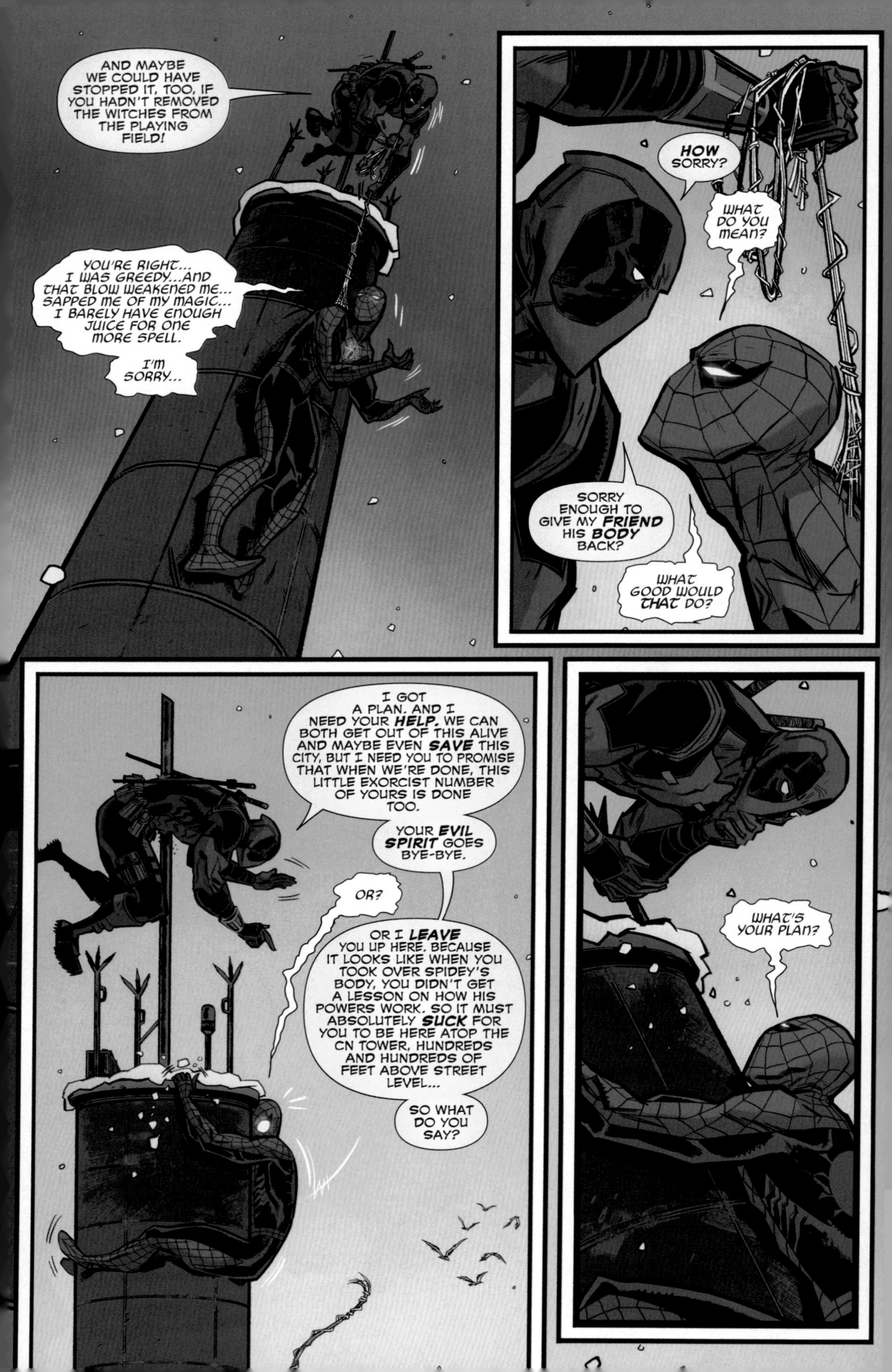
AND MAYBE WE COULD HAVE STOPPED IT, TOO, IF YOU HADN'T REMOVED THE WITCHES FROM THE PLAYING FIELD!
YOU'RE RIGHT... I WAS GREEDY...AND THAT BLOW WEAKENED ME... SAPPED ME OF MY MAGIC... I BARELY HAVE ENOUGH JUICE FOR ONE MORE SPELL.
I'M SORRY...
HOW SORRY?
WHAT DO YOU MEAN?
SORRY ENOUGH TO GIVE MY FRIEND HIS BODY BACK?
WHAT GOOD WOULD THAT DO?
I GOT A PLAN. AND I NEED YOUR HELP. WE CAN BOTH GET OUT OF THIS ALIVE AND MAYBE EVEN SAVE THIS CITY, BUT I NEED YOU TO PROMISE THAT WHEN WE'RE DONE, THIS LITTLE EXORCIST NUMBER OF YOURS IS DONE TOO.
YOUR EVIL SPIRIT GOES BYE-BYE.
OR?
OR I LEAVE YOU UP HERE. BECAUSE IT LOOKS LIKE WHEN YOU TOOK OVER SPIDEY'S BODY, YOU DIDN'T GET A LESSON ON HOW HIS POWERS WORK. SO IT MUST ABSOLUTELY SUCK FOR YOU TO BE HERE ATOP THE CN TOWER, HUNDREDS AND HUNDREDS OF FEET ABOVE STREET LEVEL...
SO WHAT DO YOU SAY?
WHAT'S YOUR PLAN?

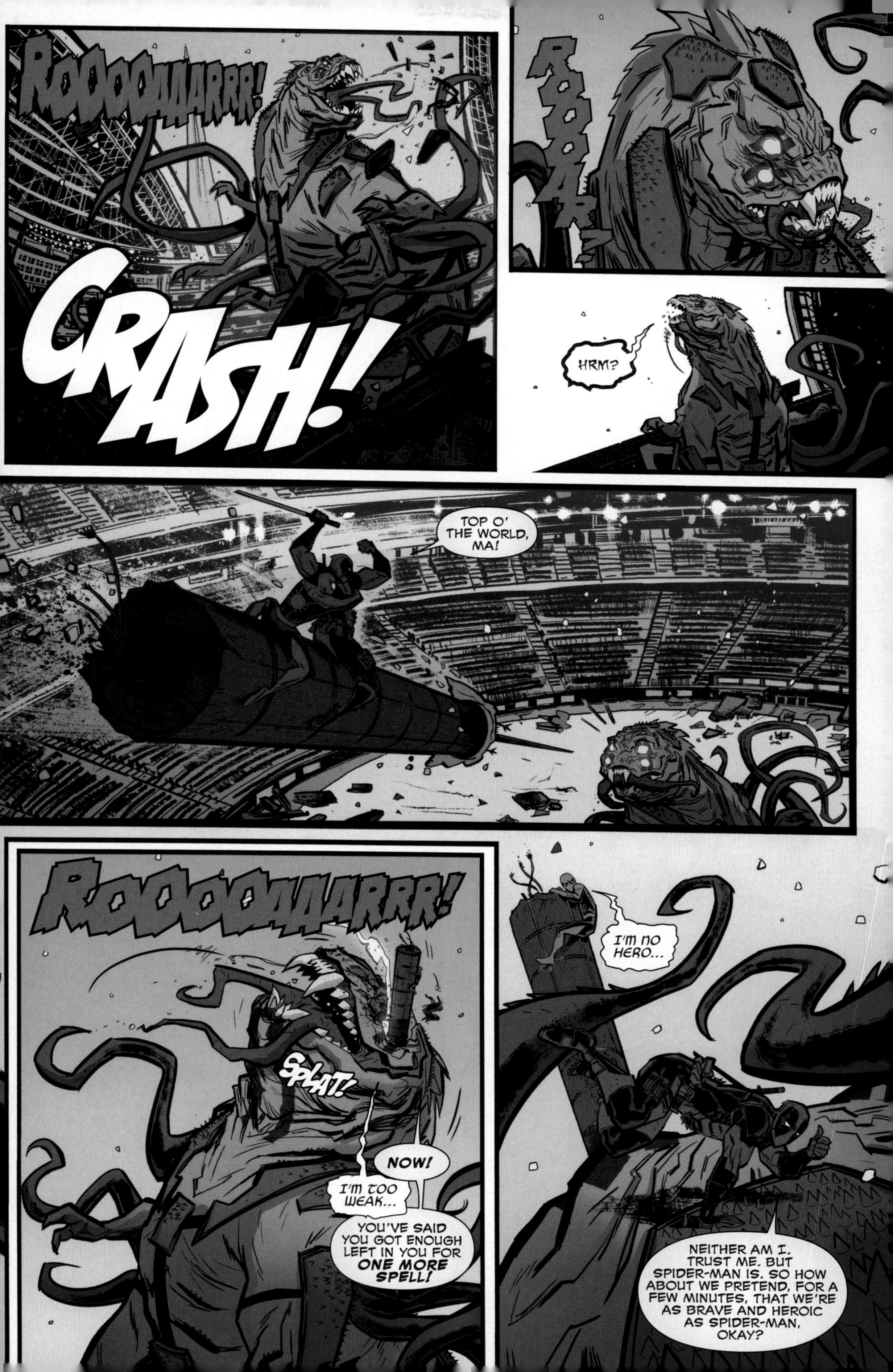
ROOOOAARRR!
CRASH!
ROOOOAR!
HRM?
TOP O' THE WORLD, MA!
ROOOOAARRR!
SPLAT!
NOW!
I'M TOO WEAK...
YOU'VE SAID YOU GOT ENOUGH LEFT IN YOU FOR ONE MORE SPELL!
I'M NO HERO...
NEITHER AM I. TRUST ME. BUT SPIDER-MAN IS. SO HOW ABOUT WE PRETEND, FOR A FEW MINUTES, THAT WE'RE AS BRAVE AND HEROIC AS SPIDER-MAN, OKAY?

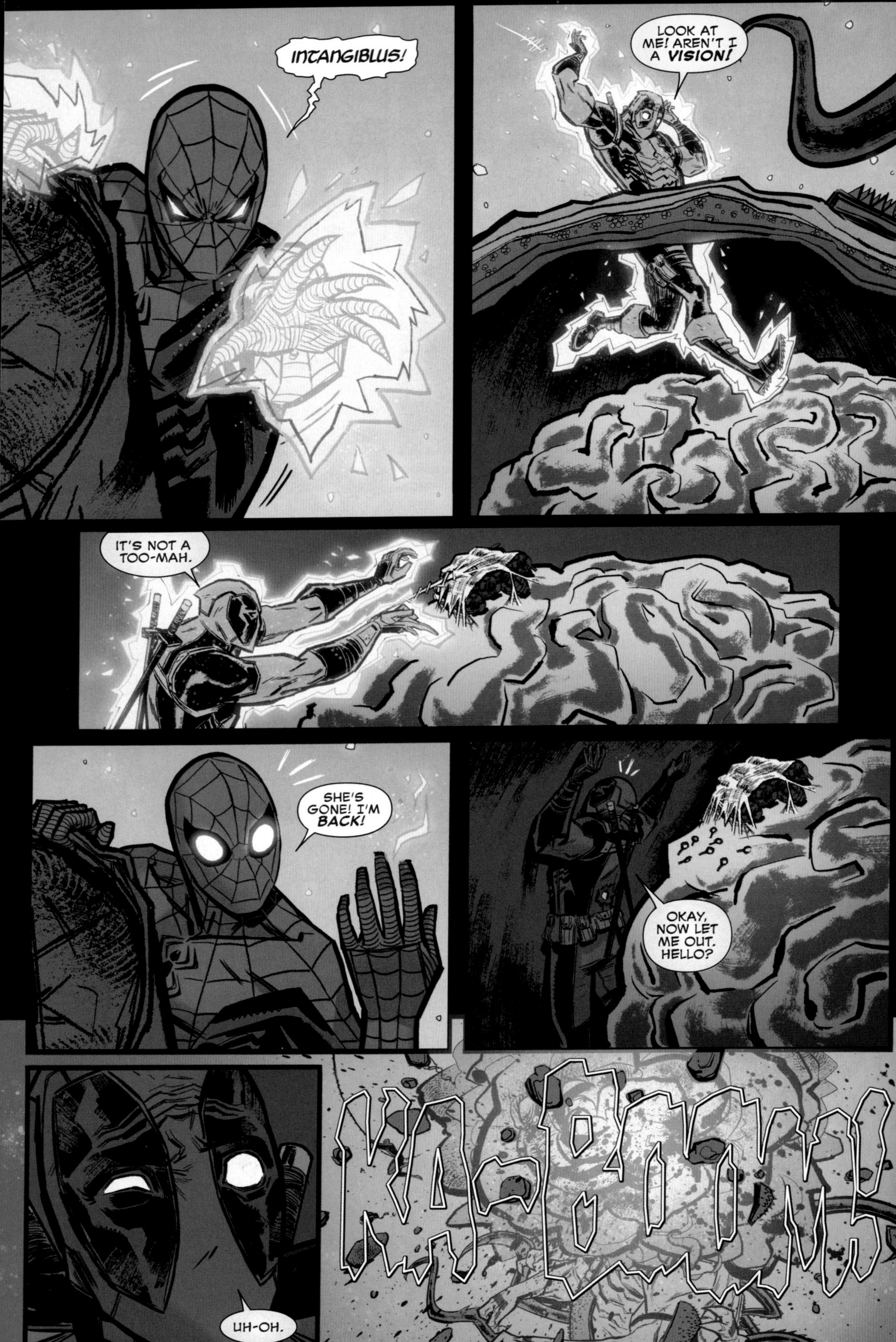
INTANGIBLUS!
LOOK AT ME! AREN'T I A VISION!
IT'S NOT A TOO-MAH.
SHE'S GONE! I'M BACK!
OKAY, NOW LET ME OUT. HELLO?
UH-OH.
KA-BOOOM!

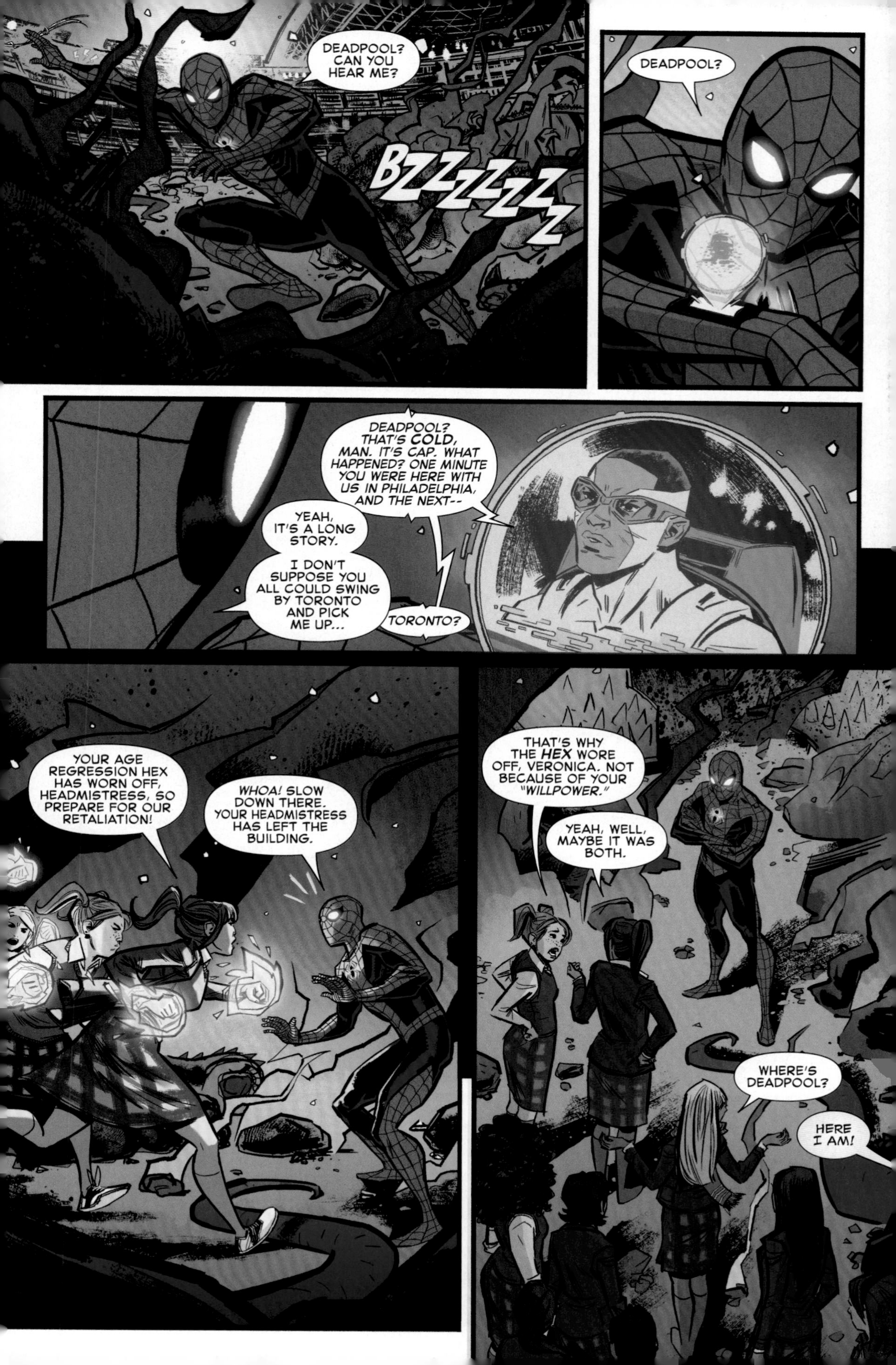
DEADPOOL? CAN YOU HEAR ME?
BZZZZZZZ
DEADPOOL?
DEADPOOL? THAT'S COLD, MAN. IT'S CAP. WHAT HAPPENED? ONE MINUTE YOU WERE HERE WITH US IN PHILADELPHIA, AND THE NEXT--
YEAH, IT'S A LONG STORY.
I DON'T SUPPOSE YOU ALL COULD SWING BY TORONTO AND PICK ME UP...
TORONTO?
YOUR AGE REGRESSION HEX HAS WORN OFF, HEADMISTRESS, SO PREPARE FOR OUR RETALIATION!
WHOA! SLOW DOWN THERE. YOUR HEADMISTRESS HAS LEFT THE BUILDING.
THAT'S WHY THE HEX WORE OFF, VERONICA. NOT BECAUSE OF YOUR "WILLPOWER."
YEAH, WELL, MAYBE IT WAS BOTH.
WHERE'S DEADPOOL?
HERE I AM!

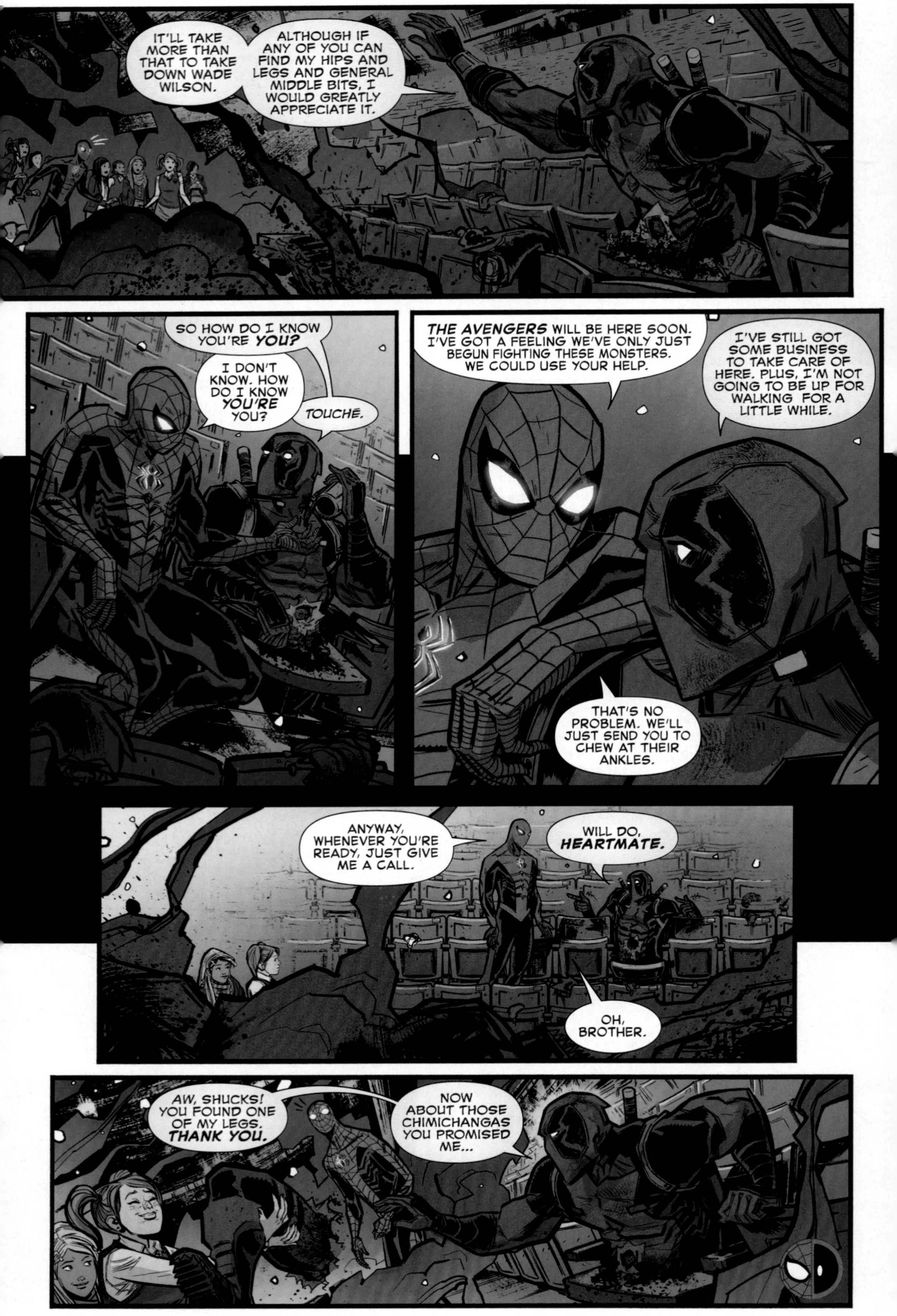
IT'LL TAKE MORE THAN THAT TO TAKE DOWN WADE WILSON.
ALTHOUGH IF ANY OF YOU CAN FIND MY HIPS AND LEGS AND GENERAL MIDDLE BITS, I WOULD GREATLY APPRECIATE IT.
SO HOW DO I KNOW YOU'RE YOU?
I DON'T KNOW. HOW DO I KNOW YOU'RE YOU?
TOUCHE.
THE AVENGERS WILL BE HERE SOON. I'VE GOT A FEELING WE'VE ONLY JUST BEGUN FIGHTING THESE MONSTERS. WE COULD USE YOUR HELP.
I'VE STILL GOT SOME BUSINESS TO TAKE CARE OF HERE. PLUS, I'M NOT GOING TO BE UP FOR WALKING FOR A LITTLE WHILE.
THAT'S NO PROBLEM. WE'LL JUST SEND YOU TO CHEW AT THEIR ANKLES.
ANYWAY, WHENEVER YOU'RE READY, JUST GIVE ME A CALL.
WILL DO, HEARTMATE.
OH, BROTHER.
AW, SHUCKS! YOU FOUND ONE OF MY LEGS. THANK YOU.
NOW ABOUT THOSE CHIMICHANGAS YOU PROMISED ME...